BEFORE AUSTEN COMES AESOP

CHERI BLOMQUIST

BEFORE AUSTEN COMES AESOP

The Children's Great Books and How to Experience Them

IGNATIUS PRESS   SAN FRANCISCO

Cover art:
Esbjörn in the Study Corner, 1912 (detail) by Carl Larsson
Photo credit: Bridgeman Images

Cover design by John Herreid

ISBN 978-1-62164-430-9 (PB)
ISBN 978-1-64229-157-5 (eBook)
Library of Congress Control Number 2020946390
Printed in the United States of America ∞

CONTENTS

Introduction 7

What You Need to Know before You Begin 12

A Note about Developing Readers 14

About the Children's Great Books 15

PART ONE
The Children's Great Books

1 Ancient Times through the Early Middle Ages 21

2 The Middle Ages through the Protestant Reformation 33

3 The Colonization of New England through the Mid-nineteenth Century 41

4 The First Golden Age of Children's Literature 55

5 The Great Depression through World War II 78

6 The Second Golden Age 92

7 The Noteworthy Books of the Late-Twentieth Century 111

PART TWO
Your Passport to Three Reading Adventures

8 Choosing Your Own Reading Adventure 135

9 The Leisurely Adventure (all ages) 137

10 The Book Club(ish) Adventure (all ages) 139

11 The Scholarly Adventure (elementary and secondary levels) 141

12 The Elementary Scholarly Adventure 145

13 The Secondary Scholarly Adventure 163

APPENDICES

A: Simplified Reading Lists 201

B: Study Method Cheat Sheets 221

C: A Secondary Scholarly Adventure Study Guide 227

D: The Scholarly Adventure Grading Rubrics 235

E: Four Short-Term Study Plans 247

F: The Children's Great Books Project 251

G: Major Awards for Children's Literature 261

H: Useful Questions for Literature Study 263

Recommended Resources 269

Selected Bibliography 271

INTRODUCTION

When I was in twelfth grade, I hit a snag in my life-long love affair with books. My English teacher led us through a study of the Thomas Hardy classic *Jude the Obscure*. Up until this point, I had made it through *Romeo and Juliet*, *Wuthering Heights*, *To Kill a Mockingbird*, *The Good Earth*, and even long selections of *The Odyssey*—all with reasonable academic success, if not much appreciation. Except for *Romeo and Juliet*, whose Franco Zeffirelli film version I knew and loved, I didn't understand any of them very well. Whether it was the quality of teaching or my limited intelligence or the book itself I am not sure, but at least the light stayed on in my mind most of the time. With *Jude the Obscure*, however, everything went dark. I lost myself so completely in its dense forest of words that I never did find my way out. To this day I can tell you exactly three things about it: it is a classic English novel (though I have no idea why); it is unbearably long; and the main character is a man named Jude (although if you assured me that he was a dog or gorilla, I wouldn't argue). In other words, I hated *Jude the Obscure* more than any other book I've encountered either before or since then. If I saw it in a bookstore today, I would probably shudder and slowly back away.

The memory of that novel didn't stay silent, as others have. Except for *Wuthering Heights* and *The Good Earth*, with which I also struggled but later reread as an adult with better success, I have mostly forgotten the other novels I endured. But the memory of those weeks (months?) with *Jude the Obscure* rumbled around and around my mind for years afterward, sparking questions about assigned literature until I became a teacher myself and was compelled to take them seriously—questions such as the following:

- Why do we continually ask students to study literature far too mature for them?
- Why is classic literature so important? Or *is* it important at all?

- Why do we rush students past juvenile classics to adult classics before they might be ready for them?

- When educators or parents decide that students are ready to read adult classics, why do so many of us feel the need to plow through as many as possible?

- Why do so many literature selections seem arbitrary? Why this one over that one?

- When—and why—should students tackle the masterpieces of Western literature, such as Shakespeare, Milton, and Homer? How fast should they read them?

- Which is better: a survey that covers many books (dip-and-sip) or a deep study of only a few books (dive-and-drink)?

- Should students study only authors of Western civilization, or is a literature program incomplete without attention to the literature of Eastern civilization, too?

- How does childhood reading (recreational or academic) affect students' ability to understand and enjoy their reading as adults? What *kind* of childhood reading helps facilitate a rich literary experience in adulthood?

- How important is poetry to a literary education, and should it be presented to students in the same way as prose? Should we study and analyze poetry or just learn the tools that help us appreciate and enjoy it?

- And finally (for now), should juvenile literature play any kind of academic role in the teen years, or should it be relegated to recreational reading only?

While I have opinions on these questions, the last one concerns me most in *Before Austen Comes Aesop*. Over the last twenty plus years, I have observed, selected, and created literature programs for both my homeschooled children and for formal classes I have taught. I have also watched many young people choose books in my five-year role as a bookseller and listened to reactions about literature from both children and adolescents. All of this has led me to three conclusions.

Far too many children grow up without reading the great classics of children's literature. Far too many have never been to Narnia, have never met Ramona Quimby or the Moffats, have never experienced what it's like to survive as did Julie amongst a pack of wolves, have never ... well, I could go on and on! Children's literature—both the classics and the contemporaries—is filled with rich and beautiful writing, incredible adventures, and characters who are just waiting to become our friends for life. When I meet teenagers who are reading books like *Wuthering Heights* without ever having met Winnie-the-Pooh, Mary Lennox, Heidi, or Tom Sawyer, I mourn a little. When will they ever do so, if they don't by the time they are grown up? Unless something compels them later, they probably never will.

Nothing much has changed since I was a child. Adolescents still often dislike the adult classics they are assigned in school. How many teens do you know who would choose to read *Wuthering Heights, Ivanhoe, Animal Farm,* or *Don Quixote* over trendy young adult picks? Of course there are some who would; there are exceptions to everything. Of course we should nudge students out of their comfort zones at times. And, of course, some students discover that they enjoy the classics forced upon them. For the most part, though, teenagers still grumble and avoid the great classics as much as they can, mainly because those books are too difficult, too unrelatable, and too boring. Could it be that many teens sidestep the adult classics we require them to read (even cheating with *CliffsNotes* to avoid the chore) not because they want to rebel against schoolwork, but because they are just not ready for them? I think so.

Adolescents differ in their ability to appreciate adult literature. Some have the maturity and intellect to sail through it, and others find themselves hopelessly lost. Some enjoy analysis and discussion, and some do not. Some relish the opportunity to write response essays and literary analyses, and others stumble over the first sentence. Nothing about these differences should surprise us, of course. Teens differ in their abilities for every subject. The boy who can't figure out the plot of *David Copperfield* may be a budding virtuoso on the oboe. The girl who can't articulate her response to *Walden* may be a natural with a microscope. With literature, though, we are dealing with the human experience and with profound themes and ideas that are often far beyond the scope of the teenager's maturity. Those who have not been prepared for literary excursions into the world of adults cannot be expected to navigate that world with any aplomb.

It may seem by now that I am advocating the kind of dumbing-down of our country's education that so many of us are trying to work against, but this is not at all true. Students *should* read the great adult classics—just not too soon. They would have a richer, deeper, more meaningful experience if we chose a gentler approach to their instruction. Such an approach would both consider students' maturity and allow teachers to ensure the sufficient mastery of literary study skills *before* leading students into the labyrinth of adult classics.

I am not suggesting that we ask teens to study only contemporary juvenile literature or that we never ask them to reach beyond their maturity level when they read a book. What I am suggesting is that instead of teaching to one extreme or the other, we need to lay a stronger foundation for their advanced literary studies, one that will help them study the difficult adult books with better success. This success can only happen when they are ready, which is later than we tend to think. To ensure this success, we must allow the Children's Great Books to take their rightful place in English courses—in the elementary grades but also beyond them in middle school and high school. In addition, we must spend more time teaching basic literary skills, such as active reading. This book attempts to do that.

Saying we should choose literature more suited to teenagers, however, doesn't address the problem of what to choose and how to organize a literature program. Here are some of the ways that have been tried.

- Make arbitrary selections based on our own opinions of what students should read.
- Choose literature that fits specific themes, such as coming-of-age or classics of the South or bullying.
- Design studies based on literary genres, such as short stories, American literature, or mysteries.
- Base our choices around a particular philosophy or approach, such as Core Knowledge or a religious worldview.
- Capitalize on our students' personal interests by choosing literature that meets those interests and designing studies based on them.
- Integrate literature with other subjects, history being the most popular.
- Focus on the works of key authors.

I have taken or admired these approaches at various times as a teacher and home educator, and they all have value. There is at least one more approach, however, that I haven't mentioned: the classical approach. The traditional classical model focuses its literary instruction on the most influential, most important authors of Western civilization, such as Sophocles, Plato, Virgil, and Shakespeare. Their works reveal and contribute to the thinking of our entire civilization. They have influenced writers of every generation, both the famous and the forgotten, which means that without these foundational works, Western literature would not exist as we know it. For those who want a classical education, which is fundamentally an education in Western civilization, these Great Books are essential reading.

The classical approach is the one I generally favor for literary study. It makes the most sense to me in the broader context of a well-rounded education. It is the most meaningful, the most valuable, the most fundamental, and the most beautiful. At the same time, however, it is not the most kid- or teen-friendly. Some of it is, of course—myths, fables, Bible stories, and even *The Odyssey* in an accessible translation. Other greats, though, are not—Milton, Dante, Chaucer, and many others. What to do about this? How do educators smoothly bridge the way from here to there without losing students to a lifelong hatred of literature on the way?

I suggest what might be considered a "sidekick" approach. This is where great works of children's literature are the primary focus during the grade-school years (including most of high school), but they actually support and lay the groundwork for the future introduction of the Great Books canon. Such an approach teaches Western children's literature from roots to leaf, leading students through the works that young people like them have enjoyed through the centuries, beginning with ancient works such as Aesop's fables and Bible stories and continuing with all the most important works from the Middle Ages to our present time.

It would be easy to put aside this body of literature with a dismissive sniff when considering adolescents. After all, this is *children's* literature we're talking about. This is all fine in the elementary grades, but middle school and high school? Teens may not be adults, but they are also not children. Should adolescents really spend even part of their few college-preparatory years on children's books?

Yes, they should. In fact, I am suggesting that they read a whole bunch of them, along with some other books and tales that were not written for children but that have been enjoyed by them for centuries (King Arthur tales, for example). If this sounds odd to you, not to mention a huge waste of time, I encourage you to consider what many children's literature experts will tell you—that children's literature is every bit as rich, meaningful, engaging, and beautiful as adult literature. In fact, they will also tell you that children's books are often better! Having read widely in both children's and adult literature myself, I emphatically agree.

This is good news for students. Because there is so much well-written children's literature available, both old and new, educators have plenty to choose from when seeking to prepare students for the challenging adult material they will *also* need to read if they want to prepare sufficiently for college. Unfortunately, many wonderful books will need to remain recreational reading; there are just too many riches to enjoy! But if we focus on the Children's Great Books, we will not only give our students the best preparation possible for the great adult classics, but also ensure that our young people do not grow up without experiencing the very best of the literature written just for them. These are the goals of *Before Austen Comes Aesop: The Children's Great Books and How to Experience Them*. Welcome!

What You Need to Know before You Begin

To begin using this book, I suggest first skimming it to get a sense of the whole, including the appendices. Copy any parts of the appendices that may be helpful throughout your chosen adventure.

This book is grounded in not just the children's classics, but the *most important* children's classics as indicated by literary history. It can be used as either a general resource for all families or as a literature program for homeschool families. When used as a literature program, the book can be used for multiple children and for multiple years. It can also replace graded literature programs until more formal instruction or group instruction is needed.

The book is divided into three main sections: a reading list, reading adventure guides, and appendices. The reading list assists parents in choosing books for their children, the adventure guides help children experience each book independently and at their own pace, and the appendices provide additional support.

There are three types of reading adventures: leisurely, book club(ish), and scholarly. The Scholarly Adventure is further divided into two parts: elementary and secondary. Although some of the book selections are appropriate for very young children, the Elementary Scholarly Adventure is best for children in grades three and up.

This book approaches literature more as an art than as an academic subject; therefore, it treats excellent picture books, poetry, short stories, nonfiction, and novels as equally worthy of attention. For this reason, older students are encouraged to read any books on the reading list that are at or below their reading level. At the same time, of course, they should still give sufficient attention to literature at or above their reading level.

As valuable as independent literature study may be, it cannot substitute for some experience of lively group discussions, peer and teacher feedback on papers, challenging exams, and creative oral presentations. Such activities develop other kinds of skills that will be useful to students in the higher grades and in college. Even if you love the freedom of independent study and the low-cost method I will introduce in this guide, I still recommend taking a formal literature class and joining a book club at some point, especially in upper high school.

Some adults consider children's classics to be inferior to adult classics and therefore not worth a teenager's or adult's time; however, this book regards them as worthy of attention at all ages. Even so, once teens have a solid foundation of children's literature beneath them, they need to study some challenging adult classics in upper high school. This is especially true if they plan to attend college. One benefit of this program is that some of the most beloved, most important children's classics are also adult classics.

A Note about Developing Readers

This book is designed to be a literature resource, meant to help parents introduce their children to the best children's stories and poetry that Western civilization has ever produced. Juvenile readers, however, are also developing readers. Some children and teens will not yet have the skills to read some of the suggested books on the list independently. Others will be able to read and comprehend all of them. Also, some books that match a child's reading level may have content that is still too mature.

To help parents determine whether a book is appropriate for a child or adolescent, most of the books listed provide a reading level. This is the grade level at which a typical American child can read and comprehend a book independently. Next to the reading level is an interest level. This is the grade range in which the book's content is developmentally appropriate. The reading level is determined by the ATOS Readability Formula, which was developed in 2000 by the educational software company Renaissance Learning and a panel of outside experts. The interest level is determined by each book's publisher or Renaissance Learning, or both.

This information has not been provided for some of the books listed. The reasons vary for entries that don't list the reading level. In some cases, the ATOS database didn't assign one, so I assigned a general reading level. In others, the titles have many translations or abridgments available for parents to choose from, so the reading level varies. Finally, some of the oldest books are included on the list because of their role in the development of children's literature, but I could not access them to estimate either a reading level or an interest level. For these books I either offered an estimate or marked them "unknown."

About the Children's Great Books

At the heart of *Before Austen Comes Aesop* is, of course, the reading list. This list presents the great books of children's literature as an important prequel to the Great Books of Western civilization. The Great Books list was developed by educators in the 1920s who sought to improve American higher education by returning it to a Western, liberal arts focus.

This does not mean that the great works of Eastern civilization are not valuable; they have made their own important contributions to the world. But in order for children in the United States to understand the cultural foundation of the society in which they live, they need to read some of the Western Great Books.

The works included in the Great Books canon are far beyond the comprehension of most grade-school students—consider the *Dialogues* of Plato and John Milton's *Paradise Lost*, for example. For classical educators and many homeschool parents, however, preparing students to read some of the Great Books is an important goal.

The Great Books of Western literature have at least four main qualities:

1. Their ideas and themes are both representative of their times and universal. Thus, they remain relevant and important to modern readers.
2. They have contributed to the "Great Conversation of Great Ideas" of Western thinkers down through the centuries.
3. They have layers of riches such that readers can return to them again and again and make valuable discoveries every time.
4. Their craftsmanship is beautiful and often exemplary.

In composing the Children's Great Books reading list, I looked for books written or adapted for children with these same qualities. The list is therefore compatible with a future study of the Great Books not only in terms of literary excellence but also in terms of how they prepare young readers for the adult books they will read later. The criteria I used, then, included the following:

- The book has played a significant role in the history of children's literature.
- It has influenced the development of Western literature— children's, adult, or both.
- It has been valued by young people for much of its existence.
- It has long been considered excellent literature. The contemporary works on the list are those currently considered excellent by literary critics and have already proven to be influential, but time will tell if they will be considered great in the long run.

I also considered how popular it has been since its publication, but I could not make long-standing popularity a deciding factor. Some important children's books were considered favorites among juvenile readers during their time period but have long been forgotten. Other books were ignored or condemned in their day but gained respect and popularity later.

The literature included on the reading list, therefore, does not reflect my own preferences. In fact, I did my best to remain as objective as possible, although I still had to make some judgment calls when my research didn't provide sufficient information. Because of my efforts to be objective, therefore, you will likely be surprised by some of the works included here. You may even be a bit annoyed to discover that your own favorites are either relegated to the "other classics" list or left out altogether. If so, know that I sympathize with you, for I was annoyed more than once that I couldn't include some of the books that I felt deserved the honor and that I had to include some books that I didn't like.

The books you are about to encounter on this list, then, are the great books of Western children's literature. To give students the best preparation possible for an advanced, classical literature program, I suggest that these books are the ones that should receive the most attention.

I must add here that all the entries on this list are *optional* for you, the parent. You already know this, of course, but sometimes it helps to be reminded that guides and curricula are there to help us, not to dictate rules. We don't fail in our parental duties if we can't do everything we would like to do. The purpose of this list is not to tell you what your child *must* study to be well prepared for adult literature; it is to help you make informed decisions without relying on a structured curriculum.

Finally, the Children's Great Books list includes literature of all genres and all reading levels. This is because great art transcends such limitations. Brilliant, beautiful literary art is found beginning with board books like *Goodnight Moon* and soars all the way up to *The Odyssey*. Let your student enjoy the whole range of children's literature, even if they are teenagers. We may grow out of the vocabulary and simplicity of baby books, but we never grow out of art.

After looking over the list, you may still feel overwhelmed by all the choices to be made. If so, consider using the Children's Great Books Project or the short-term study plans, both provided in the appendices. You might also find the two short versions of the reading list helpful for clarifying your goals and narrowing your choices, provided that you look up the fuller descriptions of the works in the complete list, especially those marked with *Parents Cautioned!* These are also in the appendices.

Here is some information about the labeling used in this book:

- *Foundational* works are those parents may want to make a priority in their student's literature program. They have been important to the development of Western children's literature, as well as to the Western child's literary experience. Not only have many of them heavily influenced children's literature, but many of them have also influenced adult literature. Although late-twentieth-century books are too contemporary as yet to have made the kind of impact that established classics have, I have applied this designation to books that seem to be heading in that direction.

- *Important* works, although not foundational, have been beloved by children and have played a role in shaping children's literature.

- *Parents Cautioned!* means the book contains mature or possibly offensive content.

- *Reading Level* is indicated by a number that refers to the grade level (year and month) at which a typical child can read and understand the book independently according to the ATOS Readability Formula (i.e., 6.2 equals sixth grade, second month). The reading level *only* measures the textual difficulty, not developmental appropriateness. For this reason, some books with mature content may be assigned a reading level much lower than what parents might expect.

- *Interest Level* indicates the grade range in which a book may be developmentally appropriate.

- *Other Children's Classics* listed at the end of each era include additional titles that were popular among children during that time. Some have been forgotten, but many are beloved classics in the traditional children's canon. Space limitations don't allow for every worthy book to be included on these lists, especially those from the twentieth century.

PART ONE

The Children's Great Books

Ancient Times through the Early Middle Ages

1500 B.C.—A.D. 1000

As much as it might perplex modern readers, the most ancient literature of Western civilization is also our most important literature; therefore, a methodical study of Western literature is best begun with the greats of that era. Throughout the centuries these works have held their place as cornerstones of not only Western literature, but also of Western culture and thought. They have also had a profound influence on many other adult and children's literary works throughout the centuries. Even in the most contemporary literature, astute readers can still find tales that either reference or retell great works and oral tales of the ancient canon.

Except for Aesop's famous fables, perhaps, the works listed below are essentially adult literature, meaning literature that was written without attention to a possible audience of children. Even so, they were introduced to the children of their time, often as part of their formal education, and they have remained a major part of the Western child's literary experience ever since. As you read the entries for every era, you will find this phenomenon to be quite common. In fact, this reading list cannot possibly include every adult work that has been popular with children; there are too many! Those that are included have been the most *important* works to the child's literary experience throughout the ages, as well as to the development of the children's literature genre. Because of their influence in the world of children, then, these adult works are included in this guide as children's literature.

The Old Testament from the Holy Bible
(roughly 1500 B.C.–100 B.C.)*
Foundational
Reading Level: varies on the edition   Interest Level: varies

The influence of the Bible on Western literature is so profound that it can hardly be exaggerated. Throughout the centuries since the birth of Christ, the Western world has been steeped in Christian teaching and culture through all the arts, and children's literature is no exception. From the invention of the first picture alphabet in the late sixteenth century to the anti-theistic subtext of Philip Pullman's His Dark Materials trilogy at the end of the twentieth century, Christianity and both testaments of the Bible have had a profound influence on children's authors.

Despite its inherent importance to Christian students, it would be a mistake for non-Christian students to ignore the Bible in their literary studies. Both classic and contemporary literature of all kinds frequently allude to Bible stories and other aspects of Christian teaching. The student who is well-grounded in the Bible, even if he regards it as mere literature, is much better equipped to make sense of biblical allusions, retellings, and direct references in other literature than the student who is not.

If you have a student who knows these stories well already, you may want to skip over this section or else find resources that allow him to dive deeper into their historical context or spiritual dimension. If your student has not grown up with Bible stories, though, you might find one of the listed resources helpful. The best source is the original source, the Bible itself, but young children and those who find the Bible confusing or intimidating will do well with orthodox adaptations or retellings.

Virtues and Themes

For Jewish and Christian students, the Old Testament is not only full of good stories that are often referenced in other literature, it is also

---

*Protestant Christians consider the last book of the Old Testament to be Malachi, which was completed circa 400 B.C. Catholic and Orthodox Christians consider the last books to be those of the Maccabees, which were completed circa 100 B.C. I have chosen to use this latter dating to include all the books considered to be part of the Old Testament canon within the Christian religion.

full of doctrinal, historical, and spiritual lessons that are key to their religious formation. For students outside these faiths, the historical, moral, and literary aspects form an essential part of a thorough education.

Resources

The titles below are only a few possibilities among many, and they do not include any of the many direct translations available, with the exception of the King James Version.** In addition, these resources were not chosen to support any particular denomination. They are only provided to get you started in your search for a resource that suits your student.

- *The Golden Children's Bible* (Based on the King James Version, this is one of the few story Bibles whose vocabulary is appropriate for an older student.)
- *The Story (Teen Edition): The Bible as One Continuing Story of God and His People*, by Zonderkidz
- *The Whole Bible Story: Everything That Happens in the Bible in Plain English*, by William H. Marty
- *Walking With God: A Journey through the Bible*, by Tim Gray and Jeff Cavins
- *Bible Stories from the Old Testament* (DVD), by The History Channel
- *The Bible* (DVD), by The History Channel

The Iliad, by Homer (c. 750 B.C.)
Foundational
Reading Level: varies   Interest Level: varies

Usually considered to be the earliest literary works of Western civilization, according to the website *Classical Literature*, the epic poems *The*

** If you choose to read a direct translation, consider using the King James Version (KJV) for your literature studies no matter what your religion, denomination, or translation preference may be. When considered from a literary standpoint, the KJV is the translation most referenced in Western literature, and it is widely considered to be the most beautiful of all the translations. Because its language is rich and poetic, it is also the easiest to memorize. I can attest to this personally, because I was required to memorize passages from both the KJV and the modern New International Version when I was in grade school. Today, the only ones that I still remember are the KJV passages. Again, this recommendation is regarding literature study only, not Bible study or church use.

Iliad and *The Odyssey* include many characters from Greek mythology. The historical facts that undergird *The Iliad* in its recounting of the Trojan War are overshadowed by the fact that the poem was written hundreds of years after it happened (c. 1184 B.C.). In addition, the context of *The Iliad* is the Greek culture that existed when the poem was written, not the Greek culture that existed when the historical events occurred.

Whatever their basis, both of Homer's epics have been a mainstay of children's literary entertainment and education since the classical era. In fact, a study of Western literature—either adult or juvenile—is incomplete without serious attention to these works. Due to their mature content, students would do well to read these tales first in age-appropriate adaptations during childhood and then again in translation in upper high school or college.

Virtues and Themes

Not only is it a powerful and timeless tale and an important example of epic poetry, *The Iliad* also sets up character types commonly found in later literature and addresses important questions without providing easy answers. Among these questions are What is courage? What are the effects of anger and pride? What is a good life? and What is justice?

Resources (in order from middle grade to adult)

- *The Trojan War*, by Olivia Coolidge (retelling, not translation)
- *The Children's Homer: The Adventures of Odysseus and the Tale of Troy*, by Padraic Colum
- *The Iliad* in translation (Acclaimed translators include Samuel Butler, Richmond Lattimore, Emile Rieu, Robert Fitzgerald, Robert Fagles, and Stanley Lombardo.)

The Odyssey, by Homer (c. 725 B.C.)
Foundational
Reading Level: varies   Interest Level: varies

After the fall of Troy, the victorious Greeks return home. One of these is Odysseus, king of Ithaca, and the obstacles he experiences on his ten-year voyage are told in *The Odyssey*. Even after he arrives at his destination, he is further put to the test before he can reclaim his family, lands, and crown.

As noted in the above entry about The Iliad, due to The Odyssey's adult content, students should read it first in age-appropriate adaptations during childhood and then again in translation in upper high school or college.

Virtues and Themes

Like The Iliad, Homer's The Odyssey is an important example of epic poetry. It presents the struggles and the temptations of life in a way that is still relevant to us today—and it does so with great beauty and elegance that continues to enchant readers nearly three thousand years later.

Resources (in order from elementary grades to adult)

- The Odyssey (Classics Starts series), abridged by Tania Zamorsky
- Tales from the Odyssey series, by Mary Pope Osborne
- The Odyssey, retold by Geraldine McCaughrean
- The Children's Homer: The Adventures of Odysseus and the Tale of Troy, by Padraic Colum
- The Odyssey in translation (Acclaimed translators include Richmond Lattimore, Alexander Pope, Allen Mandelbaum, Robert Fitzgerald, Albert Cook, Robert Fagles, and Stanley Lombardo.)

Classical mythology (first recorded between 700 B.C. and A.D. 8)

Foundational
Reading Level: varies   Interest Level: lower grades and up

For thousands of years, the world's peoples expressed their ideas and beliefs about the divine, the wonders of the natural world, and the origin and destiny of human beings through myths. In fact, myths are some of the first stories ever invented, and they are the foundation of the folklore genre. The mythology of ancient Greece and Rome is central to a study of Western literature and has formed part of the child's literary experience for centuries. Like the Bible, mythology finds its way into children's literature through allusions, retellings, and direct references. Even in the most contemporary tales, classical mythology still influences children's literature.

Ovid's *Metamorphoses* (A.D. 8) was an important work of the classical era and was likely well-known among the youth of that time. Ovid was a Roman poet who drew on the works of other writers (like Virgil, Lucretius, and Homer) to write his masterpiece. It consists of fifteen books that give a poetic narrative of the history of the world, including about 250 Greek and Roman myths. *Metamorphoses* was popular not only in its own time, it also heavily influenced medieval and Renaissance writers, including William Shakespeare.

Virtues and Themes

Like Homer's epics, classical mythology is not only relevant to a lifelong enjoyment of literature and other arts, but also rich in themes relating to human nature and to universal themes and questions. As with other classical works, Greek and Roman myths and tales are best introduced to children through age-appropriate adaptations.

Resources (in order from middle grade to adult)

- *Favorite Greek Myths*, by Mary Pope Osborne
- *D'Aulaires' Book of Greek Myths*, by Ingri and Edgar Parin d'Aulaire
- *Famous Men of Greece: Stories of Great Greek Heroes*, by John Haaren and A.B. Poland
- *The Golden Fleece and the Heroes Who Lived Before Achilles*, by Padraic Colum
- *A Wonder Book for Girls and Boys*, by Nathaniel Hawthorne
- *Tanglewood Tales*, by Nathaniel Hawthorne
- *Bulfinch's Mythology: The Age of Fable*, by Thomas Bulfinch
- *Mythology: Timeless Tales of Gods and Heroes*, by Edith Hamilton
- *World Mythology*, by Donna Rosenberg

Fables by Aesop (probably first recorded by Demetrius of Phaleron about 320 B.C. but composed closer to 600 B.C.)
Foundational
Reading Level: varies   Interest Level: lower grades and up

Facts about both Aesop and his famous fables are elusive. Scholars disagree on a variety of basic facts and details, including the true source

of the stories attributed to him, but one fact is indisputable: this collection of moral tales has had a far-reaching influence on Western
culture from popular thinking to everyday idioms to the arts, including children's literature. Although Aesop's fables were not originally
children's literature, since the genre didn't exist then, they have
been told and retold to children throughout Western history. In fact,
according to humanities professor Seth Lerer, "[Aesop's] fables have
been accepted as the core of childhood reading and instruction since
the time of Plato."[1]

Virtues and Themes

Reading the fables of any culture broadens a student's window on the
world. Reading the fables of Aesop specifically not only broadens a
student's understanding of classical Greek culture but also the many
artistic works that reference them. In addition, the fables are by their
very nature rich in lessons about life, humanity, and morality.

Resources

Choosing a collection of Aesop's fables is a matter of personal preference, rather than one of translation. Numerous editions are filled with
beautiful illustrations, and most are presented as children's books. A
brief Internet search will also offer entire websites devoted to Aesop's
fables. Allow your student to choose a resource that is appealing and
preferably at the appropriate reading level. I personally like the version by Milo Winter with his old-fashioned, charming illustrations; it
was published in 1919. His collection contains enough fables to provide a good grounding in Aesop without overwhelming the reader.

Aeneid, by Virgil (c. 20 B.C.)
Foundational
Reading Level: varies   Interest Level: middle grades and up

Just as Homer's epics were foundational literary works to classical
Greek culture, Virgil's epic of the hero Aeneas was foundational to
classical Roman culture. The Aeneid is a natural sequel to Homer's

---

[1] Seth Lerer, *Children's Literature: A Reader's History from Aesop to Harry Potter* (Chicago:
University of Chicago Press, 2009), 35.

epics, for it picks up at the fall of Troy and traces the efforts of Aeneas to found Rome. The story was intended to glorify the Roman Empire and all its virtues and to persuade its educated citizens to prefer the new imperial form of government to the republic they had previously known. In fact, Aeneas himself was characterized as the ideal Roman citizen, inspirational and impressive for his sense of duty to the state.

Of course, such a powerful testament to the glories of Rome was not meant for adults alone. Young people, too, needed to learn how to become model Roman citizens, so they, too, studied Virgil's masterpiece as part of their education. In fact, since the *Aeneid* was considered a nearly perfect poem and was so important to classical Roman culture, it became a standard text in Latin-centered schoolrooms everywhere for hundreds of years. Today it remains an indispensable part of Western culture. It has had a profound influence on some of the greats of Western literature, such as Dante's *Divine Comedy*, Milton's *Paradise Lost*, and Spenser's *The Fairie Queene*, as well as some children's literature, such as Richard Adams' *Watership Down*.

As with the Greek epics, students should read age-appropriate adaptations of the *Aeneid* first and then translations of the full work in high school.

Virtues and Themes

Some of the themes include the glory of Rome, as well as heroism, the search for a homeland and belonging, homeland as the source of one's identity, fate and divine intervention, and family bonds. The story is also an important example of epic poetry and a companion to a deep study of classical Rome.

Resources (in order from middle grade to adult)

- *Aeneas: Virgil's Epic Retold for Younger Readers*, by Emily Frenkel
- *The Aeneid for Boys and Girls*, by Alfred J. Church
- *In Search of a Homeland: The Story of the Aeneid*, by Penelope Lively
- *The Aeneid of Virgil*, by Virgil—translated by J. W. Mackail (Project Gutenberg e-book)
- *The Aeneid*, by Virgil (Penguin)—translated by Robert Fagles
- *Bulfinch's Mythology: The Age of Fable*, by Thomas Bulfinch

The New Testament from the Holy Bible
(c. A.D. 50–A.D. 95)
Foundational
Reading Level: varies   Interest Level: lower grades and up

Like the Old Testament, the stories of the New Testament are essential reading for anyone who wants a thorough grounding in Western literature. This includes both Christians and non-Christians alike. The acts and words of Jesus Christ, as well as his disciples, have had such a profound impact on our civilization that they need to be understood in the context of their source, the books of the New Testament. The stories are also essential reading for a through grounding in children's literature. Though not written *for* children, stories of the New Testament have been told and retold to children for most of Western history, primarily as part of their religious formation. Along with the works of Homer, Virgil, and Aesop, they also helped form the backbone of the Western child's literary experience.

Virtues and Themes

For Christian students, the New Testament is not only full of good stories that are often referenced in other literature, but also full of doctrinal and spiritual lessons that are key to their religious formation. For students outside of these faiths, the historical, moral, and literary aspects form an essential part of a thorough education.

Resources

See the entry for Old Testament from the Holy Bible for more information and suggested resources.

Beowulf, by anonymous (first known manuscript
c. A.D. 900–1000)
Important
Reading Level: varies   Interest Level: middle grades and up

During the Early Middle Ages, the Roman Empire in Western Europe disintegrated. Constant invasions and wars made books, which were mostly produced by monks, scarcer than ever. The tales young people commonly enjoyed, aside from whatever classical myths and poems survived, were folk stories transmitted orally from generation to generation. Among these, one of the best known is that of the hero Beowulf and his quest to destroy a horrific monster named Grendel.

While the epic we know today was written sometime between 700 and 1000 by a Christian monk, the story itself had been circulating orally for many years by that time. Because the author was Christian and thus saw the tale through a Christian lens, it is important to understand that the *Beowulf* he wrote probably differs markedly from the oral versions in their original pagan context. For those who want to experience the children's literary entertainment of this period as authentically as possible, however, *Beowulf* and other examples of European folklore are the only options available to the modern reader. *Beowulf* stands as a major work of Western literature. In fact, though the single surviving text was not discovered until the 1800s and thus did not influence authors until after that, it is commonly considered to be the first major work of English literature. Fans of J. R. R. Tolkien might be interested in his posthumously published translation edited by his son Christopher even though, according to my research, it received only a lukewarm critical reception, despite the great respect of reviewers for the man himself.

Critically acclaimed translations of *Beowulf* from the original Old English include those by the following authors:

- Michael Swanton
- Michael Alexander
- Frederick Rebsamen
- Seamus Heaney

Virtues and Themes

Not only is *Beowulf* worth reading because it's a first in English literature, it also illustrates the quintessential Anglo-Saxon hero, just as Odysseus is a hero for Greece and Aeneas is for Rome. In addition, *Beowulf* can help students gain deeper insights into Tolkien's fantasy epics, since he was inspired partly by the Anglo-Saxon world and probably *Beowulf* itself. Themes include the conflict between good and evil, loyalty, courage, honor, and revenge, among others.

Resources

If you would like a children's adaptation, try one of these:

- *The Story of Beowulf*, by Henrietta Elizabeth Marshall from Dover Children's Classics
- *Beowulf*, by Michael Morpurgo

Norse mythology (recorded c. A.D. 900–A.D. 1200 but composed much earlier)

Important

Reading Level: varies   Interest Level: lower grades and up

Norse mythology has also been deeply influential in children's literature, although it has not been as much of a part of the Western child's experience as classical mythology has been. Today, however, we can see Nordic mythological influences in both major works (e.g., *The Hobbit*, the Harry Potter series, and the Chronicles of Narnia series, which borrows just as heavily from Greek mythology) and lesser-known works (e.g., Nancy Farmer's *The Sea of Trolls* and Diana Wynne Jones' *Eight Days of Luke*). Norse mythology was not recorded as quickly and systematically as Greek and Roman mythology, so source material was difficult for later writers and scholars to piece together. The dates and authors of original sources are unknown, but the mythology of this people was rich and carefully preserved.

Norse mythology was not recorded for general use until long after it was composed. Our first sources come from the medieval period and consist of two works:

- *The Poetic Edda* (unknown date, probably somewhere between 900 and 1200)—The poems in this collection were likely written in the tenth through thirteenth centuries, possibly by Saemund the Wise or Snorri Sturluson; however, both the date and author are only speculation. This collection is not easily accessible to the average reader since relatively few translations exist, but it is the primary source of Nordic mythology.
- *The Prose Edda* (c. 1200)—Probably written by Snorri Sturluson, this collection is the other major source for Norse mythology.

It contains both genuine Nordic lore, as well as information which may only have been assumed or imagined by Sturluson. Naturally, this has made it difficult for scholars to separate the authentic material from Sturluson's own ideas. Still, *The Prose Edda* contains the most information on early Norse mythology, religion, and history.

Virtues and Themes

Nordic mythology opens a window into ancient Nordic culture and ideas. It also speaks about human nature, justice, and virtues and vices—themes that are universal and timeless for mankind.

Resources (in order from middle grade to adult)

- *D'Aulaires' Book of Norse Myths*, by Ingri and Edgar Parin d'Aulaire
- *Favorite Norse Myths*, by Mary Pope Osborne
- *The Children of Odin: Nordic Gods and Heroes*, by Padraic Colum
- *Bulfinch's Mythology: The Age of Fable*, by Thomas Bulfinch
- *World Mythology*, by Donna Rosenberg

2

The Middle Ages through the Protestant Reformation
1000–1620

Not until the late Middle Ages did the Western world first feel the birth pains of the genre known as children's literature. It seems to have begun with a book of advice written in verse, called *The Book of Curtesye* (author unknown, published in 1477). Aside from this, children enjoyed the same stories that adults enjoyed—Chaucer's *Canterbury Tales*, for example, which was made widely popular thanks to the invention of the printing press. In 1570, the first known picture alphabet was printed, and it served as a teacher resource for reading students. It was called *A Methode, or Comfortable Beginning for all Unlearned*, by John Hart. Close on its heels came *Petie Schole* in 1587, by Francis Clement, which was one of the first spellers.

Over time such books became more commonplace. Because of the Catholic Church's pervasive influence throughout Europe, most children learned to read and write mostly through primers, psalters, riddles, prayer books, and alphabets, some of which contained rhymes. These were all pious Christian works with a goal for spiritual formation as well as literacy. Books designed to entertain or develop the imagination would not exist for a long time to come.

Although this era offered relatively little child-friendly literature to its youth outside of the ancient canon of folklore and Bible stories, children did enjoy some newer tales. Mixed in with older folklore were tales of new heroes, some of which have lived on through the centuries in a variety of retellings and which are today considered classics.

Liturgical dramas also entered the arts during this era and entertained people of all ages. These were divided into three categories:

miracle plays, morality plays, and mystery plays, and all were typically performed near or inside a church. Each kind of play emphasized a different aspect of Christianity, such as Bible stories or the lives of saints.

Lullabies and nursery rhymes of Europe (composed throughout the era)
Foundational
Reading Level: varies
Interest Level: pre-school through lower grades

Mothers have no doubt been singing to their children for millennia, but the sources of our familiar English lullabies date from the Middle Ages. From this era also originated the familiar simple rhymes of modern childhood. Both lullabies and nursery rhymes are rooted in Catholic teaching and culture. For example, lullabies were often about the Virgin Mary, because of the centrality of the Nativity story in the religious formation of children. During this era, however, collections of these verses were not available to children as they are today. They mostly existed "in the margins" of medieval poetry, as Seth Lerer put it, passed along orally like mythology and folktales.[1] Although Internet research will turn up lullabies and nursery rhymes from this era, some performed in audio recordings, you may want to try finding the collection *Fleas, Flies, and Friars: Children's Poetry from the Middle Ages*, by Nicholas Orme.

You may also want to bypass the medieval sources and turn right to those with which modern society is familiar, such as Mother Goose collections. Research on individual lullabies and nursery rhymes can often turn up interesting meanings and origins, too, such as that of "Baa, Baa, Black Sheep." This is believed to be a thirteenth-century rhyme that was written not merely to entertain young children, but rather to make a political statement about the new wool taxes that King Edward I imposed after his return from the Crusades!

[1] Seth Lerer, *Children's Literature: A Reader's History from Aesop to Harry Potter* (Chicago: University of Chicago Press, 2009), 60–61.

Virtues and Themes

The rhythms and rhyme schemes of nursery rhymes help children develop an ear for language, which can then help them learn to read. Nursery rhymes also help expand the imagination with their silly nonsense and vivid images. In addition, they are perfect first stories and songs for young children. For older children, especially those who have not been exposed to nursery rhymes, they not only support their imagination and sense of rhythm, they also provide a connection with history, since many of them are hundreds of years old and provide simple windows to times gone by.

Play of Daniel, by the youth of Beauvais, France (mid-twelfth century)
Important

Reading Level: unknown   Interest Level: upper grades

For medieval children, literature was often experienced as theatrical productions, a custom that evolved out of the common liturgical traditions of the era and out of the customary schoolroom recitations often required of students. The *Play of Daniel* was one of the productions well-known among children during the Middle Ages. Two separate versions exist: one by the twelfth-century English Hilarius and the other by twelfth-century students at the cathedral school in Beauvais, France. The Beauvais version is much better known and is recommended as the children's version. It is best watched as a performance online. Because of the constantly shifting nature of Internet videos, I have not provided links here; however, students should be able to find online, CD, or DVD performances without too much trouble.

Virtues and Themes

This is one of the earliest liturgical dramas, one of the earliest operas, and one of the earliest Christmas pageants. Each of those reasons alone makes it worth watching in a literature, religion, or music program. In high medieval style, it presents the story of the prophet Daniel from the Old Testament, ending when Daniel foretells the birth of Christ.

King Arthur legends (1485 and onward)
Foundational
Reading Level: varies
Interest Level: lower grades through upper grades

The first reliable mention of King Arthur appeared in 830 in *Historia Brittonum* by the Welsh monk Nennius. In that account, however, Arthur was portrayed not as a king, but as a warrior. Legends about him existed before this historical reference and continued to develop over the centuries, until 1485 when the definitive work about King Arthur was published. This was the famous *Le Morte d'Arthur*, by Sir Thomas Malory, and it was the work that shaped our modern imagination about King Arthur.

It was not Malory who popularized the King Arthur legend, though. As essential as his saga is to a study of King Arthur, the Victorian poet Alfred, Lord Tennyson, was the one who revived the tales for his contemporaries with his poetic retelling, *Idylls of the King*. This poem influenced generations of writers, poets, playwrights, and screenwriters. Today, both adult and children's literature is rich with King Arthur tales.

Virtues and Themes

The King Arthur tales contain themes important to those studying the Middle Ages—chivalry, courtly love, heroism, loyalty, honor, and more—but these themes are also valuable to discuss for their own sake. In addition, the tales are exciting, magical, and in some cases thought-provoking, as well as appealing to children and teens.

Resources (in order from middle grade to adult)

- Picture books, such as Selina Hasting's *Sir Gawain and the Green Knight* and *Sir Gawain and the Loathly Lady*
- *The Stories of King Arthur and His Knights*, by Howard Pyle
- *King Arthur and His Knights of the Round Table*, by Roger Lancelyn Green
- *The Once and Future King*, by T. H. White
- *Sir Gawain and the Green Knight*—translations to consider include those by Bernard O'Donoghue, Simon Armitage, and Burton Raffel

- *Bulfinch's Mythology: The Age of Chivalry* (short version), by Thomas Bulfinch

Robin Hood tales (first recorded in 1500)

Foundational

Reading Level: varies

Interest Level: lower grades through upper grades

Tales of Robin Hood have enjoyed such a respectable place in the Western children's literary canon for so long that it is hard to believe that in medieval times they were looked upon with disdain by both authors and moralists. In fact, they were thought to have a corrupting influence on young minds. Robin Hood tales, however, could not be discarded. They had been passed down orally as folktales long before the first written version appeared in 1500 as *A Little Geste of Robin Hood*, by Richard Pynson. Since then, Robin Hood has lived on in Western imaginations, finding voice in all sorts of versions since then, including movies and spoofs.

Virtues and Themes

Everyone, whether they have read the Robin Hood tales or not, knows that the legendary outlaw was a principled, clever man whose mission was to rob from the rich and give to the poor during the unjust reign of Prince John, whose brother King Richard was away at the Crusades. This theme alone is worth some deep, thoughtful discussion, especially for parents who want their children to learn how to grapple with challenging moral and ethical questions. Other themes include honor, friendship, faithfulness, and loyalty to both country and family, among others. Students who read the Robin Hood tales will also be well prepared for the many allusions and references that appear in pop culture and in art, including other literature.

Resources

You can choose from many written versions today, but the best-known version is probably *The Merry Adventures of Robin Hood*, by Howard Pyle. If you enjoy getting as close to original sources as

possible, you may find *A Little Geste of Robin Hood* online, but I have
not found a translation from the Old English. If the link is still active,
one excellent Internet resource on all things Robin Hood (including
Pynson's version) is http://www.robinhoodlegend.com.

Other Children's Classics of This Era

Colloquy, by Bishop Aelfric (c. late 900s)
Reading Level: unknown   Interest Level: unknown

The Golden Legend, by Jacobus de Varagine (c. 1260s)
Reading Level: upper grades and up
Interest Level: upper grades and up

This was one of the first literary works on the lives of the saints, and
it was also one of the most popular and influential works during the
Middle Ages. The first English translation from the original Latin was
published by William Caxton in 1483.

Gesta Romanorum, author unknown
(c. early fourteenth century)
Reading Level: unknown
Interest Level: estimated middle grades and up

Translated as "Tales of the Romans," this was a favorite collection of stories in the Middle Ages, featuring all sorts of biblical and
folk characters from many places and sources, including some as
far away as the Orient. It was also the source text for some famous
authors, like Chaucer and Shakespeare. Children enjoyed these
tales through the seventeenth century. English editions exist but are
not plentiful.

Resources

Two places to start if you would like to explore this important work
are Internet Archive, https://archive.org, and *Gesta Romanorum, or
Entertaining Moral Stories*, translated by Charles Swan and Wynnard
Hooper.

Stans Puer ad Mensam (Table Manners for Children),
by John Lydgate (early 1400s)
Reading Level: unknown
Interest Level: estimated lower grades and up

Mankind, by anonymous (mid-1400s)
Reading Level: unknown   Interest Level: estimated upper grades

This is another play thought to be well-known among medieval youth. Students who would like to experience it should find a performance (video or live) if possible; the script is available, as well. Try to find a version in the original language alongside a translation.

The Book of Babees, by anonymous (c. 1475)
Reading Level: unknown   Interest Level: unknown

The Book of Curtesye, published by William Caxton (c. 1477)
Reading Level: unknown
Interest Level: estimated lower grades and up

This was one of the first manuscripts printed and sold for children, published about 1477. Presented as poetry, it is essentially a book of etiquette, covering matters of concern like table manners and good topics of conversation.

The Schoole of Vertue, by Francis Segar (1557)
Reading Level: unknown   Interest Level: unknown

*A New Interlude for Children to Play Named Jack Juggler,
Both Witty and Very Pleasant*, by anonymous (c. 1553–1558)
Reading Level: unknown
Interest Level: estimated lower grades and up

This was the first English-language play written just for children.

*Actes and Monuments (also known as Foxe's Book of
Martyrs)*, by John Foxe (1563)
Parents Cautioned!
Reading Level: unknown
Interest Level: estimated upper grades

Published in 1563, the book gives detailed accounts of mostly English and Scottish Protestants who suffered persecution under Catholic monarchs during the Protestant Reformation. Because the book is anti-Catholic, as well as gruesome, it may not be suitable reading for all student readers, but it would be a mistake to ignore its important role in the literary experience of Protestant children in the English-speaking world. It also had an influence on subsequent children's literature.

A Methode, or Comfortable Beginning for all Unlearned, by John Hart (1570)
Reading Level: unknown   Interest Level: unknown

Petie Schole, by Francis Clement (1587)
Reading Level: estimated 1–3
Interest Level: estimated lower grades

This was one of the first spellers.

3

The Colonization of New England
through the Mid-nineteenth Century
1621–1849

Observant readers will notice that the gap between the last book listed for the previous era (*Petie Schole* in 1587) and the first book listed for this one (*Orbis Sensualium Pictus* in 1658)—both entries noted in the "other classics" lists—is nearly a century. Although other books were published for or about children, they were few and far between. The children's book market on either side of the Atlantic had not yet found its footing and would not until the eighteenth century. Of course, in America the early years of settlement were mostly a time of survival and adjustment, so the establishment of a book market was not yet a priority for the colonists.

Even if it had been, though, many Protestant colonists in New England were more interested in the spiritual and moral formation of their children than in the development of their imaginations. Although they enjoyed some types of play, children were not encouraged to play creatively in the early decades of the seventeenth century. Among Puritans especially, fiction was widely considered to be spiritually dangerous. During this period most books written for the young taught manners, religion, or literacy skills. Not until the late seventeenth century, with the publication of John Locke's *Some Thoughts concerning Education* in England, do we begin to see changing attitudes toward children and their unique needs. Though Locke's assertions that children should be free to play in accordance with their "natural tempers" were not new, they only now were beginning to be widely accepted in England.[1] These ideas, of course, crossed the ocean to America, as well.

Aesop's fables and folktales were in accordance with the standards of most English-speaking people, and as this era continued and the needs of children gained more attention, other kinds of literature began to find their place in the market. Authors began to write moralistic fiction that preached strong lessons about Christian behavior and belief. Also, along with older works from previous eras, such as classical tales and *Gesta Romanorum*, children also began to enjoy more fairy tales and some adult works like *Robinson Crusoe*.

It wasn't until the mid-1700s that the children's publishing business had its true beginnings. Englishman John Newbery started out selling books and newspapers and even dealt in patent medicines. In the 1740s, though, he tried his hand at children's publishing with *A Little Pretty Pocket-Book*. Soon, he became the first to recognize the potential of children's publishing and to give it the push it needed to become a serious business. By the time this era ended, the market for children's literature had taken a firm hold in England, and it eventually did so in America, as well.

The Pilgrim's Progress, by John Bunyan (1678)
Foundational
Reading Level: 10.4   Interest Level: upper grades

Second only to the Bible in popularity in America, *The Pilgrim's Progress* was extremely important to children's literature. Though not written with children in mind, John Bunyan's allegory of Christian's journey to the Celestial City became the most influential literary work in the lives of Protestant American children throughout the eighteenth and nineteenth centuries. It was one of the only books approved for Sunday reading, and it was eventually published in various editions just for children. *The Pilgrim's Progress* was so widely read, in fact, that several fictional children in later children's books allude to it: the March girls in *Little Women*, Huckleberry Finn in *The*

---

[1] Peter Hunt, ed., *Children's Literature: An Illustrated History* (Oxford: Oxford University Press, 1995), 11.

Adventures of Huckleberry Finn, and Rebecca in *Rebecca of Sunnybrook Farm.* A study of children's literature is not complete without a reading of this classic and influential allegory.

Virtues and Themes

Within this single, short novel, readers experience the entirety of a Christian's life, from conviction to conversion to the heavenly gates, as well as the many different experiences that are often part of that journey. All the characters, settings, and events are allegorical, which provides a useful literary lesson for any student and many topics for meaningful spiritual discussions. Parents should remember that the story reflects Bunyan's Protestant theology, and it includes occasional negative references to the Catholic Church of Bunyan's time.

Resources

If you would like to introduce elementary-aged children to *The Pilgrim's Progress,* try Helen L. Taylor's excellent adaptation entitled *Little Pilgrim's Progress.* As a child I loved this book so much that I eventually replaced my battered copy and read it to my own children.

The New England Primer, edited by Benjamin Harris (1690, first version)

Important
Reading Level: varies
Interest Level: lower through middle grades

Published around 1690 by printer Benjamin Harris, this is the first textbook used by American schoolchildren, and it remained in widespread use well into the nineteenth century. In New England it was so essential to children's studies that it was called "The Little Bible of New England," and by 1830 it had been reprinted and adapted for different locations and ethnic groups in about 450 editions. There was even one printed for the Mohawk Indians in both the Mohawk and English languages. You will notice that the primer does not have an author listed. The primer was based on Harris' textbook called *The Protestant Tutor* (published in England), and it was adapted and revised many times with influences from various writers—especially John Cotton, whose short catechism was incorporated into the primer around 1700. Because of that, it is impossible to credit just one author. Facsimiles of the primer are easy to find today, however, and might be worth browsing to gain a sense of how children were entertained and educated in America's formative years.

Virtues and Themes

The primer not only contains literacy, spiritual, and behavior lessons, but also provides a way for children to understand how early American children were educated. This may be particularly interesting within the context of an American history study, so that the past can become more real and relatable.

Folktales and fairy tales of Europe (first published 1696)
Foundational
Reading Level: varies   Interest Level: lower grades and up

Folktales and fairy tales existed in oral form long before authors began to publish them in written form. The year 1729 marks the likely beginning of the English revival of these tales with the introduction of Mother Goose. The tales were originally recorded by French writer Charles Perrault in 1697 as *Histoires ou contes du temps passé: avec des moralitez*. In 1729 they were translated into English by Robert Samber as *Histories, or Tales of Past Times. Told by Mother Goose*. The first American edition was released in 1785 as *Mother Goose's Melodies*.

The *Mother Goose* anthology contained some of the stories that are today most known and loved in the Western world—"Cinderella," "Little Red Riding Hood," "Sleeping Beauty in the Wood," and "Puss in Boots"—as well as many others that have been forgotten. Retold tales by Frenchwoman Jeanne-Marie de Beaumont soon followed in the mid-eighteenth century, which included the contemporary favorite, "Beauty and the Beast."

The Grimm brothers made their entrance into literary history in the early nineteenth century with their large collection of folktales and fairy tales. They are still the most famous of all the European story collectors, and they sparked a trend in storytelling throughout

Europe. The famous Danish writer Hans Christian Andersen made his mark as part of this trend with many retold tales, some of which are still popular today—"The Little Match-Seller" (usually known as "The Little Match Girl"), "The Little Mermaid," "The Ugly Duckling," "The Snow Queen" (the source tale for the hit movie *Frozen*), and several others. By the end of the nineteenth century, the collector Andrew Lang had made his far-reaching entrance into the genre, as well, enchanting children with his famous twelve-volume Fairy Book collection. This is still available today, including such volumes as *The Blue Fairy Book*, *The Red Fairy Book*, and so on.

These collectors didn't just revive a fading oral tradition, however. Throughout the nineteenth and twentieth centuries their influence increased, for their retellings influenced new generations of writers and scriptwriters, some of whom are among the most beloved authors of children's literature. Recall Kenneth Grahame's "The Reluctant Dragon" and *The Wind in the Willows*, E. Nesbit's *The Book of Dragons* and her other fantasies, J. K. Rowling's Harry Potter series, and even J. R. R. Tolkien in his epic saga of Middle-earth.

For those students interested in exploring the realm of fairy tales and folktales as originally published, it is important to note that many of these stories were not intended for children. They are often gruesome and shocking, speaking more to the political and social issues of their home countries than to the child's imagination. This includes some of those stories that children today know best, such as "Snow White" and "Sleeping Beauty." Because of this, parents who want their children to read the original versions may want to preview them first.

Virtues and Themes

Fairy tales are the products of the nations and eras in which they arise. As such, they reflect the ideas, fears, and hopes of the people there; in fact, many fairy tales are deeply symbolic and not really children's tales at all. Reading fairy tales, however, will prepare children for the many ways in which these stories influence other literature of all eras and genres, as well as other aspects of society.

Fairy tales are worth reading for their own sake, too, for several reasons. First, fairy tales present humanity in all its many guises, and they explore the perennial conflict between good and evil and the consequences that arise out of such actions. Second, fairy tales enrich and expand the imagination. Third, they allow children to face and ponder fears in a safe context. Fourth, they provide the perfect introduction to fantasy, which is one of the major literary genres in children's literature. Finally (for now), they provide cultural windows into other nations and allow children to understand how traditional stories can spread and develop in different ways from nation to nation.

Resources

The following list contains a sampling of folk and fairy stories in their older or oldest English forms, which are appropriate for middle-grade to upper-grade readers. I have not included suggestions for lower-grade readers, because there are so many excellent retellings available. The suggestions below mostly feature the fairy tales retold by the most well-known collectors, including the Brothers Grimm, Charles Perrault, and Hans Christian Andersen. Keep in mind, though, that fairy tales abound throughout the world and have been collected by other folklorists and storytellers, as well. In addition, interested readers can find collections from individual countries, such as Ireland, England, and Norway.

- *The Classic Fairy Tales*, by Iona and Peter Opie
- The Fairy Book series, by Andrew Lang
- *The Original Folk and Fairy Tales of the Brothers Grimm: The Complete First Edition*, translated and edited by Jack Zipes
- *Hans Christian Andersen: The Complete Fairy Tales and Stories*, translated from the Danish by Erik Christian Haugaard

The One Thousand and One Nights, translated by Antoine Galland (1704–1717)

Important
Reading Level: unknown
Interest Level: estimated middle grades and up

The collection of tales widely known as *The Arabian Nights* was first published outside of the Middle East in France between 1704 and 1717. Galland translated it as a response to the widespread interest in Eastern cultures among Europeans of his day. *The One Thousand*

and One Nights was drawn from an ancient and complex collection of Middle Eastern tales that had been well-known for centuries. It had an impact in the Western world, however, not only by sending its imagination into new and exciting realms but by inspiring its writers with new literary ideas and forms, such as the frame story. It became so popular that some of its tales are familiar to many people even today. Western children know *Nights* best through tales like "Aladdin" and "Ali Baba and the Forty Thieves." In 1791, the first adaptation for children was published, called *The Oriental Moralist, or the Beauties of the Arabian Nights Entertainments.*

Virtues and Themes

Like European fairy tales, the stories in *The One Thousand and One Nights* enrich the imagination and offer many themes for discussion—luck, hospitality, greed, forgiveness, and the power of stories, for example. In addition, they provide good examples of several literary devices, such as the frame story, foreshadowing, and stories within stories.

Resources

To enjoy *The One Thousand and One Nights*, it is best to choose a retelling. The latter two below were written specifically for children:

- *The Arabian Nights*, translated by Sir Richard F. Burton (one of the earliest)
- *The Arabian Nights*, by Muhsin J. Al-Musawi
- *One Thousand and One Arabian Nights*, by Geraldine McCaughrean
- *The Storyteller's Daughter: A Retelling of* The Arabian Nights, by Cameron Dokey
- *Tales of The Arabian Nights: Stories of Adventure, Magic, Love, and Betrayal*, by Donna Jo Napoli

Robinson Crusoe, by Daniel Defoe (1719)
Foundational
Reading Level: 12.3   Interest Level: upper grades

Considered by many to be the first major English novel, the well-known island castaway story *Robinson Crusoe* has had an immense

impact on both children's and adult literature. It was published in
1719 and experienced quick success in the literary world. It became
so popular that it deeply influenced the educational philosophy of
Jean-Jacques Rousseau and spawned the entire category of island
stories. Many of the children's stories that were influenced by
Crusoe became classics themselves, including *Treasure Island*, *Swiss
Family Robinson*, *Stuart Little*, *Where the Wild Things Are*, and even
Winnie-the-Pooh.

Virtues and Themes

Because of its difficulty, *Robinson Crusoe* isn't accessible to all grade-
school students; some students may need to postpone reading it until
upper high school or college. For those who are ready, however, it
is worth reading for a couple of reasons. First, because it is the proto-
type of the island novel, *Crusoe* reverberates throughout the literary
world (and even other media), providing a kind of template for other
island tales that followed. Second, it is rich in meaningful themes,
including the importance of repentance, the struggle for survival,
the value of self-sufficiency, and the necessity of overcoming fear to
find happiness.

Gulliver's Travels, by Jonathan Swift (1726)

Important
Reading Level: varies; original edition 13.5
Interest Level: lower grades through upper grades

Although published as an adult satirical novel, *Gulliver's Travels* captured the imagination of children soon after its publication in 1726.
In fact, the wild, fantastic adventures of its hero, Gulliver, became so
popular that they have been retold in various editions many times and
have even been produced in several film versions. Despite the story's
juvenile appeal, an abridgment is recommended, for the original version is beyond a high school reading level. In fact, the first abridgment
was probably the one published by J. Stone and R. King only a year
after the original version was printed. Still, *Gulliver's Travels* is worth
reading in some form, either in childhood or in adulthood, because
of its status as one of the most important and influential works of

English literature and because of the enjoyment it has brought children since the eighteenth century.

Virtues and Themes

For older readers who are ready for it, this novel is a classic example of satire—in this case of eighteenth-century life. For younger readers, at least in an abridged form, it is a delightful fantasy. The novel also addresses several themes worth discussion. Examples include the superiority of moral authority versus physical power, the idea of a utopian society, and the limitations of the human mind.

Resources

Below is a list of several storybook versions and adaptations:

- *Gulliver's Travels* (Stepping Stone Series), adapted by Nick Eliopulos
- *Rip Van Winkle/Gulliver's Travels* (Greathall Productions audio series), retold by Jim Weiss
- *Gulliver's Travels* (Classic Starts series), abridged by Martin Woodside
- *Gulliver's Travels* (Classic Stories series), by Peter Clover
- *Jonathan Swift's Gulliver's Travels for Kids*, by Luke Hayes

The Children of the New Forest, by Captain Marryat (1847)

Important

Reading Level: 7.8   Interest Level: middle grades

During the latter half of the nineteenth century, British adventure stories that celebrated the idea of British superiority over the rest of the world became especially popular in children's literature. Captain Marryat made his mark in literary history by writing the first adventure story for children, which gave rise to adventure as a dominant genre during this century. In addition, *The Children of the New Forest* is thought to be the first historical novel written for children in English. He is known for *Masterman Ready; or, The Wreck of the Pacific*, which was his first novel for children, but he is especially celebrated for the survival tale *The Children of the New Forest*.

Virtues and Themes

Students who are studying British history may want to read this novel at the same time. Marryat wrote in strong support of the British monarchy and of patriotism during a period of revolution throughout Europe and reforms in England. Themes beyond British patriotism include wilderness survival, self-sufficiency, courage, and the character-building challenge of making the best of misfortune.

Other Children's Classics of This Era

Orbis Sensualium Pictus, by Johann Comenius (1658)
Reading Level: estimated pre-school
Interest Level: pre-school through lower grades

This was the first educational resource in which a pictorial alphabet was arranged by sound. It was reprinted in hundreds of other editions and translations for many years afterward and was influential in the production of many later textbooks. Up to this point, alphabet books had focused on conveying religious ideas with each letter.

A Token for Children: An Exact Account of the Conversion, Holy and Exemplary Lives, and Joyful Deaths of Several Young Children, by James Janeway (1671)
Reading Level: unknown
Interest Level: estimated lower grades and up

A popular book of the seventeenth century, *A Token for Children* was a morbid collection of tales about children who lived saintly lives and died young. Published in Janeway's native England in 1671, it soon found its way to American shores and into the hands of children. This was one of the first books written for children that influenced later children's literature of the eighteenth and nineteenth centuries, and it was widely read by Puritan children. It was also the first to feature contemporary characters, instead of ones from the distant past.

A Little Book for Little Children, by Thomas White (c. 1671)
Reading Level: unknown
Interest Level: estimated pre-school and up

This was one of the first books for very young children, written to instill Puritan ideals.

New Spelling-Book, by Thomas Lye (1677)
Reading Level: estimated 1–3
Interest Level: estimated lower grades

Divine Songs, Attempted in Easy Language for the Use of Children, by Isaac Watts (1715)
Reading Level: unknown   Interest Level: lower grades

Published first in England in 1715, this collection of Christian poetry became so popular that it soon crossed the ocean to America. Many editions of the book have been published, twenty of them in Watt's own lifetime. *Divine Songs* was so widely read, in fact, that it influenced the work of others, including the famous writers Benjamin Franklin, Lewis Carroll, and Emily Dickinson. The book was part of the typical Protestant childhood for about 200 years.

A Child's New Plaything, by Mary Cooper (1743)
Reading Level: estimated 1–3
Interest Level: estimated lower grades

This was one of the earliest English spellers to attempt entertainment as well as instruction.

Tommy Thumb's Song Book, by Mary Cooper (1744)
Reading Level: estimated 1–3
Interest Level: estimated pre-school and up

This was the first book of nursery rhymes in the English language.

A Little Pretty Pocket-Book, by John Newbery (1744)
Reading Level: unknown   Interest Level: estimated lower grades

An English bookseller at first, John Newbery eventually became the most successful publisher and marketer of children's literature in his time. He also wrote children's books. Though none are well-known today, his *A Little Pretty Pocket-Book* (1744) is considered the first book for children that was written for both edification and entertainment. His contribution to the genre was considered so important that in 1922 a new annual award for the most distinguished contribution to American children's literature was established and named the John Newbery Medal in his honor. Today, although children's book authors win many different awards and honors, the Newbery Medal is still considered to be the pinnacle of literary achievement for children's authors in the United States.

The Governess, or The Little Female Academy, by Sarah Fielding (1749)

Reading Level: unknown
Interest Level: estimated middle grades

This was one of the first books written for girls.

Lives of the Noble Greeks and Romans, by Plutarch (1579)

Reading Level: unknown
Interest Level: estimated middle grades

This was popular and influential among children because it was well written and exciting. Although this was published in the previous era, I include it here because it was so widely read during this era. John Newbery published an abridgment in 1762.

The History of Little Goody Two Shoes, by anonymous (1765)

Reading Level: unknown
Interest Level: estimated middle grades

The true author of this book may actually be Oliver Goldsmith, but this is just speculation. It was one of the first highly successful children's novels.

Adventures of a Bank-Note, by Thomas Bridges (1770)

Reading Level: unknown
Interest Level: estimated middle grades

Lessons for Children, by Anna Laetitia Barbauld (1778)
Reading Level: 1–2   Interest Level: estimated lower grades

This was the first series of age-adapted reading primers for children printed with large text and wide margins. It was in print for more than a century.

Hymns in Prose for Children, by Anna Barbauld (1781)
Reading Level: 5   Interest Level: middle and upper grades

Like *Lessons for Children*, this book was used widely in schoolrooms. It is also believed to have influenced the poets William Blake and William Wordsworth.

The Parent's Assistant, by Maria Edgeworth (1796)
Reading Level: 5   Interest Level: middle grades

This is a collection of children's stories that is known for giving the first realistic portrayal of children in children's literature.

Simple Susan, by Maria Edgeworth (1796)
Reading Level: 4–5   Interest Level: middle grades

Tales from Shakespeare, by Charles and Mary Lamb (1807)
Reading Level: 12.8   Interest Level: middle grades

This child-friendly collection is still used today to introduce children to Shakespeare's plays in a readable prose format. Given that the reading level is much higher than the interest level, parents may want to read these stories aloud.

The Swiss Family Robinson, by Johann Wyss (1812 in Switzerland; translated into English in 1814)
Reading Level: 9.8   Interest Level: middle grades

This was the first novel written that became widely known as a children's classic.

History of the Fairchild Family, by Mary Martha Sherwood (published in three volumes 1818–1847)
Reading Level: unknown
Interest Level: estimated middle grades

Though now forgotten among youth, both the author and her book were one of the best known of their time—despite the fact that the book contains frightening stories of children suffering the pains of the grave and of hell.

"A Visit from St. Nicholas," by Clement Clarke Moore (1823)
Reading Level: 4.3   Interest Level: lower grades

This beloved poem is known today as "The Night before Christmas" or " 'Twas the Night before Christmas." It shaped the modern conception of Santa Claus and is still well-known among American children.

Struwwelpeter, by Heinrich Hoffman (published in German, 1845; English translation, 1848)
Reading Level: unknown
Interest Level: estimated middle grades

4

The First Golden Age of Children's Literature
1850–1928

The impact that the Victorian and Edwardian eras had on the development of children's literature can hardly be exaggerated. It was during this period that two important trends converged. First, publishers produced cheaper books due to a growing market, and they also improved the quality of their publications. Second, society was beginning to give more consideration to the unique needs of children than it ever had, which meant that children were encouraged to read more and that they had more books to choose from than ever before. Despite the shameful scourge of widespread child labor in both Great Britain and the United States, childhood itself bloomed in new and beautiful ways during this era. It is within this context that children's literature entered its first golden age with fantasy (i.e., *Alice in Wonderland*) and Darwinism-inspired tales (i.e., *The Water-Babies*) taking center stage.

Those of us who want our children to know the great children's classics tend to encourage books from this golden age without realizing it—*The Secret Garden, Little Women, The Adventures of Tom Sawyer, Alice in Wonderland, The Wizard of Oz, Black Beauty, The Wind in the Willows, Winnie-the-Pooh,* and others. With the golden age novels safely under our children's belts, many of us feel that we have done our literary duty.

This is as we should feel, too. Though the writing of this era can be overly wordy and linguistically dense for many contemporary children, First Golden Age literature remains some of the most beautiful and powerful ever written for them. Not only that, but many of these classics have had a strong influence on both adult and children's literature of later eras. Some of them even made strong social or political statements that affected the development of our society, such as *Black Beauty*, one of the first animal welfare novels.

Many books have come and gone in the eras that followed, and some of them have found their own places as great children's classics, but none have usurped the special place that First Golden Age books and poetry have in the realm of children's literature. Even bookstores that place contemporary literature front and center often have shelves dedicated to beautiful editions of these classics. As you work your way through this section, I encourage you to look for ways to make your selections accessible and meaningful to your children and teens. Help them through the linguistic and historical barriers, so that the full glory of these beautiful tales can shine through.

Poetry of Edward Lear (1846–1877)
Important
Reading Level: 3–5   Interest Level: lower grades

Like many Victorians of his day, Edward Lear enjoyed wordplay and raised that pastime to new heights with his poems and limericks. Some scholars believe that he used wordplay not only for amusement but also to challenge Victorian sensibilities regarding propriety and social status. He was so innovative that even in his own time he was recognized as the creator of a brand-new literary genre: nonsense. Through his nonsense verse he could use humor, wordplay, and other devices to address difficult subjects like cruelty and pain. Lear is best remembered today for his beloved poem "The Owl and the Pussycat." He is also the poet who invented the modern form and meter of the limerick. Lear wrote four books of nonsense verse:

- *A Book of Nonsense* (1846)
- *Nonsense Songs* (1870)—contains "The Owl and the Pussycat"
- *More Nonsense* (1872)
- *Laughable Lyrics* (1877)

The nonsense genre itself has had a profound influence on the literary world. Not only does it continue to delight children and adults alike with its ability to address serious themes through humor (Lewis Carroll and Shel Silverstein being the best-known nonsense authors), it helped give rise to the movements of surrealism and theater of the absurd.

Virtues and Themes

The best reason to read nonsense poetry, in my opinion, is that it compels readers to play with words and engage their imaginations in ways they otherwise wouldn't. Little about a nonsense poem is meaningful when viewed under a microscope. Paradoxically, well-written nonsense poems such as Lear's somehow do make sense when realism is gleefully abandoned. In its own way, the nonsense genre provides all readers with a ticket to the realm of childhood, where life is often baffling, yet wondrous. Lear's poetry is the perfect introduction to this delightful genre.

Tom Brown's Schooldays, by Thomas Hughes (1857)
Important
Reading Level: 9.2   Interest Level: middle grades

Although the British classic *Tom Brown's Schooldays* was not the first school story written for children, it has the distinction of being the cornerstone work of the whole sub-genre of school stories that followed. Published in 1857, it is also one of the earliest children's novels to be written specifically for boys. Many of the novels it influenced became (or are becoming) classics themselves, such as *Goodbye, Mr. Chips*, *A Separate Peace*, and the Harry Potter series.

Virtues and Themes

Themes of *Tom Brown's Schooldays* include the meaning of being an English citizen, the author's vision of the ideal man (honesty, integrity, loyalty, strong work ethic, etc.), and nineteenth-century school life. These ideas are valuable discussion topics for students both as a literary and philosophical exercise. The novel may also provide an interesting supplement to a British history course.

The Water-Babies: A Fairy Tale for a Land Baby, by Charles Kingsley (1863)
Important
Reading Level: 8.3   Interest Level: middle grades

Charles Darwin's landmark theories on the origin of species had a profound impact on the world during the latter half of the nineteenth century and beyond, and children's literature was not exempt. In children's literature, however, Darwin's influence was felt mostly in stories in which characters grow and change—or are stunted, in the case of more racist and class-conscious stories. Though a fantasy, Charles Kingsley's *The Water-Babies* is the novel most influenced by Darwin's ideas. In it, Kingsley thematically touched on several of his personal interests and concerns. This included Darwin's theories, which he did not see as at odds with the biblical account of creation. For a long time, *The Water-Babies* was popular reading for children, but it fell out of favor over time as more readers began to object to its overt prejudices against various groups. Its critique of child labor, however, has been credited with helping to pass the Chimney Sweepers Act in 1864. This act prohibited employers from hiring minors as chimney sweeps.

Virtues and Themes

Parents may want to know up-front that this is a fairy tale about a child who drowns but has adventures in a transformed state that allows him to breathe and swim underwater. As strange as it sounds, it was a popular tale in Victorian times and is accessible to both children and adults. At the child's level it is a fantasy of underwater adventures, and at the adult level it is a strong commentary on Victorian child labor practices, education, and other issues of the day.

Parents may also want to know that Kingsley also expresses negative views toward Jewish, Irish, and American people. So why read it? Along with its fairy tale wonder and relation to Victorian English history, the novel does address Christian values and beliefs in a positive way, such as the Golden Rule, redemption, and atonement.

Alice in Wonderland, by Lewis Carroll (1865)
Foundational
Reading Level: 7.4   Interest Level: middle grades

This nonsense tale has had such a profound impact on children's literature and Western culture that most people are familiar with allusions to it, even if they have not read the book—for example, "Cheshire smile," "Mad Hatter," "Wonderland," "white rabbit," and "Off with their heads!" Carroll also has the distinction of impacting not just one genre, but two: fantasy and nonsense. In Victorian times children's literature was entering its First Golden Age, which included the rise of both fantasy and nonsense literature.

Though other Victorian authors within these genres also produced beloved classics, the *Alice* stories were probably the first important works to depart from the didactic, rational storylines that had been common up to that point. Instead, they plunged the reader into a beautiful dreamworld where nothing made sense, where rules were meant to be broken, and where children were more sensible than adults.

It is easy to substitute one of the excellent movie adaptations that have been produced over the years, but as with almost all literature, movies cannot adequately substitute for the original work. A reading of Carroll's original works with the original illustrations by Sir John Tenniel is a treat not to be missed. This includes the sequel to *Alice in Wonderland*, titled *Through the Looking-Glass, and What Alice Found There.*

Virtues and Themes

If the impact of *Alice in Wonderland* upon literature and culture isn't enough to convince readers of its value, the story itself might. The tale stretches both the imagination and the mind, gives readers a sampling of quintessential Victorian nonsense prose and poetry, and throws in intriguing themes worth some discussion, too. The most notable of these themes include the absurdities of adulthood from a child's perspective, the curiosities of etiquette and social customs, the bewildering transition between childhood and adulthood, and the struggle to understand one's identity in the world.

Little Women, by Louisa May Alcott (1868–1869)
Important

Reading Level: 7.9   Interest Level: middle grades and up

One of America's most beloved nineteenth-century writers, Alcott is best known for her novel *Little Women*, which was originally published in 1868 as *Little Women: Meg, Jo, Beth, and Amy*. Because she was under much pressure to contribute to her struggling family's income, Alcott had been writing for some time before her publisher asked her to try her hand at a juvenile novel.

Little Women was published to acclaim, but many readers may not know that the novel we love today was published in two parts. The first part tells the story of the coming-of-age of the four March sisters, who are based on Alcott's own sisters; it is the part that nineteenth-century audiences knew as *Little Women*. This book was a success, both commercially and critically, so Alcott followed it up with the second part in 1869, which was titled *Good Wives: A Story for Girls*. It was soon reissued as the second part of *Little Women* and tells the story of the March sisters as young women.

This classic is notable for being one of the first American coming-of-age stories, as well as the novel that first presented the ideal of the "all-American girl," as noted by literary historian Sarah Elbert.[1]

Virtues and Themes

One of the reasons *Little Women* is so beloved may be that it speaks deeply to the human need for family, community, security, and love. Plus, Alcott created characters that ring true and allow the reader to identify with them almost as if they are friends from afar. Themes worth discussion include growing up, sisterhood and family, finding one's place in the world, duty, sacrifice, loyalty, honor, and friendship. In addition, for those seeking classic literature featuring strong, independent girls and women, *Little Women* is an excellent choice.

---

[1] Sarah Elbert, *A Hunger for Home: Louisa May Alcott's Place in American Culture* (New Brunswick, N.J.: Rutgers University Press, 1987), 171.

Historical fiction by G. A. Henty (1871 onward)
Important

Reading Level: unknown   Interest Level: middle grades and up

A prolific writer with 122 titles to his credit, most of them for children, Henty wrote historical adventures that were particularly popular with boys. He also had a strong influence on other adventure writers of his day—so much, in fact, that such novels were said to be written in "the Henty tradition." Henty's works are still read today, though not as widely as some other classic authors. It is important for readers to be aware that Henty was an imperialist and a supporter of British colonization, and some critics of his work protest his treatment of race and class in some of his novels. However, for his important contribution to the canon of children's literature, Henty should not be overlooked. Interested readers may like to begin with his first title, *Out on the Pampas* (1871).

Virtues and Themes

For students who enjoy historical fiction, Henty novels are an excellent option. Set in various historical eras and settings, they provide much information along with their adventure narratives. Specific themes will vary from book to book, but generally they include courage, tenacity, God's faithfulness, and other traditional Christian values.

The Princess and the Goblin, by George MacDonald (1872)
Important

Reading Level: 6.1   Interest Level: middle grades

"I write, not for children," George MacDonald famously said, "but for the child-like, whether they be five or fifty or seventy-five." Indeed, his fantasies have captured the imaginations of both children and adults ever since their publication in the latter half of the nineteenth century. He is one of the most influential fantasy writers, making his mark on famous modern writers such as C. S. Lewis, Madeleine L'Engle, and J. R. R. Tolkien. The title recommended above is one of his best and most influential, though he is also well-known in children's literature for his fantasy *At the Back of the North Wind.*

Virtues and Themes

Although MacDonald's fantasy tales can be challenging for young readers, they are imagination-stretching as all fairy tales tend to be, and they contain Christian parallels. Unusual for fairy tales, *The Princess and the Goblin* also has two strong, very young child characters (one a princess, the other a miner's son) who form an unlikely friendship in the depths of a mountain crawling with goblins. A magical grandmother assists them. Themes include courage, the power of imagination, trust and obedience without full understanding, and the value of learning to see and understand in different ways.

Black Beauty, by Anna Sewell (1877)
Important
Reading Level: 6.1   Interest Level: middle grades

When Anna Sewell wrote *Black Beauty*, she not only wrote a moving fictional account of the life of a nineteenth-century American horse, she also profoundly influenced the animal rights movement. In fact, animal protection activist Bernard Unti called the novel "the most influential anticruelty novel of all time".[2] It was probably responsible for the elimination of the nineteenth-century bearing rein (replaced by the overcheck), which was used to prevent a carriage horse from lowering its head, and it inspired other anticruelty novels. And although the novel was written for adults, it has become one of the great classics of children's literature, as well as the foundation of modern children's animal stories.

Virtues and Themes

Because the story is told from a horse's point of view during times of both joy and suffering, animal welfare and the relationship between

---

[2] Quoted in *Encyclopedia of Animal Rights and Animal Welfare*, ed. Marc Bekoff (Westport, Conn.: Greenwood Press, 1998), 313.

animals and humans are the most important themes and well worth thoughtful discussion. Other themes include courage, perseverance, the power of kindness, and the dangers of ignorance. Sensitive or animal-loving readers will find it painful to follow Black Beauty's account of the abuse and suffering he experiences, but those who keep going will be rewarded with a happy ending.

Treasure Island, by Robert Louis Stevenson (serial—1881–1882; book—1883)
Foundational
Reading Level: 8.3   Interest Level: middle grades

Considered by some critics to be one of the greatest stories ever written in the English language, *Treasure Island* is also indisputably one of the most enduring novels written for children. Originally, this tale of high adventure and swashbuckling pirates was conceived as a magazine serial entitled "The Sea Cook." It ran for seventeen weekly installments in *Young Folks' Magazine* beginning in October of 1881. In 1883, however, it was published as a novel and retitled *Treasure Island*. From that point forward, *Treasure Island* became popular among adults and children alike. It has retained an honored place in the children's literature canon ever since, spawning numerous abridgments and adaptations for film, theater, radio, music, and even video games. Our modern concepts of pirates and pirate catchphrases ("Yo ho ho and a bottle of rum!") come directly from *Treasure Island*.

Virtues and Themes

The fact that it is considered to be one of the all-time children's greats is perhaps reason enough to read *Treasure Island*, but I contend that it is also worth reading to help student readers better understand popular pirate stereotypes and the pirate stories that followed *Treasure Island*. Our cultural concept of pirates is based on Stevenson's novel. More than that, though, the novel is an excellent example of good storytelling, offering complex characters, plenty of action, and several themes worth discussion—although to overdo analysis may ruin a young reader's experience of what should be a rollicking, exciting adventure. Still, for those interested, important themes worth discussing include coming of age, the consequences of greed and desire, moral ambiguity, courage, and the conflict between barbarianism and civility.

The Adventures of Huckleberry Finn, by Mark Twain (1885)
Foundational
Reading Level: 6.6   Interest Level: middle grades and up

Almost from the beginning, Twain's brilliant novel has had a rocky existence. Only a month after it was published, it was banned by the Concord, Massachusetts, Library Committee. Throughout the years it has been alternately banned with scathing criticism and hailed with gushing praise. Today it is firmly part of the American literary canon, despite the outrage it continues to provoke because of its controversial racial themes. Its greatest praise comes from two other great American authors. Ernest Hemingway once said that "all modern American literature comes from one book by Mark Twain called *Huckleberry Finn*... There was nothing before. There has been nothing as good since."[3] And William Faulkner, whose own writing was influenced by Twain's novel, said that Twain was "the father of American literature."[4]

Whether these claims are true or not, *Huckleberry Finn* is certainly notable for being one of the first American novels to be written in a dialect that accurately reflects the way Twain's characters would have spoken in real life. As a children's book, however, its appropriateness is questionable, for it wasn't really written as such. While some sources, like the Mark Twain Boyhood Home and Museum in Hannibal, Missouri, claim that it is a children's book, other sources say that Twain intended it more for adults—even though it is a direct sequel of *The Adventures of Tom Sawyer*, which was clearly written for children. Because the novel's protagonists are children, and because the novel has long been a fixture in the American high school literature curriculum, I include *Huckleberry Finn* here as a must-read for teenagers.

[3] Ernest Hemingway, *Green Hills of Africa* (New York: Charles Scribner's Sons, 2002), 23.
[4] Quoted in William Rossky, "*The Reivers* and *Huckleberry Finn*: Faulkner and Twain", *Huntington Library Quarterly* 28, no. 4 (August 1965): 373, JSTOR, https://doi.org/10.2307/3816830.

Because of its racial themes and its use of Southern colloquialisms of the time period (i.e., the n-word), I strongly suggest that readers prepare themselves with some background research about the novel.

Virtues and Themes

Because it's one of the great American novels, student readers may want to experience *Huckleberry Finn* for that reason alone. It is also an adventure story and a close look at nineteenth-century racism from an actual nineteenth-century author. This, it can be argued, is an important experience for young readers, since reading about racism only in history books affords them a too-comfortable distance. Themes worth discussion include freedom, racism, prejudice, slavery, personal growth, the conflict between civil law and moral law, hypocrisy, the human struggle with conscience, and the power of empathy to effect moral change.

Poems by Eugene Field (late 1800s)
Foundational
Reading Level: estimated 2–3   Interest Level: lower grades

Although Eugene Field wrote primarily for adults during his career, he is famous today for his contributions to children's literature. To his dismay, he was known as the "poet of childhood" and the "poet laureate" of children, and many of his poems are still some of the best-loved and most reprinted of all children's poetry. He is particularly known for "Wynken, Blynken, and Nod" (1892), "The Duel" (1894), "Little Boy Blue" (1888), and "The Sugar-Plum Tree" (1892).

Virtues and Themes

To approach these poems as a formal literary study would be to miss the point of Field's delightful rhymes. They are meant to delight and humor children, celebrating all that is bright and fanciful in the realm of imagination. That they are lovely examples of poetry is a bonus. Older readers might find it worthwhile to read them as such in a beginning poetry study that examines rhyme, rhythm, alliteration, and other poetic devices.

The Wonderful Wizard of Oz, by L. Frank Baum (1900)

Important

Reading Level: 7.0   Interest Level: middle grades

Although *The Wonderful Wizard of Oz* has been wildly popular in some form ever since its publication in 1900 and has become a fixture in American pop culture, it is not considered a model example of quality writing, and in that sense, it does not belong in a serious study of literature. The novel is important to the development of children's literature for two reasons, though. First, it is considered the first genuinely American fairy tale. Although it wasn't the first fairy tale to be written by an American, no other American fairy tale or fantasy reflected American characteristics the way *The Wonderful Wizard of Oz* did. The novel was also one of the first fairy tales to dispense with the moralistic and often dark and gruesome elements that had been characteristic of the genre. Instead of seeking to frighten children into good behavior, as children's literature often did back then, Baum simply wanted his tale to entertain and appeal to the reader's sense of wonder. More than one hundred years later, it still does.

Virtues and Themes

The Wonderful Wizard of Oz was, of course, intended to be delightful, imagination-stretching entertainment for the twentieth-century American child. As the first American fairy tale, however, it may also be worth reading in the context of an American literature or history course. Topics for discussion include courage, the meaning of home, perseverance in the face of great odds, the value of hopes and wishes, friendship, and the nature of good and evil.

The Tale of Peter Rabbit, by Beatrix Potter (1902)

Foundational

Reading Level: 4.2   Interest Level: lower grades

Few children's authors and illustrators have achieved the status of Beatrix Potter. After all, who has not heard of Peter Rabbit, Mr. McGregor, or Benjamin Bunny? Who has never seen at least a nod to her art, if not her books themselves? Potter wrote more than twenty picture books, some of them still popular today among children all over the world, and *Peter Rabbit* has never been out of print. In fact, it is the second best-selling hardcover children's book of all time in America after *The Poky Little Puppy*.[5] Potter is also known as the first children's author to consider marketing her characters in various products (toys, home goods, etc.), a venture that was extremely successful. Even today Potter merchandise is widely available.

Virtues and Themes

Potter's beautiful tale is worth reading just for its delightful drawings and its important contribution to the world of children. On the other hand, for children who are just learning how to think about and discuss literature, it provides an easy beginning. The themes of *Peter Rabbit* center on the consequences of both obedience and disobedience.

Five Children and It (1902) and The Railway Children (1906), by E. Nesbit

Important

Reading Level: 5.7 and 5.5 respectively

Interest Level: middle grades and up

Though not as widely read anymore, E. Nesbit is notable in the timeline of children's literature because she is considered one of the most "innovative" of this era's authors for children. She was even dubbed by her biographer as the "first modern writer for children."[6] These two books are representative of her best work. In fact, *Five Children and It* is said to have set the standard for British children's fantasy in the early twentieth century.

Virtues and Themes

Five Children and It is a fantasy in which magical beings and objects enter our world, and it is thought to have influenced C. S. Lewis'

---

[5] Anita Silvey, *100 Best Books for Children* (Boston: Houghton Mifflin Harcourt, 2004), 33.

[6] Julia Briggs, *A Woman of Passion: The Life of E. Nesbit, 1858–1924* (London: Hutchinson, 1987), xi.

Narnia tales. Its main theme is the consequences of making wise and unwise wishes. As the old adage goes, "Be careful what you wish for!"

Fans of family stories may want to give *The Railway Children* a try. Themes include goodness, kindness, the importance of family, self-sufficiency, and friendship. It also explores the question of what kind of responsibility people have to their neighbors, especially within a class system like England's.

Anne of Green Gables, by L. M. Montgomery (1908)
Important
Reading Level: 7.3   Interest Level: middle grades and up

Although many books of this period have become beloved classics, few have achieved the international fame that *Anne of Green Gables* has. Tourists from all over the world—and particularly Japan, which has a love affair with all things Anne—flock to Anne's "home" each year on Prince Edward Island. There they can visit the places associated with Anne and honor Montgomery's memory. Television shows, toys, and many other spin-off items have been produced for Anne fans, and the 1985 mini-series by Kevin Sullivan has become a modern classic in the film world.

That *Anne of Green Gables* is so universally treasured isn't the only reason to include it in a study of children's literature, however. After all, children's literature is full of beloved characters and tales. Along with *Little Women*, *Anne of Green Gables* is also one of the earliest examples of literature celebrating girls and girlhood. Note that I refrain from calling it an early example of feminist literature, because that term can sometimes convey a combative spirit, which *Anne of Green Gables* does not have. In a literal sense it is feminist—but in the best sense of the word. As a character Anne embodies all the admirable attributes associated with modern womanhood—intelligence, independence, imagination, strength, spirit, humor, and grit.

Boys, too, may read and appreciate *Anne of Green Gables*, of course. Anne's nemesis throughout the novel is Gilbert Blythe, whom she marries later in the series, and Anne's predicaments are so amusing that it's hard to recommend the novel only to girls. *Anne of Green*

Gables has been said to influence other authors as well, such as J. K. Rowling, author of the Harry Potter series.

Virtues and Themes

Most *Anne of Green Gables* fans would probably admit that Montgomery tends to be wordy. At the same time, nobody surpasses her for exquisite descriptions, and for this reason alone she might be considered a role model for developing writers. Of course, this is not the main reason to read *Anne of Green Gables*. The main reason, I would argue, is that Anne is one of the most delightful characters ever created. Like Sherlock Holmes, she comes so vividly to life on the page that some fans have thought her real. For students, then, she is the perfect subject for a study of characterization, along with Marilla, Matthew, and the other characters of Avonlea who also come alive on the page. Themes of *Anne of Green Gables* are many and shift as Anne grows up. Some of the overarching ones, though, are the meaning of friendship, the blessing of a secure home, growing up, the wonder of nature and the imagination, and the value of education and ambitions.

The Wind in the Willows, by Kenneth Grahame (1908)
Foundational
Reading Level: 8.2   Interest Level: middle grades

Published in 1908 at the height of the First Golden Age, this beloved novel about Rat, Mole, Toad, and Badger began as a series of bedtime stories that Grahame told his son. It went on to become not only one of the most critically acclaimed children's novels ever written, but it is also known for its more adult subtext about the English class system and a utopian vision of Edwardian bachelorhood and country life. Popular since its publication, it has been published in multiple editions and languages and has been made into films, as well. It takes one of the top places among children's classics today and also offers meaningful reading for adults.*

---

*If you enjoy movie versions of classic tales, try Disney's excellent 1949 adaptation of key portions of the novel. This film is not full-length, so it has been combined with Disney's equally worthy adaptation of Washington Irving's classic short story "The Legend of Sleepy Hollow." The double feature is titled *The Adventures of Ichabod and Mr. Toad*.

Virtues and Themes

If a child was restricted to only a handful of books to read, *The Wind in the Willows* would be a top contender for the list with its beautiful writing, almost mythical setting, gentle humor and wisdom, and memorable characters. Themes include the warmth and hospitality of home, loyalty and acceptance in friendship, the dangers of greed and consumerism, British class conflicts and divisions, the glory of adventure, the superiority and romance of country life, and the consequences of bad choices.

The Story of Mankind, by Hendrik Willem van Loon (1921)

Important

Reading Level: 9.9   Interest Level: upper grades

Though most children today have never heard of *The Story of Mankind*, let alone read it, this book represents a landmark in children's publishing. Published in 1921, *The Story of Mankind* received the first Newbery Medal (1922), which is today the most coveted award in America among children's book authors. It helped to set the standard for subsequent Newbery winners, some of which are nonfiction, some of which are poetry, and most of which are novels—but all of which are excellent works of literature. The serious student of children's literature should not bypass this important classic.

Virtues and Themes

Today in the twenty-first century, *The Story of Mankind* has much against it, even for a Newbery winner. Perhaps the most serious flaw is that van Loon intended to paint world history with a broad brush, and yet he narrowly focused on the white experience with little attention paid to other races and their contributions to the world. At the same time, it is a groundbreaking book as the first Newbery winner, and it does provide readers with the broad sweep of history, despite its flaws. Such an overview in narrative form may not only be more interesting than a history textbook but may also help students in more focused historical studies by providing an overall context. Because van Loon published his book in the early twentieth century, the book has been given updates by other writers several times. Readers may choose the original version or the updated version. Creationist readers may want to skip or discuss the sections on evolution.

Winnie-the-Pooh, by A. A. Milne (1926)
Foundational
Reading Level: 4.6   Interest Level: lower grades and up

In the history of children's literature, few characters have touched the world more than Winnie-the-Pooh. As often seems to be the case with the most beloved children's books, the Winnie-the-Pooh books weren't written *for* children at all. A. A. Milne wrote for the child within all of us and is said to have rarely read his stories to his son, the real-life Christopher Robin. Four books make up the Winnie-the-Pooh canon: two story books, *Winnie-the-Pooh* and *The House at Pooh Corner*, and two poetry collections, *When We Were Very Young* and *Now We Are Six*.

The Pooh books have been translated into at least 46 languages (and possibly more by one count). In fact, the Latin translation was the first foreign-language book to find a place on the New York Times bestseller list, and it stayed there for twenty weeks. Pooh has found such an audience with children and adults alike, in fact, that the books have spawned a huge industry of movies, toys, games, and spin-off children's books. They have even inspired adult books such as *The Tao of Pooh*, and Pooh quotes often sprinkle mugs, T-shirts, posters, and other media.

Virtues and Themes

It's hard to imagine a world without the comforting, sweet presence of Pooh, Piglet, Tigger, and the other friends in the Hundred Acre Wood. They are the very stuff of childhood innocence, even as they offer gentle wisdom that adults can appreciate. The Pooh stories celebrate childhood, freedom, nature, and friendship in ways that no other literature does, perhaps because of Milne's unique style and voice. In addition, even though they are suitable for young children, they offer much food for thought that older children and adults can ponder and discuss.

Millions of Cats, by Wanda Gág (1928)

Foundational

Reading Level: 3.5   Interest Level: lower grades

Until 1928, picture books could contain beautiful pictures, but as a genre they leaned more heavily on words than pictures to tell children a story. With *Millions of Cats*, Gág was one of the first author-illustrators to introduce the concept of letting words and pictures work interdependently to tell a story. It was also the first picture book to enjoy both literary and popular success, and it has influenced picture book authors and illustrators ever since. Gág helped set the stage for the modern concept of the picture book, where the pictures typically play a role in telling the story. It was also the first picture book to receive a Newbery Honor.

Virtues and Themes

While younger children may simply enjoy the story and striking illustrations, older children may find its position as the first modern picture book interesting. The story also has themes that parents may want to discuss with either younger or older children, such as the nature of beauty, how beauty should be judged, and how beauty relates to happiness. It also addresses loneliness and the universal longing for human companionship. A reading of *Millions of Cats* may also fit well into an art program, since picture book illustration is a valid art form in its own right. Parents may want to discuss why Gág chose to illustrate in the style she did and how her illustrations enhance the story.

Other Children's Classics of This Era

The Wide, Wide World, by Susan Warner (1850)

Reading Level: unknown   Interest Level: estimated upper grades

This was one of the earliest and best-selling American domestic novels.

The Coral Island: A Tale of the Pacific Ocean,
by R. M. Ballantyne (1858)
Reading Level: 9.3   Interest Level: upper grades

This novel was William Golding's inspiration for *Lord of the Flies* and is one of the most important examples of the boy's adventure story that was so popular in the Victorian era.

The science fiction novels of Jules Verne,
including *Journey to the Center of the Earth* (1864),
20,000 Leagues Under the Sea (1869–70), *Around the
World in 80 Days* (1872), et cetera
Reading Level: 9.6–10.8   Interest Level: middle grades and up

Verne's novels are adult novels that had a great impact on the development of science fiction. They have been widely enjoyed by children in the United States.

Hans Brinker, or The Silver Skates, by Mary Mapes Dodge
(1865)
Reading Level: 8.2   Interest Level: middle grades

Ragged Dick, by Horatio Alger (1868)
Reading Level: unknown   Interest Level: middle grades and up

The Brownies and Other Tales, by Juliana Horatia Ewing
(1870)
Reading Level: unknown   Interest Level: estimated lower grades

This forgotten book is notable for its longstanding contribution to Western culture and thus deserves a special mention here. The first tale in the book, "The Brownies," centers on dutiful and helpful children. When Girl Guides (a scouting club for girls) began in England in 1910, its junior chapter was named Brownies after the tale. In 1912 the Americans followed suit with the creation of Girl Scouts.

At the Back of the North Wind, by George MacDonald
(1871)
Reading Level: 5.4   Interest Level: upper grades

What Katy Did, by Susan Coolidge (1872)
Reading Level: 7.2   Interest Level: middle grades

The Adventures of Tom Sawyer, by Mark Twain (1876)
Reading Level: 8.1   Interest Level: middle grades and up

Heidi, by Johanna Spyri (published in two parts in German in 1880 and 1881; first published in English in 1884)
Reading Level: 8.2   Interest Level: middle grades

Uncle Remus, His Songs and Sayings, the Folk-Lore of the Old Plantation, by Joel Chandler Harris (1880)
Reading Level: unknown   Interest Level: estimated lower grades and up

This is one of the first and most notable African-American folklore collections.

Five Little Peppers and How They Grew, by Margaret Sidney (1881)
Reading Level: 7.9   Interest Level: middle grades

The Prince and the Pauper, by Mark Twain (1881)
Reading Level: 9.5   Interest Level: middle grades and up

The Adventures of Pinocchio, by Carlo Collodi (1883)
Reading Level: 5.3   Interest Level: middle grades

The publication listed here is the first child-friendly version of Collodi's original dark, adult novella.

King Solomon's Mines, by H. Rider Haggard (1885)
Reading Level: 8.9   Interest Level: middle grades

Haggard is known for pioneering the "lost world" literary sub-genre in which mysterious, uncharted lands are explored.

Little Lord Fauntleroy, by Frances Hodgson Burnett (1886)
Reading Level: 8.1   Interest Level: middle grades

Kidnapped, by Robert Louis Stevenson (1886)
Reading Level: 7.6   Interest Level: upper grades

The Jungle Book, by Rudyard Kipling (1894)
Reading Level: 7.4   Interest Level: middle grades

Moonfleet, by J. Meade Falkner (1898)
Reading Level: 8.5   Interest Level: middle grades

The Story of Little Black Sambo, by Helen Bannerman (1899)
Reading Level: 3.9   Interest Level: lower grades

The original version of this picture book is no longer easily available because it has been censored due to its racial stereotyping. I include it here because of its wide popularity for more than half a century before it came under scrutiny. It is notable not only because of this popularity, however, but also because it depicts one of the first black child-heroes in children's literature that wasn't portrayed as a buffoon.

A Child's Garden of Verses, by Robert Louis Stevenson (1900)
Reading Level: estimated 2–3   Interest Level: lower grades

This beloved poetry collection is Stevenson's only work for young children and contains many classic poems.

Kim, by Rudyard Kipling (1901)
Reading Level: 7.7   Interest Level: upper grades

Though most readers are more familiar with *Just So Stories* and *The Jungle Book*, *Kim* is widely regarded as one of Kipling's finest novels. It is also considered by some scholars and critics to be one of the finest works of children's literature, although others do not consider it a children's tale at all. *Kim* is one of the best examples of imperial adventure literature, a popular sub-genre in the Victorian era. This fascinating tale is a coming-of-age odyssey through India as the orphan of a British soldier helps a Tibetan lama seek a legendary river.

Just So Stories, by Rudyard Kipling (1902)
Reading Level: 6.4   Interest Level: middle grades

Rebecca of Sunnybrook Farm, by Kate Douglas Wiggin
(1903)
Reading Level: 8.1   Interest Level: middle grades

A Little Princess, by Frances Hodgson Burnett (1905)
Reading Level: 6.0   Interest Level: middle grades

A Girl of the Limberlost, by Gene Stratton-Porter (1909)
Reading Level: 6.1   Interest Level: upper grades

A Secret Garden, by Frances Hodgson Burnett
(first serialized in 1910; published in entirety in 1911)
Reading Level: 6.3   Interest Level: middle grades

Peter Pan and Wendy, by J. M. Barrie (1911)
Reading Level: 7.2   Interest Level: middle grades

Although I could not leave out one of childhood's most beloved literary characters, it's important to note that *Peter Pan* was originally written in 1904 as a dramatic play. The subsequent novel entitled *Peter and Wendy* was written for adults, and young people don't seem to have embraced it as much as they have stage and screen versions. With that in mind, parents might want either to bypass the novel altogether in favor of a high-quality staged production or save it for their teens.

Daddy-Long-Legs, by Jean Webster (1912)
Reading Level: 6.1   Interest Level: upper grades

Uncle Wiggily's Adventures, by Howard Garis (1912)
Reading Level: unknown   Interest Level: lower grades

This is the first of a series.

Pollyanna, by Eleanor Porter (1913)
Reading level: 5.2   Interest Level: middle grades

Understood Betsy, by Dorothy Canfield Fisher (1916)
Reading level: 5.9   Interest Level: middle grades

The Cambridge Book of Poetry for Children, edited by
Kenneth Grahame (1916)
Reading level: estimated 1–4   Interest Level: lower grades
through middle grades

Raggedy Ann Stories, by Johnny Gruelle (1918)
Reading Level: unknown   Interest Level: lower grades

This is the first of a series.

The Story of Dr. Dolittle, by Hugh Lofting (1920)
Reading Level: 5.1   Interest Level: middle grades

The Voyages of Dr. Dolittle, by Hugh Lofting (1922)
Reading Level: 5.7   Interest Level: middle grades

Rootabaga Stories, by Carl Sandburg (1922)
Reading Level: 5.5   Interest Level: middle grades

The Velveteen Rabbit, by Margery Williams (1922)
Reading Level: 4.9   Interest Level: lower grades

Bambi, A Life in the Woods, by Felix Salten (1923)
Reading Level: 4.9   Interest Level: middle grades

The Boxcar Children, by Gertrude Chandler Warner (1924)
Reading Level: 3.9   Interest Level: lower grades

The Story of Rolf and the Viking Bow, by Allen French
(1924)
Reading Level: 5   Interest Level: middle grades

Like J. R. R. Tolkien, Allen French was a fan of Norse sagas. In addition to this tale set in eleventh-century Iceland, he wrote *The Story of Grettir the Strong* and *Heroes of Iceland*.

5

The Great Depression through World War II
1929–1945

October 1929. This was the month that changed the course of not only American history, but world history. After the Great Stock Market Crash, it soon became apparent to many that the global economy had fallen apart, ushering in a depression that profoundly changed—and sometimes destroyed—millions of lives. Children's publishing did not escape the ravages of the Great Depression. Nor did it escape the effects of World War II or the rising popularity of radio and movies. The First Golden Age of children's literature was over.

And yet, this era of struggle and hardship was not as difficult for the American and British publishing industry as one might expect. Publishers did pare down their lists during the most difficult years, but they also began publishing paperback editions, which were cheaper to make and to buy. These editions were easier to carry, which was especially important to soldiers during World War II. Reading was one of the few diversions they could enjoy while on active duty.

Despite (or perhaps because of) the unique challenges of this era, publishers managed to produce some of the most powerful literature ever written for children. Both realism and fantasy rose to new heights. During these sixteen years the industry introduced the world to authors who are still beloved and widely read: Laura Ingalls Wilder, J. R. R. Tolkien, E. B. White, and Antoine de Saint-Exupéry, among others. Not only did these authors add their own brilliance to the children's literary genre, their work also had a profound influence on the Second Golden Age that soon followed. Because of them, the children's book market would never be the same.

The Story of Babar, by Jean de Brunhoff (1931)
Foundational
Reading Level: 4   Interest Level: lower grades

Published in 1931, *The Story of Babar* is the first book in the longest-running picture book series ever published. The fiftieth book in the series was published in 2014. Babar the elephant is an iconic figure in children's literature today, but according to scholars the stories about Babar have influenced children's literature itself. Like *Millions of Cats*, the Babar books have been said to be the origin of the modern picture book. Beloved author-illustrator Maurice Sendak (*Where the Wild Things Are*, etc.) was deeply influenced by the series. "Babar," he said, "is at the very heart of my conception of what turns a picture book into a work of art. The graphics are tightly linked to the 'loose' prose-poetry, remarkable for its ease of expression."[1] Although some scholars have pointed out that some of the series' outdated themes (like social elitism) are potentially offensive to modern audiences, Babar continues to delight children today.

Virtues and Themes

Adult reactions to this story can vary between extremes, from warmth to shocked indignation. Children will likely just enjoy the story the way children always have, so parents may want to determine whether Babar conflicts with their values before bringing him home. Those who choose to read it will encounter not only a time-tested tale and charming illustrations, but also emotion-laden themes of death, courage, optimism, and endurance in the face of trials.

Little House series, by Laura Ingalls Wilder (1932 onward)
Foundational
Reading Level: 4.6–5.8   Interest Level: middle grades

It is hard to overstate the impact that these novels about a young girl's youth on the American frontier have had on American culture. Told in simple language, Wilder's tales made this bygone era come

---

[1] Quoted in "Babar," Encyclopedia.com.

alive in such fascinating detail that they are still read across the nation both for fun and education. Of all the children's books published since the 1932 edition of *Little House in the Big Woods*, few of them are as well-known or widely read as the Little House series. So influential was Wilder's series, in fact, that in 1954 the American Library Association created a new award for lasting achievements in children's literature—the Laura Ingalls Wilder Award—and named her its first recipient (although it has since been renamed). The series has not only entertained three generations of young readers, it has also delighted adults, challenged scholars, inspired several movies and a nine-season television series, and served as the basis for a commercial industry that includes tourist sites and commercial products associated with Laura's life and her books. Even highways were renamed in her honor!

Virtues and Themes

The Little House books are special in that they were written by a woman who didn't need to research pioneer life as some other authors do, because she lived it herself. Each of Laura's nine novels, except for *Farmer Boy*, is based on her own memories of growing up in the days when Kansas was still a territory and young men yearned to find their golden destinies in the Wild West. *Farmer Boy* is based on the real-life memories of Laura's husband, Almanzo, who grew up in upstate New York. In her series, Laura gives modern readers a vivid, remarkably detailed picture of life on the frontier while still telling memorable stories that children have loved for decades. Themes for discussion are many, such as the importance of family, man versus nature, courage, honor, and growing up.

The Hobbit, or There and Back Again, by J. R. R. Tolkien (1937)
Foundational
Reading Level: 6.6   Interest Level: upper grades

When *The Hobbit* reached the public in 1937 as a children's book, it wasn't an overnight sensation, but it did earn enough acclaim for the publisher to ask for a sequel. This resulted in the adult epic saga

The Lord of the Rings. More importantly, though, *The Hobbit* was a breakthrough in fantasy literature that has influenced both adult and children's literature ever since. Indeed, Tolkien's tales of Middle-earth opened a market for high fantasy where one had not previously existed. They also established the structures and elements of the genre, which have influenced fantasy writers ever since. Indeed, some readers and scholars doubt that some of today's most acclaimed children and adult fantasy novels would exist if it were not for the works of J. R. R. Tolkien.

Virtues and Themes

Tolkien's saga of Middle-earth (all four books together, plus related books) is arguably both the beginning and end of high fantasy. Nothing has surpassed it in beauty, scope, or adventure. Although Tolkien's language can be challenging and wordy, *The Hobbit* is the perfect introduction to high fantasy for both fantasy-lovers and for those who prefer other genres. It is also rich in themes worth pondering, such as the quest, courage, greed and temptation, heroism, power, and personal growth.

The Yearling, by Marjorie Kinnan Rawlings (1938)
Foundational
Reading Level: 5.0   Interest Level: upper grades

When *The Yearling* was published in 1938, it was fortunate to have been marketed as an adult novel; this was what Rawlings intended when she wrote it. If it had been marketed as the children's book it is known as today, it would have likely never received the phenomenal attention that helped turn it into one of the most important American classics ever written. Not only was it a Book-of-the-Month Club selection, translated into many languages, and made into a movie in 1946, it was also the winner of the 1939 Pulitzer Prize for the Novel. Even now, it is the only children's (formerly adult) novel to have won that prize. In addition, it contributed to the Florida environmental movement, inspiring activists to protect the land about which Rawlings wrote. Today, the area is known as the Marjorie Kinnan Rawlings State Park and is on the National Register of Historic Places.

Rawlings was a regional writer, and her coming-of-age tale is firmly set in post-Civil War, rural Florida. What makes *The Yearling* special, though, is the way it transcends its regional setting to touch upon universal themes of love, loss, grief, and growing up that are important to all readers. Newbery-winner Lois Lowry once described how the novel had influenced her as a writer: "It was the first book that allowed me to see how the writer could elicit an emotional reaction—she made my mother cry.... *The Yearling* made me understand what fiction could accomplish and what a writer could do with words."[2] As a work of literary art, *The Yearling* holds a special place in American children's literature.

Virtues and Themes

In a practical sense, *The Yearling* is an excellent supplement to an American history course, because it helps bring the people of 1870s rural Florida to vivid life. This is may be especially illuminating for readers who don't live in Florida, since this region gets little attention in most American history courses. *The Yearling* is also worthwhile reading for its literary beauty and moving coming-of-age story. It's important to note, however, that animal lovers or very sensitive readers may find the novel emotionally painful, because one of the important themes is the human conflict between a love for animals and our need to kill them sometimes for self-preservation. Some other themes include growing up and the loss of childhood innocence, the necessity of learning to cope with death, and the importance of family in the struggle for survival.

Curious George, by Margret and Hans Rey (1941)
Foundational
Reading Level: 2.6   Interest Level: lower grades

While he is yet another iconic children's book character in America, the lovable monkey Curious George is beloved all over the world. In

---

[2] Quoted in Anita Silvey, *Children's Book-a-Day Almanac* (New York: Roaring Book Press, 2012), 221.

some countries he is even known by different names, such as Peter Pedal in Denmark. In America, of course, he will always be known as Curious George. Many stories have been written about Curious George, but originally the Reys wrote just seven, beginning with the classic *Curious George*. Today, the story has been made into three movies, a television series, and a commercial product line, and it is considered one of the most important contributions to children's literature of the twentieth century. In 2012 *Curious George* was inducted into the Indie Choice Book Awards Picture Book Hall of Fame. The original story has never been out of print.

Virtues and Themes

These tales about lovable George are great fun for children because he is always getting into perilous scrapes yet cheerily manages to come out on top every time. He is one of the great literary friends that every child should have. Of course, the overarching theme of *Curious George* is none other than curiosity, and George's adventures provide good discussion topics about the value of curiosity and exploration, as well as how to follow curiosity wisely.

A Tree Grows in Brooklyn, by Betty Smith (1943)
Important   Parents Cautioned!
Reading Level: 5.8   Interest Level: upper grades

In addition to its enormous popularity as soon as it was published, *A Tree Grows in Brooklyn* is considered one of the great American novels. It was enormously popular with soldiers during World War II, and it has been embraced by both adults and teens because its themes and characters appeal to both groups. Because it is a coming-of-age novel about a young girl in early twentieth-century Brooklyn, it is best suited for older adolescents. However, as a window into history, a compelling story, and a model of powerful, beautiful writing, *A Tree Grows in Brooklyn* is an American treasure.

Parents should be aware that despite its lyrical writing, this novel is partly a gritty examination of American poverty, which may be shocking to some young readers. Although it was written at a time when writers weren't as explicit as they often are now, Smith does

touch on alcoholism and sexuality, and the novel contains some vulgar language and a near-rape.

Virtues and Themes

This novel can be enjoyed on several levels—as a richly detailed window into the lives of poor Americans (many of them immigrants) in
the early twentieth century, as a tender young adult tale about a girl
trying to mature into womanhood in a challenging environment,
and as a collection of character studies within the context of old
Brooklyn. Some themes include American poverty, the early immi-
grant experience, the role of "old-world" religion and customs in the
context of the "new world," coming-of-age, the need for life beyond
mere survival, and the effects of alcoholism.

The Little Prince, by Antoine de Saint-Exupéry (1943)
Foundational
Reading Level: 5.0
Interest Level: middle grades through upper grades

Written by a French military pilot during the most volatile period
of the twentieth century, *The Little Prince* is an unusual publishing
phenomenon. Saint-Exupéry indicated that he wrote and illustrated
it *as* a children's story but *for* grown-ups. Perhaps because of that, it is
accessible to both adults and children just as the best books often are;
therefore, it can be enjoyed and understood on several levels. The
novella is also unusual in that it appears on nearly every "best books
for children" list, even though it is deeply philosophical and thus
perhaps most meaningful for teens and adults.

   The Little Prince was originally published in both French and English
here in the United States. It was published in France later, after the
Liberation and after the author's death. Although its author never
lived to see his tale become a beloved classic—he was shot down in
1944 while flying a reconnaissance mission—it has been translated
into a whopping 253 languages.

Virtues and Themes

Like the best children's books, this tale is timeless and can be enjoyed
on several different levels; both younger and older readers alike may

find it meaningful and easy to understand. Themes include greed, compassion, true beauty, the search for beauty, and the necessity of learning to see with the heart, not just the eyes.

Johnny Tremain, by Esther Forbes (1943)
Important
Reading Level: 5.9   Interest Level: middle grades

One of the best-selling children's books of all time, Esther Forbes' 1943 classic is enjoyed both for recreational reading and for academic studies across the United States. It holds a special place in the children's canon for at least two reasons. First, as literary historian Seth Lerer observed, "it is a story of both personal and national coming of age."[3] Children and teenagers had some coming-of-age stories to enjoy by 1943, but *Johnny Tremain* invited them to go deeper in a way that other books hadn't, because of its focus on the war that won American independence. Second, consciously or unconsciously, Esther Forbes was the first children's author to take readers into the heart of war through an eyewitness-style account, rather than in the traditional style of an objective reporter.

Virtues and Themes

It would be a mistake to think of *Johnny Tremain* as just as a useful addition to a history program; it is also a meaningful coming-of-age tale. Some of the themes include the journey from boyhood to manhood, the resistance of tyranny, the right to stand up for one's beliefs, the value of hard work, and the struggle to find one's place in life.

Strawberry Girl, by Lois Lenski (1945)
Important
Reading Level: 4.8   Interest Level: middle grades

This Newbery-winning novel is only a small sample of the profound contribution that Lois Lenski made to children's literature. She is the prolific author of many, many books spanning multiple series,

---

[3] Seth Lerer, *Children's Literature: A Reader's History from Aesop to Harry Potter* (Chicago: University of Chicago Press, 2008), 282.

and she is also known for her charming illustrations in both her own books and the books of other authors (i.e., the Betsy-Tacy series, etc.). As an influence on the development of children's literature, however, Lenski's work is particularly valued for her regional novels. These novels, like another classic novel of this era, *Blue Willow*, depicted the lives of children with stark reality and were based on meticulous research that often included intensive visits to the regions she featured. Because much of Lenski's work focused on the lives of real children in various places and circumstances, she is known as an early promoter of understanding, empathy, and tolerance for our nation's cultural diversity.

Virtues and Themes

For her beautifully vivid and realistic depiction of early twentieth-century life in Florida—or any other region of the United States, for that matter—it's hard to beat Lois Lenski. Not only that, but *Strawberry Girl* is an absorbing story with interesting characters. At the center is a feud between neighboring families, and themes include man versus nature, the pursuit of education, alcoholism, hard work, and the possibility of people changing for the better.

Stuart Little, by E. B. White (1945)
Important
Reading Level: 6.0   Interest Level: middle grades

Acclaimed author E. B. White received the gamut of response for *Stuart Little*, which was his first children's book. Some critics turned up their noses at it, and others felt it deserved high praise. To read *Stuart Little* on one level is to follow the story of a mouse on a grand adventure. On a deeper level, though, it is (in the words of White himself) the story of "the continuing journey that everybody takes—in search of what is perfect and unattainable."[4] This may be one reason for its enduring popularity, despite the criticism it has received. Seth Lerer has another theory about why it has captured the imaginations of so many readers. Noting that Stuart's journey takes him away from the

---

[4] Quoted in "E. B. White," Encyclopedia.com.

bustle of city life and toward upstate New York to "the heart of old America," he wonders if perhaps the novel "makes all of its readers long for a collective, national childhood."[5] Whatever the reason, the novel has found its place in American literature as a central and beloved children's classic and has been made into a full-length movie. It is a winner of the Laura Ingalls Wilder Medal.

Virtues and Themes

One of the defining features of the fantasy genre is the hero's quest, and this invariably makes the hero stronger and wiser as he fulfills the purpose of the quest. *Stuart Little* is not a fantasy in the usual sense, but at its heart lies the quest of a little mouse to find a dear friend, as well as himself. One thing that makes this novel unusual, though, is the open ending, which may encourage meaningful discussion about the ongoing nature of life and the fact that sometimes stories don't have neat and tidy endings. Themes include standing strong in the face of forces larger than oneself, the best of human nature, and the struggles of those who are different.

Other Children's Classics of This Era

Smoky the Cowhorse, by Will James (1926)
Reading Level: 6.5   Interest Level: middle grades

Emil and the Detectives, by Erich Kästner (1929)
Reading Level: unknown   Interest Level: middle grades

This is a pre-Nazi German novel that was possibly the first to feature child detectives.

Hitty, Her First Hundred Years, by Rachel Field (1929)
Reading Level: 7.1   Interest Level: middle grades

This novel follows the imagined adventures of a real-life doll owned by Field, which today resides at the Stockbridge Library Museum in

---

[5] Lerer, *Children's Literature*, 297.

Stockbridge, Massachusetts. Her tale is particularly notable in that Field was the first woman to receive the Newbery Medal.

The Little Engine That Could, by Watty Piper (1930)
Reading Level: 3.5   Interest Level: lower grades

The Secret of the Old Clock, by Carolyn Keene (1930)
Reading Level: 5.4
Interest Level: middle grades to upper grades

This is the first book in the iconic Nancy Drew series.

Young Fu of the Upper Yangtze, by Elizabeth Foreman Lewis (1932)
Reading Level: 6.4   Interest Level: middle grades

The Story About Ping, by Marjorie Flack (1933)
Reading Level: 4.3   Interest Level: lower grades

Mary Poppins, by P. L. Travers (1934)
Reading Level: 6.1   Interest Level: middle grades

Caddie Woodlawn, by Carol Ryrie Brink (1935)
Reading Level: 6.0   Interest Level: middle grades

National Velvet, by Enid Bagnold (1935)
Reading Level: 5.5   Interest Level: middle grades

Ballet Shoes, by Noel Streatfeild (1936)
Reading Level: 5.7   Interest Level: middle grades

Ballet Shoes was cutting-edge when it was first published in 1936. Although the orphan-benefactor premise wasn't unusual, it was the first children's novel to feature children who were employed as professional performers. This is the first of a series of stand-alone novels about children in various professions.

The Story of Ferdinand, by Munro Leaf (1936)
Reading Level: 3.7   Interest Level: lower grades

Roller Skates, by Ruth Sawyer (1936)
Reading Level: 6.3   Interest Level: middle grades

The Sword in the Stone, by T. H. White (1938)
Reading Level: 7.5   Interest Level: middle grades

Mr. Popper's Penguins, by Richard and Florence Atwater (1938)
Reading Level: 5.6   Interest Level: middle grades

Thimble Summer, by Elizabeth Enright (1938)
Reading Level: 5.7   Interest Level: middle grades

B is for Betsy, by Carolyn Haywood (1939)
Reading Level: 4.3   Interest Level: middle grades

Madeline, Ludwig Bemelmans (1939)
Reading Level: 3.1   Interest Level: lower grades

Mike Mulligan and His Steam Shovel, by Virginia Lee Burton (1939)
Reading Level: 4.4   Interest Level: lower grades

Betsy-Tacy series, by Maud Hart Lovelace (1940–1955)
Reading Level: 4.0–5.8
Interest Level: middle grades through upper grades

Like the Little House series, the Betsy-Tacy series has been loved by generations of children and praised by scholars for its accurate portrayal of a child's life in early twentieth-century America. *Betsy-Tacy* and its sequels are also some of the most enduring children's novels about a primary subject in children's literature: friendship. In 1980, Minnesota named its state children's book award after Lovelace with the purpose of encouraging recreational reading among children.

Call It Courage, by Armstrong Sperry (1940)
Reading Level: 6.2   Interest Level: middle grades

Pat the Bunny, by Dorothy Kunhardt (1940)
Reading Level: estimated K–1   Interest Level: pre-school

This was the first interactive book for babies.

Caps for Sale, by Esphyr Slobodkina (1940)
Reading Level: 3.1   Interest Level: lower grades

Blue Willow, by Doris Gates (1940)
Reading Level: 6.5   Interest Level: middle grades

This novel was considered a landmark novel for two reasons. First, it is one of the first novels about American migrant farm workers. Second, and most important for the development of children's literature, it is one of the first novels published for children to present stark reality. Because of these two qualities, the novel earned the nickname "the children's *Grapes of Wrath*." It won a Newbery Honor in 1941.

Make Way for Ducklings, by Robert McCloskey (1941)
Reading Level: 4.1   Interest Level: lower grades

The Moffats, by Eleanor Estes (1941)
Reading Level: 5.2   Interest Level: middle grades

Paddle-to-the-Sea, by Holling Clancy Holling (1941)
Reading Level: 5.4   Interest Level: middle grades

Seventeenth Summer, by Maureen Daly (1942)
Reading Level: 5.9   Interest Level: upper grades

This book was notable for being one of the first novels written for young adults, long before the genre was established, as well as for its honesty and frankness about sexuality and desire.

The Poky Little Puppy, by Janette Lowrey (1942)
Reading Level: 4.0   Interest Level: lower grades

This was the number one best-selling children's book of the twentieth century for domestic sales. Published in 1942 as the twelfth book in the beloved Little Golden Books series, it is still in print with its original text and illustrations.

Many Moons, by James Thurber (1943)
Reading Level: 4.5   Interest Level: lower grades

Homer Price, by Robert McCloskey (1943)
Reading Level: 6.6   Interest Level: middle grades

Rabbit Hill, by Robert Lawson (1944)
Reading Level: 6.4   Interest Level: middle grades

Lawson is notable in that he is the only author-illustrator to win both the Newbery and Caldecott awards.

The Hundred Dresses, by Eleanor Estes (1944)
Reading Level: 5.4   Interest Level: middle grades

This novella may be the first children's story to address prejudice.

The Moved-Outers, by Florence Crannell Means (1945)
Reading Level: unknown   Interest Level: estimated upper grades

Pippi Longstocking, by Astrid Lindgren (1945)
Reading Level: 5.2   Interest Level: middle grades

The Pippi series has been loved by American children for decades, but they had an even stronger impact in their native Sweden. Pippi became an iconic character, helping to promote gender equality and igniting controversy over its anti-authoritarian themes. Because of her prolific body of work, which has been popular worldwide in more than seventy languages, Lindgren won the international Hans Christian Andersen Award in 1958.

6

The Second Golden Age
1946–1965

As we enter the modern era in children's literature, young readers will encounter books that take them into worlds and lives that seem much like their own. Even in the fantasies, the characters will often seem familiar and relatable, perhaps since we live in a similar world and could know them in real life were they flesh and blood. Because of that and our fond memories of our own childhood favorites, parents may have a more emotional response to the selections featured here than they have with those of previous eras. For many of us, certain books give us joy, and we want to pass them on to our own children.

In addition to books with nostalgic significance, some readers may find books with content that offends them. It is in this era that some literary taboos were first broken by authors who included vulgar language, sexual references, countercultural and disturbing thematic content, and rebellious protagonists (aside from a few early predecessors, like Mary Lennox in *The Secret Garden*).

Many parents do not want to see such books recommended in study guides, so it is here that I would like to remind readers that this list is not a collection of recommendations. The books selected were chosen for their accepted status as the best of the best in the genre of children's literature. This designation is based on their influence and importance to children and to the children's genre, as well as on their overall literary quality. The term "literary quality" here refers to the art of writing and the craft of stoytelling, not the morality of an author's characters. Parents must therefore decide whether a given book is appropriate for their children. Most parents will want to bypass at least a couple of them or read them with their children.

For better or for worse, this era is the first divisive one, a problem that will only increase as we proceed toward the twenty-first century.

Still, the era is called the Second Golden Age for good reason. It produced many beloved novels, and it also broke away from traditional storytelling in important ways. For example, it began addressing the darker side of childhood and introducing new kinds of fantasy. In fact, children's literature flowered so spectacularly during these years that composing the list was particularly challenging. Some that I expected (and wanted, in some cases) to rise to the top did not do so at all, such as *The Chronicles of Prydain* and *Bedtime for Frances*. The same is true of the next era. There are just too many good books!

The Diary of a Young Girl, by Anne Frank (1947)
Foundational
Reading Level: 6.5   Interest Level: middle grades and up

Although the diary of this teenage girl was never intended to be read, it made its way into literary history soon after World War II. Otto Frank, Anne's father, was the sole survivor of his family after they were caught hiding in Amsterdam and sent to Nazi concentration camps. After the Liberation, Miep Gies, the family friend who had helped them survive their years of hiding, found Anne's diary. Otto felt that it should be shared with the world, and it was published in 1947 (1952 in the U.S.). Since then, it has become one of the most widely read works of nonfiction in the world and is considered to be both an important contribution to twentieth-century literature and an important World War II document. Not only has it been translated into sixty-seven languages and has sold more than thirty million copies, it has also been adapted into a Pulitzer Prize-winning play, a television mini-series, and an Academy Award-winning movie.

Virtues and Themes

Anne's diary gives readers a unique window into both the Jewish experience during World War II and into the mind of a 1940s teenager. Although wonderful novels are available about the same subject, the diary adds a moving and important dimension to a study of the

Holocaust. Some themes include puberty, coming-of-age, parent-teen conflict, friendship, the Nazi regime, fear, and romance.

Goodnight Moon, by Margaret Wise Brown (1947)
Important
Reading Level: 1.8   Interest Level: lower grades

Included on at least eleven "best books for children" lists, this beloved classic is one of the best-selling picture books in history and is still in print after seventy years. Margaret Wise Brown was a prolific children's author and produced several classics besides *Goodnight Moon*—most notably *The Runaway Bunny*—but *Goodnight Moon* seems to hold a special place in the hearts of parents and children as they enjoy the book together at bedtime and then grow up to share it with the next generation.

Virtues and Themes

Children will love this story's gentle, rocking rhythm, as well as the soothing illustrations. Themes include bedtime rituals, peace, and security.

The Chronicles of Narnia series, especially *The Lion, the Witch and the Wardrobe*, by C.S. Lewis (1950–1956)
Foundational
Reading Level: 5.4–5.9   Interest Level: middle grades

Few children's books are as influential and beloved as C.S. Lewis' magical series about the world of Narnia. Not only has it impacted the children's book world by influencing the work of major authors like Katherine Paterson and J.K. Rowling, it has also become a global phenomenon among readers of all ages with one hundred million copies sold in at least forty-seven languages. As one reviewer wrote, Narnia is "one of the gold standards for great children's literature *and* great literature."[1] It is enjoyed by all ages on several levels—sometimes as

---

[1] Chris Meadows, "Children's Literature Is Anything but Childish," *Teleread*, June 7, 2014, http://teleread.com/c-s-lewis-reading-childrens-literature-is-anything-but-childish/.

an enchanting bedtime tale, sometimes as a literature study in schools of all levels, and sometimes as a religious study of its Christian themes. It is one of the few works for children—in secular and religious circles alike—that has been the subject of serious analysis and scholarship.

In 1956, the final book in the series, *The Last Battle*, was awarded the Carnegie Medal (England's version of the Newbery Medal), but it is beloved on both sides of the Atlantic. The whole series, especially *The Lion, the Witch and the Wardrobe*, has been adapted for stage, screen, radio, audiobooks, and picture books. In 1980 the Christian band 2nd Chapter of Acts even released a concept album based on *The Lion, the Witch and the Wardrobe* titled *The Roar of Love*.

Virtues and Themes

Part of the brilliance of the Narnia books is their appeal to both children and adults. For that reason, they make a perfect family read-aloud series, as well as an ideal introduction to fantasy. For Christians they also feature a spiritual dimension that promises meaningful pondering and discussion, for the books are rich in Christian parallels and symbolism.

The Catcher in the Rye, by J. D. Salinger (1951)
Foundational   Parents Cautioned!
Reading Level: 4.7   Interest Level: upper grades

Few juvenile novels raise quite as much ire among parents as this one, and yet few have been as influential among teen readers. Parents should be aware that *The Catcher in the Rye* contains much vulgar language, as well as some references to sex.

One of the earliest novels that might be legitimately classified as "young adult" (YA) although it was intended for adults, *The Catcher in the Rye* introduces readers to one of the most enduring literary characters of all time, Holden Caulfield. Vulgar, angry, and alienated, Holden Caulfield is no role model, but Salinger broke new literary ground by making him more real and honest than any other previous teen protagonist. For the first time, many teenagers saw themselves, their complex emotions, and their torturous angst reflected in a character. In fact, no other author of the twentieth century affected teen readers the same way as Salinger did, and even now *The Catcher in the Rye* is frequently read both in and out of school. The novel continues to be so influential among teen readers that YA author John Green once said that "anybody who writes about teenagers does so in the shadow of Salinger."[2]

Virtues and Themes

Whatever one thinks about the novel in general, the character Holden Caulfield resonates deeply with readers everywhere and has for decades. He has been described as a "teenage everyman," relatable to boys and girls alike. For teenagers struggling to process all the new emotions and confusion they feel as they grow up, *The Catcher in the Rye* may be cathartic. Parents who are concerned about the mature content but think the novel could be valuable may want to read it alongside their teens and then discuss it. Some of the themes include the need for and consequences of self-protection, the need to protect childhood innocence, the struggles of growing up, cynicism about the adult world, and the struggle to accept death and its inevitability.

Charlotte's Web, by E. B. White (1952)
Foundational
Reading Level: 4.4   Interest Level: middle grades

Called "one of the best-loved and most perfectly crafted children's books of all time" by children's book expert Anita Silvey, *Charlotte's Web* is included on virtually every children's "best books" list.[3] Classic author Eudora Welty concurs with Silvey. "As a piece of work, it is just about perfect, and just about magical in the way it is done," she once said.[4] And Newbery-winner Kate DiCamillo went a step

---

[2] Quoted in Emma Michelle and Anne Maxwell, "Six Years On: The Enduring Influence of J. D. Salinger," *Conversation*, January 26, 2016, https://theconversation.com/six-years-on-the-enduring-influence-of-j-d-salinger-53495.

[3] Anita Silvey, *100 Best Books for Children* (Boston: Houghton Mifflin, 2004), 131.

[4] Quoted in Karen MacPherson, "Children's Corner: *Charlotte's Web* Has Been Spinning Magic for Sixty Years," *Pittsburgh Post-Gazette*, April 17, 2012, https://www.post-gazette.com/ae/books/2012/04/17/Children-s-Corner-Charlotte-s-Web-has-been-spinning-magic-for-60-years/stories/201204170222.

further when she suggested, "I would leave off the phrase 'for children.' I think it's a book that you can put in anybody's hands—adults or children—and they will get something out of it."[5] Perhaps it is the timelessness and cross-generational appeal of the novel that makes it a masterpiece, or perhaps it is the literary quality itself. Either way, *Charlotte's Web* is essential reading not only for those who seek beautiful stories with depth and humor, but also anyone who wants to experience the best that children's literature has to offer.

Virtues and Themes

Like all the best stories, *Charlotte's Web* is timeless, resonating with readers across the years and miles—perhaps because it is really a story about life itself and what is truly important during our time on earth. Although it is not the only book to focus on the entire scope of life from birth to death, the genius of E. B. White is, perhaps, his ability to explore such a lofty theme in a way that is meaningful, beautiful, and moving to adults and children alike. Themes include friendship, loyalty, sacrificial love, the power of words, birth, death, and growing up.

Lord of the Flies, by William Golding (1954)

Important   Parents Cautioned!
Reading Level: 5.0   Interest Level: upper grades

First published in England, this short novel has been read by millions on both sides of the Atlantic. It is widely considered to be one of the most important works of Western literature ever written. As so many of the most enduring tales are, it was published for the adult market but is also of interest to younger readers because of its exciting adventure plot about a group of English schoolboys. With its thought-provoking themes, child-focused tale, and high-quality writing, *Lord of the Flies* has influenced both teens and adults and has been an important part of many high school English programs for over fifty years. It has been translated into several languages and has inspired discussions, tributes, other stories, and even television shows.

[5] Ibid.

Parents should be aware that this novel contains some disturbing violence, including two murders. Because of the heavy philosophical themes in this novel, discussion is particularly important to help young readers understand and process them.

Virtues and Themes

Lord of the Flies is at its core a study of the complexities of human nature and behavior. It is also a profound examination of societies—how they are formed, how they develop, and how they can either succeed or fall apart. Major themes include civilization versus savagery, loss of innocence, the inborn evil of mankind, the power of mob mentality, the power of the strong over the weak, and human nature.

The Cat in the Hat, by Dr. Seuss (1957)
Foundational
Reading Level: 2.1   Interest Level: lower grades

Before Dr. Seuss, *Dick and Jane* ruled literacy education. Then, one day Theodor Seuss Geisel, already the author of a dozen children's books, was challenged to write a fun story for beginning readers that used only 250 words. The result was *The Cat in the Hat*. To say that this simple tale of nonsense and wordplay revolutionized the children's book world is no exaggeration. For the first time beginning readers had a storybook written just for them—and not just any book, but one that was *fun* without featuring children who were too perfect to seem real. After *The Cat in the Hat*, there was no going back to the *Dick and Jane* standard. The *Cat in the Hat* phenomenon was the turning point that launched a whole new sub-genre of storybooks just for beginning readers.

Dr. Seuss, in fact, has been so profoundly influential in children's literature that he has been called the "savior of children's literacy." The writer and critic Louis Menand once said, "*The Cat in the Hat* transformed the nature of primary education and the nature of children's books."[6] Indeed, it was Dr. Seuss' favorite book of the

---

[6]Louis Menand, "Cat People: What Dr. Seuss Really Taught Us," *New Yorker*, December 23, 2002, https://www.newyorker.com/magazine/2002/12/23/cat-people.

many he produced during his career, because, he said, "it is the book I'm proudest of because it had something to do with the death of the *Dick and Jane* primers."[7]

Virtues and Themes

With vivid, memorable illustrations, a rhyming story full of silliness, and easy words for the earliest reader, what is there not to like? The main theme might be how fun it can be to break rules, so long as you clean up the mess afterward. It is conveyed through the nonsense and the rambunctious antics of one crazy cat.

Tom's Midnight Garden, by Philippa Pearce (1958)
Important
Reading Level: 6.1   Interest Level: middle grades

Although it was awarded the Carnegie Medal in 1958 (England's version of the Newbery Medal), Philippa Pearce's classic novel is often forgotten among today's children, teachers, and parents. The reasons for this are debatable, perhaps, but one thing is not. According to critics and children's literature experts, *Tom's Midnight Garden* is an undeniable masterpiece and deserves a prominent place in the children's canon. In fact, the reviewer John Rowe Townsend, who was known for being hard-to-please, said this upon reading it soon after its release: "It is as near to being perfect in its construction and its writing as any book I know...I have no reservations to make about it. If I were asked to name a single masterpiece of English children's literature since the last war it would be this outstandingly beautiful and absorbing book."[8]

Virtues and Themes

At once a sort of ghost and time-travel story, this fantasy is both meaningful and beautifully written. It's even set on the grounds of an old English mansion, which is arguably the best setting ever for

---

[7] "Dr. Seuss: The Story behind *The Cat in the Hat*," Biography.com, February 28, 2019, https://www.biography.com/news/story-behind-dr-seuss-cat-in-the-hat.

[8] Quoted in Gordon Campbell, "Classics: Tom's Midnight Garden (1958)," *Werewolf*, February 9, 2012, http://werewolf.co.nz/2012/02/classics-toms-midnight-garden-1958/.

stories of a mysterious nature. Some themes include growing up, change, loss, aging, time, and the beauty of childhood, making this a good read-aloud for parents looking for discussion-worthy stories.

To Kill a Mockingbird, by Harper Lee (1960)
Foundational   *Parents Cautioned!*
Reading Level: 5.6   Interest Level: upper grades

With more than forty million copies sold since its publication, Pulitzer Prize-winning masterpiece *To Kill a Mockingbird* has had a powerful impact on both adults and adolescents. It is one of the most important American novels ever written, and it is frequently taught in high school literature programs across the nation and as far away as Australia. The novel has become so important in American literature that some consider it to be an archetypal novel about both race and coming-of-age. When it was published, it was also unique because of its feminine perspective and authentic depiction of the modern South. Not only has the novel achieved lasting acclaim, it also became a triple Oscar-winning movie in 1962, starring Gregory Peck. Because of the novel's lasting impact on American society, President George W. Bush awarded Harper Lee the Presidential Medal of Freedom in 2007, and President Barack Obama awarded her the National Medal of Arts in 2010.

Parents should be aware that the central conflict of the novel is a legal case in which a black man is accused of raping a white woman in segregated Alabama during the Great Depression. It also contains a little violence and some mild swearing and derogatory language against black people, including the n-word.

Virtues and Themes

Although *To Kill a Mockingbird* is an adult novel, it has had a strong influence on young readers because of its unusual combination of a child's point of view and a profoundly moving story. For some young readers, the novel has been a formative, even transformative, experience. It has been called a morality tale without preachiness, its major themes being racism, prejudice, social injustice, honor and courage, and the conflict between good and evil.

Island of the Blue Dolphins, by Scott O'Dell (1960)
Important

Reading Level: 5.4   Interest Level: middle grades

Like most of the other twentieth-century authors featured in this guide, *Island of the Blue Dolphins* is featured on many "best books" lists and is a multiple award-winner, including the Newbery Medal. However, like other twentieth-century authors mentioned here, he is not included just for those reasons. O'Dell has written many novels for children, and through them he has passed down two legacies to the children's book world. First, he is credited for being one of the first children's authors to move away from the survival story as "man taming nature" and toward the more realistic premise of "man adapting to nature." In his biography of O'Dell, David Russell credited him with "raising the social conscience of young readers" through tales that dealt with difficult themes, such as the unjust treatment of minorities by whites in the Americas, the need to recognize gender equality, the importance of ecological concerns, and the corruption of civilization through selfish motives.[9] Beautiful and spare, his writing has been compared to Ernest Hemingway's. *Island of the Blue Dolphins* is the first and best known of his many books and has been said to be his masterpiece.

Virtues and Themes

Although this novel is somewhat challenging and best saved for older children and teens, it is a well-written, dramatic story about a young girl forced to survive alone on an island. Themes include survival, man versus nature, adaptation to environment, loneliness, forgiveness, respect for all animals, and the roles of men and women in society.

The Phantom Tollbooth, by Norton Juster (1961)
Important

Reading Level: 6.7   Interest Level: middle grades

When it was first published, a reviewer wrote, "*The Phantom Tollbooth* is something every adult seems sure will turn into a modern

[9] Quoted on the Scott O'Dell website.

Alice."[10] More than fifty years later, it has become classic in its own right and appears on many "best books" lists. Paradoxically, it has also become largely overlooked by today's readers. As a philosophical fantasy in the tradition of *Alice in Wonderland*, critics have complained from the time it was published that the sophisticated wordplay and complex themes are too difficult for children. Despite these concerns, however, the children who have discovered it have been entranced by the magical, delightful tale and are the ones who have given the book its important place in the children's canon.

Virtues and Themes

A fantasy unlike any other, *The Phantom Tollbooth* is at heart a celebration of language and numbers, of the world's many wonders, and of the richness of life. It has been compared to *Alice in Wonderland*. Some themes include the value of education, the wonders of everyday life, the problem with boredom, and the power of imagination.

A Wrinkle in Time, by Madeleine L'Engle (1962)
Foundational
Reading Level: 4.7   Interest Level: middle grades

Today, this Newbery-winning novel is considered an essential fixture in the children's literature canon, so it's hard to believe that is was rejected by publishers twenty-six times and has been on the American Library Association's One Hundred Most Frequently Challenged Books list for years. But L'Engle's classic isn't impressive only for its almost miraculous success; it is also one of the most influential novels in contemporary children's literature. Said to have changed science fiction itself by her biographer Leonard S. Marcus, L'Engle opened "the American juvenile tradition to the literature of 'What if?' as a rewarding and honorable alternative to realism in storytelling."[11] In doing so, she helped pave the way for

---

[10] Quoted in Chelsey Philpot, "Books That Made Us: *The Phantom Tollbooth*," *Los Angeles Review of Books*, November 17, 2011, https://lareviewofbooks.org/article/books-that-made-us-the-phantom-tollbooth/.

[11] Jen Doll, "How *A Wrinkle in Time* Changed Sci-fi Forever," *Mental Floss*, July 28, 2015, https://www.mentalfloss.com/article/66705/how-wrinkle-time-changed-sci-fi-forever.

major children's fantasy authors who followed in her wake, such as Lloyd Alexander and Ursula K. Le Guin. The novel has been adapted for screen and stage several times and has also been produced as a graphic novel.

Virtues and Themes

A science-fiction fantasy, *A Wrinkle in Time* takes the reader on an amazing journey through space and time with young Meg as she seeks to rescue her father in another part of the universe. Although it appeals to all readers, some Christians may particularly appreciate L'Engle's allusions to Christian theology, although others may not like L'Engle's fantastical, witch-like creatures or her mixing of science and religion. Some themes include the triumph of love, creativity, individuality, and good versus evil.

The Snowy Day, by Ezra Jack Keats (1962)
Important
Reading Level: 2.5   Interest Level: lower grades

Many people are familiar with *The Snowy Day*, even after fifty years. It is easy to find in bookstores and libraries, and on household shelves. What most people don't know, however, is that this gentle story was one of the most controversial and groundbreaking books of the 1960s, for its white author chose to do something in his story that no other children's author had done before: utilizing a black protagonist, he described and illustrated the universal joys of childhood and the beauty of all children. Although Peter lives in an urban landscape, his little world bursts with color and delight. *The Snowy Day* has been translated into at least ten languages and is a winner of the Caldecott Medal.

Virtues and Themes

In its simplicity and celebration of winter, *The Snowy Day* captures the essence of childhood delight and encourages children to explore the natural world with wonder. Themes include childhood innocence, the beauty of nature, and simple joys.

Where the Wild Things Are, by Maurice Sendak (1963)
Foundational
Reading Level: 3.4   Interest Level: lower grades

Maurice Sendak is to children's literature what peanut butter is to jelly. To imagine the genre without his work is difficult, for he is the one who took children's literature on a voyage from the sanitized waters of earlier picture books into the uncharted territory of the child psyche's dark side. Although he touched on this new topic in several of his books, children's book expert Anita Silvey wrote that his masterpiece, *Where the Wild Things Are,* "brought the picture book to new levels of psychological realism."[12] Many authors have followed his example in the decades since, so that exploring all aspects of juvenile life is now considered important. In the 1960s, however, *Where the Wild Things Are* caused much controversy and was often challenged. In fact, some librarians wouldn't add it to their collections because the story contained monsters and a naughty child who had a great adventure anyway.

Even so, the tale has endured and has been called the most influential picture book of the 1960s and 1970s. It is included on virtually every "best books" list for children. As for Sendak himself, he won not only the 1964 Caldecott Medal for *Where the Wild Things Are,* he also won other prestigious awards for his body of work: the Hans Christian Andersen International Medal (1970), the Laura Ingalls Wilder Award (1983), the first Astrid Lindgren Memorial Award for Literature (2003, shared with Austrian author Christine Nöstlinger), and the National Award of Arts, an honor given by the President of the United States.

Virtues and Themes

Sendak's masterpiece is different from most children's books in that it's all about the internal life of children—what happens to them inside, rather than the adventures they experience out in the world. The story speaks especially to the sense of powerlessness that children often experience and to the emotions they feel, so it resonates with young readers on a deep level that they may not be able to articulate.

[12] Silvey, *100 Best Books,* 38.

Some themes include the power of imagination, the struggle for control between parent and child, coping with anger and frustration, imagination versus reality, and forgiveness.

Charlie and the Chocolate Factory, by Roald Dahl (1964)
Important
Reading Level: 4.8   Interest Level: middle grades

Although Dahl wrote many well-known children's novels, this beloved tale about a boy who wins a magical chocolate factory in a contest is his best known and most widely acclaimed. It has not only sold over twenty million copies in at least fifty-five languages, it has become a part of both American and British pop culture. In addition, it appears on most "best books" lists and has been made into two major movies, an opera, and a musical. Today, more than fifty years after its publication, *Charlie and the Chocolate Factory* holds a prominent place in the canon of children's literature.

Virtues and Themes

Perhaps the main reason to read *Charlie and the Chocolate Factory* is that it is just plain fun, not to mention charming and wildly imaginative with a relatable character that readers can't help but root for. On top of that, the tale has some delightfully awful characters that readers love watching get their just desserts. Some themes include humility, kindness, greed, reaping what we sow, wonder, and impossible dreams coming true.

Harriet the Spy, by Louise Fitzhugh (1964)
Important   Parents Cautioned!
Reading Level: 4.5   Interest Level: middle grades

Despite the fact that Fitzhugh's classic has upset parents, teachers, and critics since its publication (I wasn't allowed to read it as a child, in fact), *Harriet the Spy* has nevertheless secured a place at the top of the children's canon for good reasons. Harriet may not be the likable, admirable child-hero that was expected in the 1960s—or even today, for that matter—but she has been inspirational to both young and adult readers ever since, especially to the many children who feel like they never fit in anywhere.

The novel also represents an important turning-point in children's literature. Today, its themes and topics are common in books intended for both middle and upper grades, but back then authors didn't often tackle the issues of diversity, challenges to gender norms, juvenile psychotherapy, bullying, peer pressure, and the negative consequences of honesty. It also wasn't common in the 1960s for female protagonists to be strong and independent or for them to be unlikable and morally suspect. Despite or perhaps *because* of these traits, *Harriet the Spy* inspired not just misfits like Harriet, but also the many new writers who followed in Fitzhugh's daring, groundbreaking steps.

Virtues and Themes

Although Harriet is no literary role model, she is a realistic character that still resonates with children today, more than fifty years later. Through her eyes, readers can view life with its ups and downs and human struggles. Parents may also find Harriet herself worth discussing, since her behavior and comments are sometimes questionable or unethical. Some themes include growing up, the meaning of family, the many ways of living life, truth, and being true to oneself.

Other Children's Classics of This Era

Mrs. Piggle-Wiggle, by Betty MacDonald (1947)
Reading Level: 5.2   Interest Level: middle grades

Happy Little Family, by Rebecca Caudill (1947)
Reading Level: 3–4   Interest Level: estimated lower grades

Caudill is a multi-award-winning children's author with a large body of work. This book is the first in a charming four-part series about the Fairchild family.

White Snow, Bright Snow, by Alvin Tresselt (1947)
Reading Level: 4.2   Interest Level: lower grades

The Twenty-One Balloons, by William Pène du Bois
(1947)
Reading Level: 6.8   Interest Level: middle grades

This was the first Canadian Library Association Book of the Year
Award for Children.

Blueberries for Sal, by Robert McCloskey (1948)
Reading Level: 4.1   Interest Level: lower grades

My Father's Dragon, by Ruth Stiles Gannett (1948)
Reading Level: 5.6   Interest Level: lower grades

The Jennifer Wish, by Eunice Young Smith (1949)
Reading Level: 4–5   Interest Level: middle grades

This is the first of a popular series for girls.

The Door in the Wall, by Marguerite de Angeli (1949)
Reading Level: 6.2   Interest Level: middle grades

The Borrowers, by Mary Norton (1952)
Reading Level: 5.3   Interest Level: middle grades

Secret of the Andes, by Ann Nolan Clark (1952)
Reading Level: 4.7   Interest Level: middle grades

Children of Green Knowe, by Lucy M. Boston (1954)
Reading Level: 5.3   Interest Level: middle grades

The Eagle of the Ninth, by Rosemary Sutcliff (1954)
Reading Level: 7.1   Interest Level: middle grades and up

Harold and the Purple Crayon, by Crockett Johnson (1955)
Reading Level: 3.0   Interest Level: lower grades

Frog Went A-Courtin', by John Langstaff (1955)
Reading Level: 2.7   Interest Level: lower grades

The Hundred and One Dalmatians, by Dodie Smith (1956)
Reading Level: 5.4   Interest Level: middle grades

Little Bear series, by Else Holmelund Minarik (1957)
Reading Level: 1.5–3.1   Interest Level: lower grades

Little Bear appeared the same year as *The Cat in the Hat* and helped change the template for beginning readers in America.

A Bear Called Paddington, by Michael Bond (1958)
Reading Level: 4.7
Interest Level: lower grades through middle grades

This is the first book in a series about the iconic English character.

Chanticleer and the Fox, by Barbara Cooney (1958)
Reading Level: 4.6   Interest Level: lower grades

The Witch of Blackbird Pond, by Elizabeth George Speare (1958)
Reading Level: 5.7   Interest Level: middle grades

This was one of the few novels published without first needing extensive corrections or revisions. It was a unanimous Newbery Medal choice from the first ballot.

A Separate Peace, by John Knowles (1959)
Reading Level: 6.9   Interest Level: upper grades

My Side of the Mountain, by Jean Craighead George (1959)
Reading Level: 5.2   Interest Level: middle grades

Bedtime for Frances, by Russell Hoban (1960)
Reading Level: 2.7   Interest Level: lower grades

See other early-reader Frances books.

The Cricket in Times Square, by George Selden (1960)
Reading Level: 4.9   Interest Level: middle grades

Green Eggs and Ham, **by Dr. Seuss (1960)**
Reading Level: 1.5   Interest Level: lower grades

Are You My Mother?, **by P. D. Eastman (1960)**
Reading Level: 1.6   Interest Level: lower grades

This book and *Go, Dog. Go!* below are representative works of Eastman, a major author of early readers.

Go, Dog. Go!, **by P. D. Eastman (1961)**
Reading Level: 1.2   Interest Level: lower grades

James and the Giant Peach, **by Roald Dahl (1961)**
Reading Level: 4.8   Interest Level: middle grades

D'Aulaires' Book of Greek Myths, **by Ingri and Edgar Parin d'Aulaire (1962)**
Reading Level: 6.6   Interest Level: middle grades

The Winged Watchman, **by Hilda van Stockum (1962)**
Reading Level: 5   Interest Level: middle grades

This novel set in Nazi-occupied Holland is the most famous of van Stockum's many stories for children published between 1934 and 1975. She won the Newbery Honor in 1935 for her picture book *A Day on Skates*.

The Wolves of Willoughby Chase, **by Joan Aiken (1962)**
Reading Level: 6.5   Interest Level: middle grades

Swimmy, **by Leo Lionni (1963)**
Reading Level: 2.9   Interest Level: lower grades

Amelia Bedelia, **by Peggy Parish (1963)**
Reading Level: 2.5   Interest Level: lower grades

The Chronicles of Prydain, **by Lloyd Alexander (1964–1968)**
Reading Level: 5.2–6.2   Interest Level: middle grades

The Dark Is Rising series, by Susan Cooper (1965–1977)
Parents Cautioned!
Reading Level: 5.4–6.2   Interest Level: middle grades

Although this is a modern children's classic for good reasons, religious parents may want to read reviews first to ensure that its thematic content is appropriate for their children.

7

The Noteworthy Books of the
Late-Twentieth Century
1966–2000

As we saw in the previous era, one hallmark of contemporary children's literature is the way authors and publishers began to cross long-protected boundaries. For centuries, American society seemed to share an unspoken agreement that adults should shelter minors from certain experiences and language until they were adults, but in the last forty years or so, this idea has all but dissolved. Today, sheltering is often viewed as unhealthy for children, and the juvenile book market has increasingly reflected this new thinking since 1965.

Many noteworthy books for young people published in the late-twentieth century include rawness, honesty, and realism, and with increasing intensity. Well into the twenty-first century, authors and publishers of children's and young adult (YA) fiction continually push social boundaries that were probably unimaginable back in the 1960s and 1970s and perhaps even the 1980s. Swearing, sex, abuse, drinking, and the like are all common today, although they are mostly limited to YA literature and are usually less explicit than what appears in adult novels. Middle-grade publishers can still be trusted to give realism a careful hand, such that most books for the under-twelve set are still "safe" in that regard. This may not be the case with fantasy stories, however, especially those that include the occult, as we can see with middle-grade fiction like Philip Pullman's His Dark Materials trilogy and J.K. Rowling's Harry Potter series. LGBTQ themes are also increasing in the middle-grade category. Wary parents, therefore, should examine any contemporary middle-grade novels their children would like to read, even the most noteworthy.

These concerns aside, however, the late-twentieth century offers some wonderful, greatly beloved children's books that are quickly becoming classics. These books, especially, are the ones that many of today's parents know best from their own childhoods, and it is their privilege to share them with the new generation. If you prefer older classics for the bulk of your literature study, the books from this era would be ideal for cozy read-alouds and informal discussion of important contemporary issues.

On the question of whether older books are preferable to newer books, a quick note is in order. Some parents feel that the only books their children should be reading are the older classics, because contemporary literature is morally suspect or badly written. In fact, this era offers so many wonderful books that I had to curtail the list, which meant that many worthy books could not be included.

In our zeal to choose the best literature for our children, we sometimes forget that even the greatest classics were once contemporary themselves. Some of them were harshly questioned and criticized in their day, yet they lived on because of their quality and the way they spoke to the readers of subsequent generations.

As you design your student's literature program or reading list, I encourage you to make your choices based on their overall merit, not whether they are older or newer. If you have moral concerns about a novel simply because it is newer, I encourage you to research it a little before you reject it. Every era has gifted us with its share of outstanding literature.

The Giving Tree (1964) and *Where the Sidewalk Ends* (1974), by Shel Silverstein

Foundational
Reading Level: 2.6 and 3–4 respectively
Interest Level: lower grades through middle grades

Few authors can say that one of their titles is one of the best-selling books ever, yet two of Shel Silverstein's books made the 2001 *Publisher's Weekly* list of the top twenty best-selling children's books of all time: *The Giving Tree* was number fourteen and *Where the Sidewalk Ends* was number twelve. Though that number may change the next time they update the list, the fact remains that Silverstein is one of juvenile literature's most important—and beloved—contemporary authors.

Both children and adults love his work for its humor, quirkiness, gentle philosophy, and delightful, cartoonish illustrations. Though his many books did receive their share of criticism and censorship, Silverstein was an innovator who introduced a new kind of poetry that helped many children enjoy poetry for the first time. In fact, his work has often been used in schools to introduce poetry to students. In the words of children's book author Eric A. Kimmel, Silverstein's greatest contribution was in "convincing millions of children that poetry is neither difficult nor threatening."[1]

Virtues and Themes

There is something about Silverstein's work that celebrates childhood in a unique way. It's sometimes silly, sometimes thought-provoking, and sometimes nonsense—but it always has a delightful, innocent whimsy that is uniquely Silverstein. *Where the Sidewalk Ends* is a poetry anthology that children have loved for decades, and its themes vary. The central themes of *The Giving Tree* are love, generosity, and self-giving, contrasted with dependency, dissatisfaction, and self-centeredness.

The Outsiders, by S. E. Hinton (1967)
Foundational   Parents Cautioned!
Reading Level: 4.7   Interest Level: upper grades

Written while Hinton was still in high school, *The Outsiders* is one of the most important contemporary novels in children's literature. Not only is it widely seen as an excellent literary work, which has been taught in schools for decades, it is also the book that marked the birth of the young adult (YA) category of children's literature. Compared to many contemporary YA novels this novel is fairly tame, but parents should be aware that it does contain some swearing, violence,

---

[1] Quoted in "Shel Silverstein," Encyclopedia.com.

and other mature content. Although it didn't sell well among the other adult books with which it was placed in stores, Hinton's publisher soon realized that teachers were buying it and teaching it in their classes. For the first time they saw that a real market existed for teenagers.

It would not be accurate to say that it is the first novel written with teen protagonists, of course. Before *The Outsiders* was published, a few other books appealed to teens as well, such as *The Catcher in the Rye* and *Seventeenth Summer*. This debut novel of Hinton's, though, changed the way such books were marketed. *The Outsiders* is considered a YA classic today, and Hinton wrote other critically acclaimed YA novels as well. To honor her contribution to American young adult literature, Hinton was awarded the Margaret Edwards Young Adult Author Achievement Award in 1988 by the American Library Association.

Virtues and Themes

For teenagers who are ready to grapple with serious issues through reading and discussion, *The Outsiders* may be a good novel to start with. Although it is more than fifty years old now, it still resonates with teens as both entertaining and meaningful. Some of its themes include family relationships, class conflict, loyalty, and isolation from society.

Ramona the Pest and other stories, by Beverly Cleary (1968–1999)
Foundational
Reading Level: 4.8–5.6   Interest Level: middle grades

Ramona Quimby was born in Cleary's imagination long before she had her own series. She was introduced in Cleary's first series about Henry Huggins as the preschool sister of Beezus Quimby. She came to such vivid life, in fact, that Cleary wrote another book about Beezus' relationship with Ramona. Readers were so charmed by Ramona that Cleary went on to write an entire series about her, the first and most representative of which is probably *Ramona the Pest* (1968). Few characters in children's literature are as well-known as Ramona. She is as alive in the children's canon as Mary Lennox (*The Secret Garden*), the Pevensie children (The Chronicles of Narnia series), and Anne Shirley (*Anne of Green Gables*). But Cleary's work is much bigger than Ramona. She wrote forty-two books, always focusing on the real-life, everyday adventures that are meaningful to most children.

This and her simple, comfortable style have earned her so many awards that there is not enough room here to list them all. Some of the most prestigious ones include the Newbery Medal (*Dear Mr. Henshaw*), the Laura Ingalls Wilder Award, a Newbery Honor (*Ramona Quimby, Age 8*), and an honor from the National Endowment of the Arts for her contribution to children's literature. She was also a nominee for the international Hans Christian Andersen Award and was declared a Living Legend by the Library of Congress. Her work has been translated into many languages and appears in at least 20 countries.

Virtues and Themes

Few people can speak directly to and about children the way Beverly Cleary can, conveying their real emotions and concerns accurately and without condescension. Although most of the series is so outdated that children may be confused by some of Cleary's diction, they still delight in Ramona's day-to-day misadventures as she tries to grow up and find a place in her world. Some themes include school, sibling relationships, growing up, and discovering personal identity.

A Wizard of Earthsea, by Ursula K. Le Guin (1968)
Important   Parents Cautioned!
Reading Level: 6.7   Interest Level: upper grades

With *A Wizard of Earthsea* Ursula K. Le Guin threw a literary stone that caused a ripple effect we can still see today in authors of both juvenile and adult fiction—most notably J. K. Rowling and Neil Gaiman. She furthered the Tolkien-style fantasy genre in children's literature, but she broke with convention by introducing a non-white hero and using an Eastern focus on balance in the universe instead of a Western focus on the battle between good and evil. Some parents may want to know that Le Guin herself once stated that the philosophy behind the Earthsea books is "not only non-Christian but anti-Christian."[2] Its spiritual elements are fantastical but founded in Daoism.

A Wizard of Earthsea did not break through the rules of children's fantasy that were common at the time, but it was the foundation of her groundbreaking six-part series called The Earthsea Cycle, as well as many more novels and short stories for both teens and adults.

Le Guin has won many prestigious awards. For books in the Earthsea series alone, she collected a Newbery Honor, a National Book Award for Children's Books, a Boston Globe-Horn Book Award, a Nebula Award, a World Fantasy Award for Best Novel, a Hugo Award, and a Lewis Carroll Shelf Award. She also appears on a number of "best books for children" lists.

Virtues and Themes

As one of the most critically acclaimed high fantasies of the twentieth century, *A Wizard of Earthsea* may be worth reading just for that reason, especially if your teen enjoys fantasy. Also, for those seeking something different in fantasy, *A Wizard of Earthsea* may be what you're looking for. It departs from the standard white-skinned characters, gives a different take on the hero's journey and quest that are typical of high fantasy, does not pit good against evil the way most fantasies do, and is decidedly feminist. In addition to growing up, some themes include community, trust, courage, self-acceptance, and the proper use of power.

The Very Hungry Caterpillar, by Eric Carle (1969)
Important
Reading Level: 2.9   Interest Level: lower grades

One of the most prolific picture book authors ever, Eric Carle is best known for one of his earliest works, *The Very Hungry Caterpillar*. With his signature technique of colorful tissue-paper collage and his occasional inclusion of special effects like tiny lights and die-cut

---

[2] *Conversations with Ursula K. Le Guin,* ed. Karl Freedman (Jackson, Miss.: University Press of Mississippi, 2008), 44.

pages, he is known for stretching the boundaries of picture-book art. Carle's talent goes beyond his illustrations, though, for his stories, too, are beloved by children. Carle has a way of connecting with children, and he always manages to entertain them while giving them a little deeper understanding of the world around them. Collectively, his work has sold over 139 million copies around the world. *The Very Hungry Caterpillar* alone has been translated into sixty-two languages and sold more than forty-four million copies.

Virtues and Themes

Playing upon the young child's love of repetition, Carle takes the reader on a journey through a caterpillar's week when he does nothing but eat and eat and eat. Children will love hearing about all the things the little caterpillar eats and examining the colorful collage illustrations for which Carle is beloved. The best part, of course, is the surprise ending. Children will love turning the last page again and again. The main theme of this simple book is the life cycle of caterpillars.

Are You There, God? It's Me, Margaret, by **Judy Blume** (1970)
Important   Parents Cautioned!
Reading Level: 3.6   Interest Level: middle grades

One of the earliest YA authors, Judy Blume made waves in the children's book world in 1970 with her groundbreaking novel, *Are You There, God? It's Me, Margaret*. As much as she was praised for her honest portrayal of a young girl's coming-of-age struggles, she was also widely criticized and often censored for *Margaret* and subsequent novels. Whichever side parents and readers may take on the value of her work, Blume remains one of the most important writers in contemporary children's literature. She helped create the problem novel, which centers on a crisis or struggle in the protagonist's life. She also approached previously taboo topics, such as puberty, more openly than writers had in the past. This is a big reason she was and is so often censored, in fact.

Over the years, Blume has crossed age levels, writing popular books for middle-grade children, young adults, and adults, but she is best known for her realistic, taboo-busting novels of which *Margaret* is probably the most classic. Despite the frequent censorship of her work, Judy Blume's books have sold more than eighty-five million copies and have been translated into many languages. Her work (especially *Margaret*) also appears on many "best books for children" lists. She herself has won multiple prestigious awards, such as the Library of Congress Living Legend Award and the American Library Association's Margaret A. Edwards Award for Lifetime Achievement.

Virtues and Themes

Because this novel is a somewhat gritty, realistic tale about maturing into puberty, many parents will want to screen it first. Some parents think it's wonderful, perfect for helping girls through this confusing time of life, and others feel it's highly inappropriate. *Margaret* does have some content that all parents should be aware of—menstruation, kissing, sexual interest, crushes, spiritual searching, and other honest takes on the facts of life.

Watership Down, by Richard Adams (1972)
Foundational
Reading Level: 6.2   Interest Level: upper grades

When Adams sought a publisher for his now-classic novel, the most common complaint about it was that it would be hard to sell to either younger or older children. Exasperated, Adams once commented in an interview, "I used to say, 'But I didn't mean it to be a children's book! Who's talking about children's books? It's a book!' "[3] This cross-generational appeal is one of the main reasons that *Watership Down* plays such an important role in children's literature. It was one of the first novels to enthrall both children and adults—so much so that it became a publishing phenomenon in its native Britain. More than that, it is critically acclaimed as fine literature, for it is an epic

[3] S. F. Said, "The Godfather of Harry Potter," *Telegraph*, October 15, 2002.

drawn from mythic adventure tales like the *Aeneid*. The novel appears on many "best books for children" lists, and it has also won the Carnegie Medal and the Guardian children's fiction prize, both prestigious juvenile book awards in Britain.

Virtues and Themes

While younger children won't be ready for the gritty realities of *Watership Down* (minus the talking rabbits, of course), older children and especially adolescents may find the novel a safe way to learn about and discuss them. It is also a good introduction to political theory for young people because of the complex rabbit societies portrayed in the novel. Important themes include nature, the epic journey, home and belonging, leadership, politics, and individual freedom versus restrictions for the good of community.

The Chocolate War, by Robert Cormier (1974)

Important   Parents Cautioned!
Reading Level: 5.4   Interest Level: upper grades

Although *The Outsiders* marked the birth of the YA genre as we know it, Robert Cormier's gritty classic is also considered an important milestone in YA literature. *The Chocolate War* was noted for its stark realism, weighty themes, and unhappy ending—all traits that have influenced the development of the genre ever since. Parents should be aware that it contains significant mature content, such as vulgar language and sexual situations.

Before the novel was published, realism had already found its footing in YA literature, but happy endings were still the expected norm. Cormier pushed through this expectation so that YA became a genre in which authors could write whatever ending seemed appropriate to them and in which teenage readers had to consider the truth that happy endings are uncertain—not only in novels, but in life itself. *The Chocolate War* has been heavily criticized and banned. Despite this, the novel won several awards, is featured on many "best books for children" lists, has been taught in schools, and is widely regarded by critics as an important literary work.

Virtues and Themes

This is not a book recommended for entertainment. It is literary fiction best suited to group or parent-teen discussion. Despite the swearing and other crude content, *The Chocolate War* is a realistic and cynical, yet (perhaps) safe way for mature teens to examine moral and ethical issues that are relevant to them, such as peer pressure, the conflict between the desire for individuality and the pressure to conform, psychological bullying, fear, and power. Its bleak, unsatisfying ending is also a subject for mature discussion.

Roll of Thunder, Hear My Cry, by Mildred D. Taylor (1976)

Important

Reading Level: 5.7   Interest Level: middle grades

This 1977 Newbery winner is not only one of the first contemporary children's novels to be written by an author of color, it is also one of the finest. *Roll of Thunder, Hear My Cry* is a powerful novel about race and prejudice largely because Taylor wrote honestly about the African-American experience of the 1930s. Because this required using authentic language, she has been harshly criticized because of the pain such language inflicts on some readers. Taylor has said that she doesn't want to cause her readers pain but doesn't see any other way to help children understand what life was really like for African-Americans in the past and sometimes even today. To her, telling the truth is the only option.

It is this unflinching honesty, as well as her beautiful writing, that has made her one of the most important twentieth-century children's writers. In fact, she was one of the first children's authors to write so realistically about African-American life and culture. *Roll of Thunder, Hear My Cry* isn't her only novel, however. It is actually the second in the multi-volume series about the Logan family, and every novel in the series is award-winning. Because it is a Newbery winner, however, *Roll of Thunder, Hear My Cry* is her best-known work.

Virtues and Themes

For black readers *Roll of Thunder, Hear My Cry* can be a particularly meaningful, bonding experience because of its exploration of racism during the Great Depression, told through the eyes of a nine-year-old girl. For all readers, however, the novel is illuminating and eye-opening, especially for children who don't yet understand the history of racism in our country or perhaps even the concept of racism itself. Some themes include prejudice, racial violence, poverty, and the importance of dignity, land ownership, and community.

Bridge to Terabithia, by Katherine Paterson (1977)
Important
Reading Level: 4.6   Interest Level: middle grades

Paterson is the author of many well-known novels, picture books, short stories, and essays. It wasn't until her fourth novel, however, that she began her rise as one of children's literature's most important authors. *Bridge to Terabithia* was the first of many novels in which she dealt with difficult themes and life challenges from which adults often want to protect children. Like Mildred D. Taylor, Paterson has touched many young readers through her honest but child-appropriate stories, but also like Taylor, her work has been banned countless times. This may be particularly interesting to parents looking for Christian children's authors, for Paterson is one of the most notable Christian authors writing for the secular market. She is also the winner of many prestigious awards, including two Newbery Awards (one of them for *Bridge to Terabithia*), two National Book Awards, and *both* international awards—The Hans Christian Andersen Award and the Astrid Lindgren Memorial Award. In addition, she served as the second U.S. Ambassador for Young People's Literature (2010–11).

Virtues and Themes

Well written and memorable, *Bridge to Terabithia* is an excellent novel in its own right. It is also a safe way to introduce children to the reality of death and mortality at any age. Parents may want to read and discuss the novel with sensitive children or children who are already struggling with the concept of death. Some themes include imagination, friendship, courage, mortality, personal transformation, and the conflict between the pressure to conform to society and the need for individuality.

The House on Mango Street, by Sandra Cisneros (1984)
Important   Parents Cautioned!
Reading Level: 4.5   Interest Level: upper grades

In 1984 Sandra Cisneros surprised the literary community with this coming-of-age novel. It was so well received and so highly praised that before long it became required reading in high schools and colleges across the United States. Perhaps because it was not written specifically for a young audience, *The House on Mango Street* has some mature content, including sexual assault, that has upset many parents. It also contains only negative male characters.

Although the age-appropriateness of the book has been hotly debated, it is generally considered to be a novel for teens and adults. In fact, it is widely considered to be one of the most important contemporary novels for teens to read. This is not only because of the excellent writing, but because the novel made Cisneros a pioneer in contemporary literature.

She was the first female, Mexican-American writer to be published by a major publisher, which paved the way for a new literary sub-genre: Chicana literature. She is a multi-award-winner and has received several prestigious fellowships, including two from the National Endowment of the Arts (1981 and 1988).

Virtues and Themes

This novel gives an illuminating look at underprivileged Hispanic-American culture and the struggles of growing up in that world. It is also an example of a novel written without a clear plot; the story is told through a series of vignettes. Some themes include coming-of-age, determining self-identity, moral struggles, dreams for a better life, and the longing for a home of one's own.

Lincoln: A Photobiography, by Russell Freedman (1987)
Important
Reading Level: 7.7   Interest Level: middle grades

Lincoln: A Photobiography is one of only a handful of nonfiction books to win the Newbery Award, and it has had an extraordinary influence on children's nonfiction ever since. Although he is best known for *Lincoln*, Freedman has written many books for children and is considered "influential in the revitalization of non-fiction over the last 25 years."[4] Anita Silvey concurs, saying that *Lincoln: A Photobiography* "brought renewed focus and attention to information books by writers and publishers; in fact, it has become the standard of excellence for all contemporary children's biographies."[5]

Virtues and Themes

Biographies can be dry, but *Lincoln* is an example of how interesting, compelling, and memorable a biography can be to children. The writing is engaging, providing a well-rounded portrait of Abraham Lincoln as both man and president, and the book includes many well-chosen photographs that enhance each page. In addition, it contains several useful appendices, such as a list of other good books about Lincoln.

Hatchet, by Gary Paulsen (1987)
Important
Reading Level: 5.7   Interest Level: middle grades

Author Gary Paulsen is widely considered one of the most important children's writers in recent decades. His body of work is awe-inspiring with more than 175 books and around 200 articles and short stories to his credit. He has written for both children and adults, but it is his multi-award-winning children's fiction that has earned him a fixed place in the children's canon. *Hatchet* is his most famous novel, the first in a series of five called Brian's Saga or the Hatchet Adventures. A Newbery Honor book, *Hatchet* has been called the best modern survival story for children and is featured on many "best books for children" lists. For more than thirty years, it has been one of the most popular novels for reluctant readers and avid readers alike.

[4]Emer O'Sullivan, *Historical Dictionary of Children's Literature* (Lanham, Md.: Scarecrow Press, 2010), 104.
[5]Silvey, *100 Best Books*, 94.

Virtues and Themes

So removed are most children from raw nature in the twenty-first century that they will identify closely with the protagonist Brian, himself a modern child more used to cars and skyscrapers than the natural world. Unlike his readers, though, Brian must learn how to survive in the wilderness on his own, and this allows readers to learn along with him realistically and without sugar-coating. They also get to experience his harrowing adventures vicariously and in a way that is both entertaining and educational. Through his ordeal Brian becomes one with nature and learns to recognize, use, and appreciate the many gifts of the world around him. Some themes include wilderness survival and appreciation, loneliness, man versus nature, the power of hope and optimism, and personal transformation.

The Giver, by Lois Lowry (1993)
Foundational
Reading Level: 5.7   Interest Level: middle grades

Lois Lowry has been writing award-winning fiction for children since the 1970s, her first novel being *A Summer to Die*. With the light-hearted Anastasia Krupnik series, beginning in 1979, she gained popularity, but it wasn't until her 1989 Newbery award-winner *Number the Stars* that she staked her claim in children's literary history. In 1993, she published her most important novel yet, a second Newbery winner titled *The Giver*, which is the first in a series of four.

    The Giver is featured on virtually every "best books for children" list and has won not only the Newbery Award but also the Margaret Edwards Award. The novel is not included here only for those reasons. It has the distinction of being the first children's dystopian novel, a genre that has become wildly popular in recent years with YA works such as *The Hunger Games* and *Divergent*. It is also known for its skillful treatment of complex and controversial themes, which have caused it either to be banned or critically acclaimed, as well as taught widely in schools.

    Today, it is considered one of the most important novels in contemporary children's literature. In fact, Anita Silvey went so far as to state that *The Giver* is "not only one of the greatest novels of the 1990s for children but also one of the greatest science-fiction novels for young readers of all time."[6] The novel has been adapted into several theatrical formats, as well as a major movie production, and it has sold more than twelve million copies.

Virtues and Themes

This novel is fast-paced and engaging, as well as fascinating in its portrayal of a future utopia, while also meaningful and thought-provoking. It is worth reading for both entertainment and analysis, especially since the YA dystopian genre began with this novel. Those who enjoy *The Giver* will also be pleased to learn that it is the first of a four-book series. Some themes include utopia versus dystopia, individuality versus freedom, the importance of human emotion, the power and value of memory, the value of old age, and the dangers of unquestioned physical security.

His Dark Materials trilogy, by Philip Pullman (1995–2000)

Important   Parents Extremely Cautioned!
Reading Level: 6.2–7.1   Interest Level: upper grades

Of all the literature included in this guide, this series is probably the most offensive to the largest number of parents, including myself. In fact, I nearly deleted it from the list because I do not want to glorify it in any way. In the end I included it here in the complete list for two reasons. First, it is an important work of children's literature in an objective sense, and my goal in compiling this reading list was to be as objective as possible. Second, parents need to know about this series, especially because it is marketed to children ages ten and up and has been made into feature films and a television series. The trilogy includes *The Golden Compass*, *The Subtle Knife*, and *The Amber Spyglass*. *The Golden Compass* is the mildest of the three books and should not be the one parents use for discernment.

Although the tale is a fantasy and was published around the same time as the Harry Potter series, few parents are aware of it. However, it is far more insidious as it relates to morality, faith, religion, and the occult. Although its far-reaching influence is not yet clear, the critical reception and awards it has received indicate that the series

---

[6] Ibid., 147.

will eventually take its place among the most important works of the children's fantasy genre. It appears on most "best books for children" lists, has received high praise from scholarly critics, and has won many prestigious awards, including the Carnegie Medal and the international Astrid Lindgren Memorial Award.

Much of the reason for Pullman's popularity is that his tale is unusually rich and well written, and it appeals to both children and adults. Another reason is that it includes "themes rarely found in children's fantasy, for example the shortcomings of religion."[7] In fact, the trilogy is often called "anti-Narnian," making it probably the most atheistic, secular humanistic children's tale ever written. It is notable that Philip Pullman himself has expressed surprise at the weak parent outcry.

Like many of the most celebrated children's novels, it has frequently been banned, but also like many such novels, this notoriety has not dampened enthusiasm for it or altered its status as an emerging classic in children's literature. All parents, especially those of Judeo-Christian faiths, should be very cautious about allowing their children to read this trilogy. I strongly recommend that they examine it first, even if they think they might want to read it with their children.

Virtues and Themes

Except for its overall literary quality and excellent storytelling, which can be found in equally great measure in other classics, I consider this trilogy to have no virtues. Some themes include the struggle for free will, the importance of sex in the process of growing up and gaining complete independence, the conflict between authority and personal freedom, the nonexistence of sin, the glorification of mankind, the death of God, and the dangers of religion, particularly Catholicism.

Harry Potter series, by J. K. Rowling (1997-2007)
Foundational   Parents Cautioned!
Reading Level: 5.5–7.2
Interest Level: middle grades through upper grades

---

[7] Farah Mendlesohn and Michael Levy, "The Most Influential Children's Fantasy Books," *fifteeneightyfour: Academic Perspectives from Cambridge University Press*, June 13 2016, http://www .cambridgeblog.org/2016/06/the-most-influential-childrens-fantasy-books/.

Whether parents approve or disapprove of the Harry Potter books, no one can deny the powerful effect they have had on global pop culture or on children's literature as a whole. In fact, because I am a former bookseller who personally witnessed the birth of the Harry Potter phenomenon, this is the one series that I hardly needed to research to discuss its impact. Even though it has been widely challenged and debated, Harry Potter has become an unprecedented literary *and* cultural superstar. It has been said to be "the equivalent of the Beatles in children's publishing."[8]

Rowling's series did more than just capture the imaginations of children across the globe. It had a revolutionary effect on children's literature—both middle grade and young adult. Children's publishing was suddenly taken more seriously than ever before, as publishers rushed to recreate the magic of the series with new authors. The series also sparked a push to develop more crossover series, meaning those that straddled the children's, YA, and adult markets. Its appeal to both children and adults is yet another reason Harry Potter is important to children's literature, for it drew them together through a shared literary experience like no book ever had before. Finally, Harry Potter had a powerful impact on the reading habits of children. According to fan fiction author Tanaqui, many parents have noted that their children not only want to read more but are doing better in school because of it.[9]

Scholarly reception is mixed, with some critics praising the series' literary virtues and others finding many flaws in it. Flawed or not, Harry Potter changed the face of children's literature and has already secured its future place in the children's classics canon.

Most parents are aware of the controversy surrounding the Harry Potter series. Those who aren't should know that the series is an epic fantasy that centers on a school for witchcraft and wizardry in the heart of England for children who are born with magical powers. There is some violence and coming-of-age content, including intense battles between good and evil forces.

---

[8] Catherine Gray, "How JK Changed the Face of Literature," *Stylist*, https://www.stylist .co.uk/people/interviews-and-profiles/how-jk-changed-the-face-of-literature/173288.

[9] Tanaqui, "Harry Potter and the Literacy Phenomenon," *Leaky-Cauldron*, http://www .the-leaky-cauldron.org/features/essays/issue10/literacy/.

Virtues and Themes

This series' many virtues and vices are so controversial that I will not discuss them here. It is helpful to know, however, that most critics would agree that Rowling's seven-volume tale is a masterpiece of originality, imagination, and plotting. Some themes include love and friendship, good versus evil, magic and witchcraft, alternate or parallel worlds, choice and free will, power, courage, and the necessity of rebellion in some situations.

Other Noteworthy Books of This Era

The Mouse and His Child, by Russell Hoban (1967)
Reading Level: 6.6   Interest Level: middle grades

From the Mixed-up Files of Mrs. Basil E. Frankweiler, by E. L. Konigsburg (1967)
Reading Level: 4.7   Interest Level: middle grades

Brown Bear, Brown Bear, What Do You See?, by Bill Martin, Jr. (1967)
Reading Level: 1.5   Interest Level: lower grades

Corduroy, by Don Freeman (1968)
Reading Level: 3.5   Interest Level: lower grades

The Pigman, by Paul Zindel (1968)
Reading Level: 5.6   Interest Level: upper grades

Sylvester and the Magic Pebble, by William Steig (1969)
Reading Level: 4.0   Interest Level: lower grades

Frog and Toad Are Friends, by Arnold Lobel (1970)
Reading Level: 2.9   Interest Level: lower grades

See also other Frog and Toad books.

Summer of the Swans, by Betsy Byars (1970)
Reading Level: 4.9   Interest Level: middle grades

Corgiville Fair, by Tasha Tudor (1971)
Reading Level: estimated 3–4   Interest Level: lower grades

This is only a representative work of this important children's author-illustrator.

The Best Christmas Pageant Ever, by Barbara Robinson (1971)
Reading Level: 5.1   Interest Level: middle grades

Mrs. Frisby and the Rats of NIMH, by Robert C. O'Brien (1971)
Reading Level: 5.1   Interest Level: middle grades

George and Martha, by James Marshall (1972)
Reading Level: 2.7   Interest Level: lower grades

Julie of the Wolves, by Jean Craighead George (1972)
Reading Level: 5.8   Interest Level: middle grades

Alexander and the Terrible, Horrible, No Good, Very Bad Day, by Judith Viorst (1972)
Reading Level: 3.7   Interest Level: lower grades

Summer of My German Soldier, by Bette Greene (1973)
Reading Level: 5.2   Interest Level: middle grades

M. C. Higgins, the Great, by Virginia Hamilton (1974)
Reading Level: 4.4   Interest Level: middle grades

This novel won the National Book Award and the Newbery Medal, as well as other awards. It was the first Newbery to be awarded to a black author.

Strega Nona, by Tomie dePaola (1975)
Reading Level: 3.7   Interest Level: lower grades

In total, dePaola wrote and illustrated more than 250 children's books. He won many awards from the Caldecott Honor to the Laura Ingalls

Wilder Medal. Many of his titles have special interest for Catholics and other Christians. Some of these for children in the lower to middle grades are *Brother Francis of Assisi*, *The Clown of God*, *The Good Samaritan and Other Parables*, *The Holy Twins*, *The Lady of Guadalupe*, *Mary, the Mother of Jesus*, *Saint Patrick*, and *Petook*.

Tuck Everlasting, by Natalie Babbitt (1975)
Reading Level: 5.0   Interest Level: middle grades

The Snowman, by Raymond Briggs (1978)
Reading Level: 2.5   Interest Level: lower grades

Freight Train, by Donald Crews (1978)
Reading Level: 1–2
Interest Level: pre-school through Kindergarten

The Westing Game, by Ellen Raskin (1978)
Reading Level: 5.3   Interest Level: middle grades and up

The Neverending Story, by Michael Ende (German—1979; English—1983)
Reading Level: 5.9   Interest Level: upper grades

Anastasia Krupnik, by Lois Lowry (1979)
Reading Level: 4.5   Interest Level: middle grades

Jumanji, by Chris Van Allsburg (1981)
Reading Level: 3.9   Interest Level: lower grades

Sweet Whispers, Brother Rush, by Virginia Hamilton (1982)
Reading Level: 3.8   Interest Level: middle grades and up

The Polar Express, by Chris Van Allsburg (1985)
Reading Level: 3.8   Interest Level: lower grades

If You Give a Mouse a Cookie, by Laura Numeroff (1985)
Reading Level: 2.7   Interest Level: lower grades

The People Could Fly: American Black Folktales, by Virginia Hamilton (1985)
Reading Level: 2.9   Interest Level: middle grades

Redwall series, by Brian Jacques (1986–2011)
Reading Level: 5.0–6.3   Interest Level: middle grades

Owl Moon, by Jane Yolen (1987)
Reading Level: 3.2   Interest Level: lower grades

Yolen, like dePaola, is a well-known, prolific children's book author who has published more than 250 books. I have listed this picture book and the middle-grade novel that follows as two representative works. She has won many awards, including the Caldecott Medal.

The Devil's Arithmetic, by Jane Yolen (1988)
Reading Level: 4.6   Interest Level: middle grades

The True Story of the Three Little Pigs!, by Jon Scieszka (1989)
Reading Level: 3.0   Interest Level: lower grades

The Stinky Cheese Man and Other Fairly Stupid Tales, by Jon Scieszka (1992)
Reading Level: 3.4   Interest Level: lower grades

The Watsons Go to Birmingham–1963, by Christopher Paul Curtis (1995)
Reading Level: 5.0   Interest Level: middle grades

Lily's Purple Plastic Purse, by Kevin Henkes (1996)
Reading Level: 3.1   Interest Level: lower grades

A Series of Unfortunate Events series, by Lemony Snicket (1999–2006)
Parents Cautioned!
Reading Level: 6.2–7.4   Interest Level: middle grades

These tales of orphans always in danger are extremely popular with both children and adults and have been made into a Netflix series.

The children's woeful circumstances and misadventures are exaggerated to the point of hilarity, but not everyone will find them amusing.

Because of Winn-Dixie, by Kate DiCamillo (2000)
Reading Level: 3.9   Interest Level: middle grades

Yes, they should. In fact, I am suggesting that they read a whole bunch of them, along with some other books and tales that were not written for children but that have been enjoyed by them for centuries (King Arthur tales, for example). If this sounds odd to you, not to mention a huge waste of time, I encourage you to consider what many children's literature experts will tell you—that children's literature is every bit as rich, meaningful, engaging, and beautiful as adult literature. In fact, they will also tell you that children's books are often better! Having read widely in both children's and adult literature myself, I emphatically agree.

This is good news for students. Because there is so much well-written children's literature available, both old and new, educators have plenty to choose from when seeking to prepare students for the challenging adult material they will *also* need to read if they want to prepare sufficiently for college. Unfortunately, many wonderful books will need to remain recreational reading; there are just too many riches to enjoy! But if we focus on the Children's Great Books, we will not only give our students the best preparation possible for the great adult classics, but also ensure that our young people do not grow up without experiencing the very best of the literature written just for them. These are the goals of *Before Austen Comes Aesop: The Children's Great Books and How to Experience Them.* Welcome!

What You Need to Know before You Begin

To begin using this book, I suggest first skimming it to get a sense of the whole, including the appendices. Copy any parts of the appendices that may be helpful throughout your chosen adventure.

This book is grounded in not just the children's classics, but the *most important* children's classics as indicated by literary history. It can be used as either a general resource for all families or as a literature program for homeschool families. When used as a literature program, the book can be used for multiple children and for multiple years. It can also replace graded literature programs until more formal instruction or group instruction is needed.

The book is divided into three main sections: a reading list, reading adventure guides, and appendices. The reading list assists parents

I have taken or admired these approaches at various times as a teacher and home educator, and they all have value. There is at least one more approach, however, that I haven't mentioned: the classical approach. The traditional classical model focuses its literary instruction on the most influential, most important authors of Western civilization, such as Sophocles, Plato, Virgil, and Shakespeare. Their works reveal and contribute to the thinking of our entire civilization. They have influenced writers of every generation, both the famous and the forgotten, which means that without these foundational works, Western literature would not exist as we know it. For those who want a classical education, which is fundamentally an education in Western civilization, these Great Books are essential reading.

The classical approach is the one I generally favor for literary study. It makes the most sense to me in the broader context of a well-rounded education. It is the most meaningful, the most valuable, the most fundamental, and the most beautiful. At the same time, however, it is not the most kid- or teen-friendly. Some of it is, of course—myths, fables, Bible stories, and even *The Odyssey* in an accessible translation. Other greats, though, are not—Milton, Dante, Chaucer, and many others. What to do about this? How do educators smoothly bridge the way from here to there without losing students to a lifelong hatred of literature on the way?

I suggest what might be considered a "sidekick" approach. This is where great works of children's literature are the primary focus during the grade-school years (including most of high school), but they actually support and lay the groundwork for the future introduction of the Great Books canon. Such an approach teaches Western children's literature from roots to leaf, leading students through the works that young people like them have enjoyed through the centuries, beginning with ancient works such as Aesop's fables and Bible stories and continuing with all the most important works from the Middle Ages to our present time.

It would be easy to put aside this body of literature with a dismissive sniff when considering adolescents. After all, this is *children's* literature we're talking about. This is all fine in the elementary grades, but middle school and high school? Teens may not be adults, but they are also not children. Should adolescents really spend even part of their few college-preparatory years on children's books?

PART TWO

Your Passport to
Three Reading Adventures

8

Choosing Your Own
Reading Adventure

This book is primarily intended to ground grade-school students in what I've termed the Children's Great Books. At the same time, its purpose is to give students the tools for enjoying literature to its fullest, as well as to prepare them for deeper explorations in more challenging courses. Many literature programs are appreciation courses, but *Before Austen Comes Aesop* is designed to show parents and students how to guide themselves in their literary adventures.

To plan their courses, teachers, publishers, and curriculum designers use certain principles to develop lesson plans that teachers and parents can follow. Anyone can access these principles, though; being a trained teacher isn't a requirement! This doesn't mean that trained teachers aren't valuable. Their expertise allows them to take students deeper into literature than those students might otherwise go; therefore, we will always need good teachers. Still, when families want to experience literature independently, such as in a homeschool curriculum, they can use general literature appreciation principles to enjoy a rich and meaningful experience of any poem, short story, play, or book they choose.

Literature can be experienced in several ways, and in *Before Austen Comes Aesop* I will present three ways that grade school students can best understand. The three ways, or adventures, are relevant and easily accessible to children and adolescents. They may be used in a leisurely or intensive way, as needed, but the primary goal is the same—to immerse them in the Children's Great Books, the most important literature written for or beloved by young people from the classical era through the second millennium.

To begin, choose one of the adventures in the following chapters:

- *The Leisurely Adventure*—if you are interested in experiencing the Children's Great Books for pure delight at any age or reading level, go to the next page.
- *The Book Club(ish) Adventure*—if you are interested in a meaningful experience of the Children's Great Books with some informal accountability, go to page 139.
- *The Scholarly Adventure*—if you are interested in a formal, academic study of the Children's Great Books, begin with the introduction to the Scholarly Adventure that starts on page 141. For elementary students, then turn to page 145. For secondary students, the Scholarly Adventure begins on page 163.

In addition, the appendices include information and aids that you may find helpful throughout your studies. Enjoy your adventures with the Children's Great Books!

9

The Leisurely Adventure (all ages)

Fun, delight, excitement, enchantment, inspiration, and lots of new heroes and friends—this is what the leisurely path is for! Whether your student is a pre-reader or ready for Homer, the wonderful adventures found in the Children's Great Books belong to everyone. Best of all, we can enjoy them anytime, anyplace. That's the magic of a good book!

Sometimes it's hard to know where to start, because so many good books fill our libraries and bookstores and often even our bookshelves at home. Still, some of us want to choose only the very best literature, and sometimes it's challenging to tell which books fit that description.

Although already published guides are available to help you, *Before Austen Comes Aesop* is unique in that it emphasizes the *crème de la crème* of children's and young adult books according to literary history. Though the reading list may be fairly debated among literature buffs, my goal was to make it as objective and trustworthy as possible.

I don't promise you will like all the books on the list. You may want to avoid some of them, because they may be too much at odds with your personal values or religious convictions. In making my selections, I had to put aside this concern in order to pursue objectivity. Like them or not, though, these are the books that have been the most important and influential in the world of children's literature— and even, in some cases, in the world of adult literature, as well.

To enjoy the Leisurely Adventure to the fullest, follow one of these two plans:

1. Have your child do the Children's Great Books Project in appendix F, on pages 251-58.
2. Have your child follow the Leisurely Adventure instructions on the next page.

The Leisurely Adventure

Step 1: Skim through the reading list to get a sense of the whole. The list is organized chronologically, so choose the era in which you would like to begin.

Step 2: Choose a book that interests you.

Step 3: Purchase a notebook in which you will enjoy writing. Make sure the pages are blank. You will probably find it easier to use a lined notebook, but unlined pages are okay, too, especially if you enjoy drawing pictures or diagrams that relate to your reading.

Step 4: Choose a writing utensil you enjoy using, and keep it attached to your notebook, so that you always have it ready.

Step 5: On the cover of your notebook, add a title such as "Reading Notebook" or "Reading Record" or perhaps something more creative.

Step 6: Label the first page on the inside with the same title. On the next page, write "Table of Contents" at the top. For your first entry, write the title and author of the book you will read. Every time you read another book, add it to your table of contents.

Step 7: Read the book and from time to time write down your thoughts about it.

Step 8: After you finish the book, jot down your general reactions and thoughts about it. If you don't have much to say, at least write what you liked and disliked about the book. Someday you will enjoy having this record, so fill it up and store it with your mementoes.

Step 9: Repeat steps 1–8 for as many books as you like!

10

The Book Club(ish) Adventure (all ages)

While taking off on literary adventures is always exciting, sometimes we might want to share them with other adventurers. It's fun to discuss and celebrate books together, sharing ideas and insights that come to us, musing over events or characters, and asking questions about things we didn't understand. Sometimes, too, we might find that having a little accountability pushes us to finish and contemplate books that we might otherwise put down when life distracts us.

People of all ages enjoy belonging to book clubs. They meet in a variety of settings, from a living room to a bookstore's back corner, and they often focus on a specific genre, such as mysteries or historical fiction. In some book clubs, members take turns choosing monthly selections. At an appointed day and time, they come together to discuss that month's selection and perhaps eat a meal or light refreshments.

Years ago, I attended a book club that met in a children's bookstore. It was for adults who loved children's books, so its emphasis was new children's fiction. During the meeting we would discuss that month's selection, which included both a picture book and a novel. Later in the meeting, we were offered a snack or drink that related to the books. It was far away from my house, unfortunately, so I couldn't attend often, but it was fun to celebrate children's literature with other adults.

If you and your child choose this reading adventure, it doesn't mean that you must join or start a book club. It is ideal, of course, but you can also enjoy the principles of book clubs in a more private way. All you need is at least one person to join in periodic meetings to discuss the books, and perhaps a yummy snack or meal. You can make it even more fun by decorating the meeting space or searching for activities related to the books. For example, if you read *From the Mixed-up Files of Mrs. Basil E. Frankweiler,* you could add an outing to your local art museum.

To begin a Book Club(ish) Adventure, follow these steps.

The Book Club(ish) Adventure

Step 1: Find one or more members who will agree to meet regularly, participate faithfully, and hold you accountable for your reading.

Step 2: Decide what kind of books you'll read. Perhaps you might pick a certain genre or era, for example.

Step 3: Decide who will choose the first book. Then set a regular location and time for your meetings.

Step 4: Decide who will lead the meetings. That member could be responsible for preparing some discussion questions and providing snacks—or perhaps one member could host and the other members could provide food, etc. Alternatively, you could all sign up for different tasks, varying them from meeting to meeting. At minimum, you will need a leader to moderate each meeting, even if it's just an informal chat on a living room couch.

Step 5: Be faithful in keeping up your end of the agreement. If you don't, your book club won't be much fun. But if you do, you will not only deepen your appreciation of literature, but also deepen your friendships with the other members.

Step 6: Do an extension activity. Extension activities are meant to be just plain fun. You can find lots of ideas on the Internet or at your library, but these books offer a variety of foods, games, and activities related to classic children's books.

Cherry Cake and Ginger Beer: A Golden Treasury of Classic Treats, by Jane Brocket

Ripping Things to Do: The Best Games and Ideas from Children's Books, by Jane Brocket

Storybook Parties, by Penn Warner and Liya Lev Oertel

Turkish Delight and Treasure Hunts: Delightful Treats and Games from Classic Children's Books, by Jane Brocket

The Scholarly Adventure
(elementary and secondary levels)

For the Scholarly Adventure you will use no suggested workbooks or textbooks. That doesn't mean I don't think they are worth trying. In fact, I do use and admire several programs. The discussion questions and information they provide can be invaluable in the study of a literary work. The goal of *Before Austen Comes Aesop*, however, is to offer a path to literary independence. I will show you how your students can study a book on their own without relying on a special curriculum or workbook. This is a skill they can use throughout their lives to experience great literature. Group discussion, collaborative projects, teacher feedback, and other activities that only a class can provide have their own intrinsic value. Solitary study cannot replace them. But solitary study also has intrinsic value, and that is what we will discuss for this adventure.

To study literature without a teacher or a class or even a curriculum, you will follow a simple method and need only a few supplies for both levels. Your goals at each level, however, will be a little different. At the elementary level, your focus should be on establishing fluency and active reading skills, so that your child is prepared for analytical reading in the secondary grades. You'll also want to nurture your child's interest and delight in reading. At the secondary level, your focus should be on improving active reading skills and mastering analytical skills, as well as nudging your student into more challenging, mature literature. This will prepare him for literary study at the college level.

Each time your student sits down to study his chosen literature, he will need his book, reading notebook, and writing utensil, along with this guide. Each book should have its own corresponding set of pages in his notebook with clear headings at the top of the first page.

When your student has prepared the page and added it to his table of contents, he is ready to read and engage with the text.

Using a reading notebook not only provides your student with a simple, natural approach to studying literature, but also frees him to develop more creative and meaningful responses to what he reads compared to what workbooks and textbooks may encourage. If your student puts his best efforts into keeping the notebook, it may also serve as a helpful study guide for assessments. In addition, all these notes and responses may be valuable to your student later in life, much like a diary might. I'll explain more about the notebook and other supplies in the step-by-step guides below.

Help from Bloom and Adler

The study method I'll give you in the Scholarly Adventure is based on Bloom's Taxonomy of Learning and Mortimer Adler's *How to Read a Book: The Classic Guide to Intelligent Reading* (1972, revised and co-authored with Charles Van Doren). I'll explain each one in turn.

The Value of Bloom's Taxonomy

Bloom's Taxonomy is a learning theory developed by Benjamin Bloom in 1956 about how humans tend to learn. In 2001 it was revised by Lorin Anderson and David Krathwohl to reflect new research and updated vocabulary. It is important to understand that this taxonomy provides only a framework for how a subject is mastered. The actual process of learning does not always march in a straight line up the hierarchy; sometimes the levels can dovetail or progress in reverse order.

The taxonomy is shown below in both its original and revised forms. They both begin with the lowest level and ascend to the highest level. Because they show essentially the same concepts, I have added definitions for only the revised version, which I will use in this book.

Original Bloom's Taxonomy

1. Knowledge
2. Comprehension

3. Application
4. Analysis
5. Synthesis
6. Evaluation

Revised Bloom's Taxonomy

1. Remembering—basic knowledge of the facts, rules, concepts, and ideas presented
2. Understanding—full comprehension of the presented material
3. Applying—making use of new knowledge and comprehension
4. Analyzing—deconstructing and examining individual parts of a whole
5. Evaluating—making judgments and critiques of a work, such as a novel
6. Creating—using what has been learned about individual parts to construct a new whole

This is a model that I find helpful for understanding how we master a subject. You might find it helpful, too, if you are devising your own study of literature or any other subject.

The Value of Mortimer Adler's Reading Theories

Mortimer Adler was a twentieth-century professor, philosopher, and author who was a strong advocate for a liberal arts education that emphasized the Great Books of Western civilization. He wrote and edited more than fifty books, among them the original version of *How to Read a Book*, which was then subtitled *The Art of Getting a Liberal Education* (1940). Adler divided meaningful reading into four distinct levels, which again ascend in order:

1. Elementary—basic literacy and fluency
2. Inspectional—two stages of what we today call prereading (gathering context information and skimming)
3. Analytical—studying, deconstructing, discussing, and interpreting a book
4. Syntopical—examining two or more books to gain deeper insight on a particular symbol, idea, theme, etc.

I used Adler's reading levels and Bloom's Taxonomy as a simple framework to design the self-study methods for elementary and secondary students. For both the elementary and secondary methods we will stick to Bloom's Taxonomy, 1 through 4, and Adler's levels, 1 through 3. Secondary students, however, will go deeper into all of the levels than elementary students.

12

The Elementary Scholarly Adventure

For future easy reference, all the steps in the Elementary Scholarly Adventure are condensed into one page in appendix B (see page 224).

The Elementary Scholarly Adventure, Step-by-Step

Step 1: Gather Supplies

Preparing for a next literary adventure is kind of like packing a field kit for a nature hike. In the elementary stage, this doesn't require a lot. Students need only a notebook, writing utensils, and a dictionary.

Reading Notebook

In the elementary years, the use of the reading notebook may vary widely depending on the student's reading and writing ability, as well as the selection itself. You may assign many activities in the notebook, or you may find that your student really needs oral work more than written work. Either way, the reading notebook can be useful in several ways at the elementary level:

- record of literature read
- list of books to read
- responses to literature
- graphic organizers
- discussion question responses
- vocabulary words to learn
- prewriting activities for literature-related essays

Even if a student cannot make much use of the reading notebook for whatever reason, I encourage keeping a log of each book read and the student's general reactions to it. You might also add your observations of the student's progress. Not only will this become a helpful academic record, it will also become a valued personal record that your student may someday like to have.

You may choose any notebook you like from a three-ring binder to an expensive hardbound journal, but I recommend a standard college-ruled composition book. The pages are sewn together for durability, the price is low, the size is easy to handle and transport, and the smooth binding allows for easy storage on a shelf or in a stack.

Label the front with "Reading Notebook." Do not use the notebook for any other purpose. Make a contents page, and add to it every book that is read.

Writing Utensils

The writing utensils your student uses are solely a matter of preference. Color, style, and size do not matter, so long as your child is comfortable using them. That said, consider using a distinctive color to record new vocabulary or a highlighter to make them stand out. It will help your student find them quickly in his notebook when it's time to practice them. More on that later.

Dictionary

Learning new vocabulary is an important component of literature study, particularly at the elementary level when fluency is still a priority. Find a good dictionary and teach your child how to use it. I encourage you to use a book dictionary for basic instruction before you introduce Internet dictionaries. It is never a good idea to depend entirely on computers. That said, keep in mind that some Internet dictionaries provide at least one benefit that book dictionaries do not: audio files that provide word pronunciations. When you need help with pronunciation, try the written key in the book version first. Learning how to read this is a basic skill in itself—but when this is not enough, feel free to make use of audio files.

Reader's Handbook, green and yellow levels (optional)

One of the benefits of a formal reading program is that it will likely teach specific reading skills that parents may otherwise overlook, such as making predictions and inferences. These reading skills are important for preparing students for literary study that goes beyond basic comprehension. I address these skills in step 6, which is about answering discussion questions well. Some parents may want to teach these skills directly before attempting discussion questions, and for them I recommend a book by Great Source called *Reader's Handbook*. This is a wonderful resource for both parents and students that was written for classroom use but is useful to homeschool families as well. I wish everyone knew about it!

Reader's Handbook is full of helpful features designed to help students become strong, active readers. The book includes instruction on how to approach different kinds of literature, explanations of basic reading skills, and definitions of many literary elements. Be aware, though, that since it is published for schools, it is most easily obtained through the used-book market.

Step 2: Choose a Book

Of course, the literature selection is the most important item, so choose carefully. You may want to use the Children's Great Books Project in appendix F to narrow down the choices. Also, consider giving your student some ownership of his study by offering several options. Encourage selections that present some challenge, so that he can improve his fluency and stretch his mind, but don't forbid easier books. Both simple and complex literature can be worth experiencing for readers of all ages. Some picture books are even beautiful and unforgettable works of art, such as those by Tomie dePaola, Jan Brett, and Tasha Tudor.

While both classic and contemporary children's literature are appropriate for recreational reading, I encourage the classics for formal study. Not only are they proven through their popularity over time, they are also often influential in more advanced literature. *Alice in Wonderland*, for example, has profoundly impacted Western culture, as well as both juvenile and adult literature. By making the classics your focus throughout your student's school years, you will lay the ideal foundation for your student's high school and college studies.

If you aren't sure about a selection, have your student read a chapter or two. Some books take time to engage one's interest, especially older books, so it's important to give your choice a fair chance.

However, if the student dislikes it after that—or if it proves to be too challenging—choose another book without guilt. In another year or so, the discarded book might be just right. I remember when my mother read portions of *Anne of Green Gables* to me as a child. I found it a bit boring and tedious. A few years later, I gave it another try on my own. This time it became one of my favorites and has remained so ever since.

For older students, consider buying not borrowing the book so that they can write in it. For both younger and older students, choose an edition that is visually beautiful, if possible, to enhance their enjoyment of the book.

Step 3: Do an Inspectional Reading

In Mortimer Adler's reading theory, fluency takes top priority. This includes a basic comprehension of the literature being read, including vocabulary and the connections between ideas. Throughout the elementary years, fluency is a primary goal. Working on the next stage is also valuable, though; this is what Adler called "inspectional reading."

This stage is quite simple and brief. Its purpose is to establish a surface familiarity with the text, so that the reader can determine whether the book is worth a deep reading. It can also provide a clear sense of the whole work as preparation for a deep reading. In the elementary years, an inspectional reading can be helpful for orienting readers to a new book, as well as give them practice in identifying key parts of a book.

Adler divided this stage of reading into two levels: prereading and superficial reading. Superficial reading is for high school and college students attempting to read a book above their reading level. Elementary students need to do only prereading, also called systematic skimming, by following these steps.

1. With your student read all the text on the front and back covers.
2. Open to the title page and read it.
3. Study the copyright page to understand when it was *originally* published. Note how many editions it has had since the first edition, if any. Also note where the original publisher was

located and whether it has been re-published in other countries. This information will provide insight into how old the book is, the culture in which it was written, where it was originally written and for whom, and how important it has been to the literary world overall. Help your student understand the book's broader context in literary history by showing them on a history timeline and map where the book would fit.

4. Read the table of contents to get a sense of the book's structure and content.

5. If there is a preface or introduction, skim it (read it quickly) to get any general information about the book and its author.

6. Look in the table of contents to see if the book contains an index. If so, skim the index to get a sense of the specific concepts covered in the book.

7. If the book is complex, you may want to identify chapters that seem to cover key aspects of the plot, characters, or setting (if it's fiction) or key concepts and ideas (if it's nonfiction). Skim any introductory material, chapter titles, and subheadings.

Step 4: Do a Slow Reading

Now that you and your student have familiarized yourselves with the book by examining and skimming its outer edges, so to speak, it is time to experience it fully through a slow, thoughtful reading in one or more of the following ways:

- *Read-aloud*—For this kind of reading, the teacher reads aloud, and the student practices listening skills. (Plus, it's a great way for parents and their children to cuddle!)
- *Silent reading*—The student reads independently to himself. In this way he practices concentrating on the material and comprehending it without also having to decode and pronounce words aloud.
- *Oral reading*—The student reads aloud to the teacher, in this way practicing fluency, pronunciation, and expressive inflections.
- *Shared reading*—The student and the teacher read the book together. The teacher takes the lead, modeling good oral reading skills while the student follows along. Periodically, the

teacher pauses to ask open-ended questions, such as "What do you think will happen next?" This allows the student to build vocabulary and comprehension by reading along silently and thinking through the questions posed. It also gives practice with discussion.

Recording Vocabulary

The first level of Mortimer Adler's reading theory is fluency, which requires gaining the ability to read literature of increasing difficulty, until the student can read challenging adult literature. This ability depends on building vocabulary.

When a student encounters an unknown word, he should pause to mark it in the book or to jot it down in his notebook. Later, when he is finished with that reading session, he should take some time to look up the definition and the part of speech and record them in his notebook, along with the page number where he found the word.

To keep vocabulary words separate from other notes in the reading notebook, the student can create a special section for them or use a colored pen or highlighter to make them stand out. Also, to make sure the student understands how to pronounce a word, he could ask someone who knows or listen to an audio file in an online dictionary.

Several times per week, the student should practice a few words by covering up the definitions and trying to remember them. He should also practice spelling them. Periodically, quiz your student on his vocabulary words. Every time he gets a word right, place a checkmark next to it in the notebook until it has three checkmarks. This will mean that word has been mastered.

Step 5: Summarize or Narrate the Story

Once the student has completed a slow reading of the chosen literature, it is a good idea to test and strengthen his comprehension through a narration or a summary. You may even want to do this chapter by chapter, instead of after he has finished the whole thing. For children in the primary grades, summaries and narrations can be done orally.

Summary

A summary is a kind of essay that has the typical introduction-body-conclusion structure. Its purpose is to describe briefly the beginning, middle, and end of a literary work, presenting only its key characters and events. Here is an example:

> In the story "William Tell," retold by James Baldwin, a Swiss tyrant demands that everyone who enters the town must bow down before a pole on which was set his cap. William Tell refused to do this, which made Gessler, the tyrant, so angry that he decided to punish William as an example to others. Knowing that William was a great hunter, Gessler forced him to shoot an arrow into an apple sitting on his young son's head. If William refused or missed, the tyrant threatened, his soldiers would kill the son. Yet William did not miss and thus saved his son's life that day. Not long after this, William killed the tyrant and freed his country.

Narration

A narration is a retelling of a story that is written by someone else but retold as if it is the student's own creation. The student tells the story in his own way and uses as many details as possible without making any changes to the original story. Here is an example:

> Once there was a man named William Tell, who lived in a kingdom of Switzerland that was ruled by a wicked tyrant named Gessler. Wanting to ensure his power over every citizen of his kingdom, he decided to force everyone entering the public square to bow to his cap, which was set atop a tall pole. William Tell only laughed, however, refusing to give the tyrant what he wanted. Fearing that he would lose power if other people followed suit, Gessler tried to think of a way to bring Tell to misery.
>
> Now, William Tell was a great hunter in those parts, so Gessler decided to put his skill to the ultimate test. One day he ordered William Tell's young son to stand in the public square with an apple on his head. If Tell did not shoot an arrow into the apple squarely on the first try, Gessler threatened, the boy

would immediately be killed by his soldiers. Tell begged for mercy but received none, so with a prayer he took aim and shot the apple right in the center. Then a second arrow fell from his coat, and Gessler fumed. "What is this under your coat?" he cried. Tell replied, "It is the arrow I would have shot you with if I had missed and harmed my child." Soon afterward, William Tell did, in fact, kill the tyrant Gessler with an arrow and finally freed his country.

Similarities between Narrations and Summaries

- Both convey a sense of the entire story—the beginning, middle, and end.
- Both may be done as an oral or written exercise.
- Both focus on a single literary work.
- Both are completely objective writing forms and thus don't allow the writer to insert personal opinions or other commentary.
- Neither may quote from the original literature or from any sources outside of the literature.
- Both must remain true to the original work without copying the author's words, and they never add or change anything.

Differences between Narrations and Summaries

Summary	Narration
Good for testing basic comprehension but also for sharpening skills in discerning main, supporting, and detail parts of a literary work.	Good for testing comprehension thoroughly, for developing skills in identifying all the important elements of a literary work, and for developing the ability to expand a composition with details.
Must be brief—perhaps one paragraph to a couple of pages, depending on the length of the literature; gives only key characters, events, and information.	May be as long as necessary to retell the story or information in detail.
Is a type of formal, analytical essay.	Is an informal retelling in the same genre as the original literature.

Writer speaks from outside the story, because he or she is writing *about* it.	Writer speaks from inside the story, because he or she is *retelling* it.
Has an impersonal, formal voice.	Has an engaging storyteller voice.
Refers to the title and author of the original work in the topic sentence.	Does not refer to the title and author of the original work anywhere.
Begins with a topic sentence that provides the title, author, and a general statement about the work.	Begins with an opening sentence that pulls reader into the beginning of the story—not a topic sentence.

Step 6: Discuss the Story

One of the most important literary study activities is responding to discussion questions. Every reading and literature teacher values discussion, because it is difficult, if not impossible, to mine the treasures of a book without discussing it in some way. Unfortunately, discussion is also one of the most challenging activities for teachers and parents to do well. This is because it can be so open-ended. It's not always easy to know how to guide a student to logical, coherent thinking about a book or even to come up with meaningful discussion questions.

Easy or not, though, students need the benefit of discussion about books and other literature. Through discussions they cement their knowledge and understanding of the literature, and eventually discussions give them opportunities to grapple with the subtext of literature and the many themes and ideas that may not confront us so directly in real life.

Discussions are used in a variety of ways, but their purposes boil down to a basic three:

1. Helping students develop the various skills required for deep and insightful reading. Such skills include (but are not limited to) comprehension, making inferences and predictions, examining character traits and motives, extracting themes and symbols, making interpretations, making comparisons and contrasts, and drawing conclusions.

2. Deepening students' experiences of the work because discussions introduce the ideas and insights of others who are reading the same literature.
3. Helping students apply the literature to themselves and their own lives, which further deepens their reading experience.

Students need to become skilled at answering three main types of discussion questions in complete sentences, whether written or spoken aloud:

1. *Factual questions ask who, what, when, and where, and sometimes why and how.* These generally have one right answer, which can be given in one or two sentences. Factual questions about literature often focus on the literary elements in the story, such as plot, characters, setting, and so on. To be prepared for the more analytical, complex literary studies of high school and college, students need to have a solid grasp of these elements. This is equivalent in importance to basic arithmetic before moving on to algebra or geometry. For a list of the most basic elements of narrative literature and their definitions, see page 155.

2. *Interpretive questions ask why and how.* They require thinking about actions, conversations, or events in the story and determining their meaning or significance. Such questions often have more than one right or good answer, as long as those answers are thorough, specific, and supported by the text.

3. *Evaluative questions ask the reader what he thinks about the story.* These involve considering the actions of the characters in the light of one's own reasoning.

For a complete guide to discussion questions see appendix H on pages 263–67.

The Basic Elements of Narrative Literature

Narrative literature tells a story. The list on the next page covers the basic elements of a narrative with which *all* literature students need to be familiar. Students need to begin identifying them in the

The Basic Elements of Narrative Literature

Characters   The people, animals, or animated objects in the story. They can be categorized as main characters (or protagonist), supporting characters, and minor characters. The protagonist often has an antagonist, a character or a force that works against the protagonist.

Point of View   The vantage point from which the story is told. Several possibilities:

First person—a character telling the story through his own eyes (I did, thought, said)

Second person—a character telling the story from the reader's or another character's perspective (You did, thought, said)

Third person omniscient—a non-character narrator telling the story through the eyes of multiple characters (He or they did, thought, said)

Third person limited—a non-character narrator telling the story through the eyes of only one character, sometimes switching between a small number of selected characters in separate chapters.

Setting   When and where the story takes place; can include one or more of the following: historical era, time of year, time of day, time of week, place on the planet, and place in the character's world.

Conflict or Inciting Incident   The problem that drives the story; what happens in the story to begin the plot; usually a struggle between the protagonist and the antagonist.

Plot   The main events of the story, usually told in chronological order.

Dialogue   The words spoken by the story's characters; usually set off by quotation marks.

Mood   The feelings that the story evokes in the reader such as sadness, joy, or fear.

Theme   The underlying message or universal ideas of a story; usually must be inferred by the reader through careful reading.

elementary grades so that they have that foundational knowledge when they enter the secondary grades.

The Four Rules for Written Answers to Discussion Questions

Once students have the skills to write a complete sentence, they can begin to answer discussions in writing by following these four rules:

1. *Answer in complete sentences with a subject that does not use a pronoun and without a yes or no lead-in.* This will not only help prevent confusing responses, but also help prepare students for the more complex responses of harder questions.
   Example Question: What are Anne Shirley's main goals in *Anne of Green Gables*?
   Example of a Good Answer: Anne's main goals are...

2. *Give not only a correct answer but also a thorough one.* One of the most important skills to cultivate in writing about any subject is how to support and expand upon a main idea. If students give correct responses to a discussion question, they have done well, but they are not yet finished. They must also consider whether they have supported their answer with details from the text that explain or defend their answer. Sometimes questions are so simple there is nothing more to say.
   In the primary grades, this is a skill that will not yet be developed. Focus on a clear, correct answer and feel free to add guiding questions to draw out deeper responses from your student. In the intermediate grades, however, learning how to give strong support to an answer without guiding questions is good preparation for secondary-level study.

3. *Answer the question directly.* This means examining the question to determine exactly what it is asking and then answering only that.

4. *Avoid opinion phrases, such as "I believe ..." or "I think ...".* Whether answers are opinion or fact, they should be stated as facts. This air of confidence will strengthen a student's writing.

In the primary grades I encourage parents to focus more on oral discussion, adding in written answers to discussion questions in the intermediate grades. But oral discussions of books is good for children at any age. Sometimes they lead you to discuss topics about the literature that you didn't expect, which may be both rewarding and beneficial. Feel free to follow your student's lead if your discussion heads in unexpected directions. The best part about literature discussions is thinking deeply about meaning and ideas in the literature, especially when they can be applied to one's own life.

How to Prepare Good Discussions

By now you may be wondering how to come up with discussion questions to ask your child if you are studying a literary work without a formal curriculum. You can use several strategies:

1. Appendix H (page 263) is a selection of general discussion questions that can be applied to many different literary works and answered in a reading notebook. Move progressively from simple factual questions to complex factual questions to interpretive questions to evaluative questions.

2. Read the novel alongside your student, and ask each other questions. Don't feel that you must complete a preplanned set of questions or you have failed the whole exercise. Do, however, focus mainly on questions that address the first two levels of Bloom's Taxonomy: remembering and understanding. Your student needs to comprehend the material before analyzing it.

3. If your student is ready for it, ask him to pretend he is a teacher who must create a test for a class. Ask him to develop questions based on the Five Ws (Who, What, When, Where, Why) and One H (How), as well as any other questions that probe parts of the book that seem important to him. When he has developed the questions, he can answer them in writing. This is an excellent study technique for any subject, by the way! Formulating meaningful questions deepens learning.

4. Some homeschool literature programs and online resources offer study guides for individual novels. Of course, this pulls you back to a formal program, but if you need that support, there is nothing wrong with using it.

Step 7: Write about the Story

Beginning in the middle primary grades, no meaningful literature study is complete without relevant writing assignments. Going beyond mere discussion questions to full essays or stories draws students deeper into the literature, helping them to experience it more fully and to learn how to wrestle with more complex ideas than what discussion questions allow.

Early literary writing doesn't need to be formal, as it does in the upper grades and college, but it does need to challenge students at least a little. To put the value of early literary writing in perspective, consider this sequence of literary writing throughout an education:

Elementary students are capable of

- retelling
- explaining
- storytelling
- responding

With the above skills mastered *middle school* students are capable of

- expanded and more complex retelling, explaining, storytelling, and responding
- summarizing
- arguing an opinion logically
- applying ideas to real life
- analyzing simple elements of literature

With the above skills mastered *high school* students are capable of

- expanded, more complex essays
- writing analytical essays according to Modern Language Association (MLA) standards
- writing full research papers according to MLA standards

With the above skills mastered *college* students are capable of

- writing scholarly papers of considerable length
- syntopical analysis
- literary theory and criticism

As you can see, the development of these higher skills begins in the elementary grades. Give your student many opportunities to write about literature, and give him constructive feedback on his work. At the same time, the kind of formal writing and grading that secondary students are ready for isn't necessary in the elementary grades. Let the writing assignments be casual and pleasant. Focus on helping your student learn how to express ideas easily and coherently. Refrain from picky criticism; this will help your student preserve his natural voice and keep him from fear of "doing it wrong." Help him learn how to express his ideas in sequential order and to add interesting details. Logical arguments, complex explanations, formal organization, and in-depth grading can wait until middle school, when he is developmentally ready for those skills.

Finally, avoid focusing on grammar, spelling, and mechanics in rough drafts. Although these elements are all essential to polished writing and need to be mastered by upper high school, pointing out technical mistakes during the drafting phase is a mistake in itself, because it stunts the creative process of developing ideas. Wait until it's time to guide your student through a final draft, if you choose to carry a writing assignment that far.

But what should you ask your student to write about if you don't have a curriculum to prompt you? The possibilities vary with every story, and you may have to create some interesting prompts yourself. An Internet search for "writing prompts on (name of novel)" may give you some ideas, too. Here are some all-purpose basics to get you started:

1. *Narrate the story or a chapter in the story.* As explained in Step 5, this simply means to retell a story in one's own words in as much detail as time and space allows. Narrations require the student to practice remembering and sequencing, to show comprehension, and to choose appropriate and sufficient details to develop the story. They can be done as oral or written exercises.

2. *Write a book report.* Traditionally, this refers to a short paper written to provide objective information about a book, as well as the writer's reactions to it. You can find many creative book report ideas on the Internet, however, if you want to let your student have more fun with the project.

3. *Create an original story based on the book.* For example, you might have your student write an alternate ending or imagine how the story might have been different if a key event had not occurred. If the book was a fantasy, perhaps your student might imagine a magical world of his own and write an original story about it.

4. *Write a letter to the author.* For most classic books the author will no longer be living, but your student can still write one as a way to express his thoughts, feelings, and opinions about the book. If the author is still alive, this letter will be more meaningful—and better written—if you help your student send the letter. Many authors have their own websites with contact information, or you might be able to send the letter through the author's agent or publisher, if you can locate that information.

5. *Write a like-dislike essay.* This is a simple essay that will give your student a non-intimidating introduction to personal response writing. In the first paragraph (or in the first half of the paragraph, if your student is too young to write more than one) the student should discuss what he liked about the story. In the second paragraph he should write about what he disliked about it (or vice versa).

Step 8: Do One or More Enrichment Projects

Sometimes in your literary studies, you may have limited time to devote to a book. That's okay. Just complete the activities you feel are important, and then move on to the next book. In my opinion, though, the best kind of literary study includes a little fun— especially when it comes to children's literature! In fact, you may want to change your focus with every book. Perhaps with some books you might focus on comprehension and writing, and with others you might focus on casual discussion and extension activities. Extension activities, which enrich the literary experience, are what this final step is about.

Every good book is rich in possibilities for all kinds of enrichment activities, and these will vary from book to book. It is impossible for me to cover every possible idea, so I encourage you to come up with some of your own as you read your selections. Here are some general ideas to get you and your student started.

Creative Enrichment Activities

- Draw portraits of the main characters the way you remember them.
- Draw a storyboard or cartoon version of the story.

- Make a poster that shares the important elements of a story in creative, fun ways.
- Extend the story by telling what you think might happen next if the story continued.
- Write a poem about something you really liked or disliked in the story.
- Write an alternate ending to the story.
- Draw a picture of a scene in the novel, and then cut it into puzzle pieces for a family member to put together.
- Learn about the genre of the story. Then write your own story in that genre.
- Try the storyteller's craft. Learn some techniques of professional storytellers, and then gather your family and friends together to tell them the story in your own words.
- Tell the story through a different character's point of view.
- Create a board game based on the story, and then play it with someone.
- Draw a map of your story's world.
- Create a short newspaper featuring important stories and columns that reflect parts of the story. These might include a weather report, an advice column, a crossword puzzle, advertisements, and, of course, feature stories.
- Turn the story or a scene from it into a script for a play.

Practical Enrichment Activities

- Find a recipe for a food that was mentioned in the story, and then make it for your family.
- Research the setting of the story, and study photographs of it. Write a report about the culture, landscape, and other aspects of the setting.
- Make a timeline of the story's events.
- Listen to some music that came from the era in which your story is set. Try to choose music that the main character might have chosen, and explain your choices.
- If the main character belongs to a different religion or culture from yours, research it and write a report about what you learn.
- Make a collection of your favorite lines from the story, and explain why you liked each one.

- If your story is set in another era, plan and make a menu for a meal or tea party typical of that era and invite your friends to enjoy it with you.
- Make a poster about the historical background of the story, and give a presentation to your family.
- Research the fashions of the story's historical era, and make an illustrated booklet.
- Sew or make a handicraft that is related to your book.

And if none of these ideas inspire you, try the Internet or these wonderful books for more ideas:

Cherry Cake and Ginger Beer: A Golden Treasury of Classic Treats, by Jane Brocket
Ripping Things to Do: The Best Games and Ideas from Children's Books, by Jane Brocket
Storybook Parties, by Penny Warner and Liya Lev Oertel
Turkish Delight and Treasure Hunts: Delightful Treats and Games from Classic Children's Books, by Jane Brocket

13

The Secondary Scholarly Adventure

In chapter 11, the Scholarly Adventure was introduced with descriptions of elements common to both elementary and secondary levels. This chapter builds on that information and presents the steps involved in the Secondary Scholarly Adventure, which are addressed to the student. For future easy reference, all of these steps are condensed into one page in appendix B (see page 225).

A Note about Juniors and Seniors

Upperclassmen who are not well-read in the Children's Great Books should take the time to read as many as they can. These are foundational works of Western literature worth reading at all ages. However, these students also need to spend time preparing for postsecondary education by reading more adult literature. While a few of the Children's Great Books were originally written for adults, such as *The Odyssey* and *The Pilgrim's Progress*, most were not. In addition, upperclassmen may need more formal teaching at this point in their education; self-directed study may not be enough. I encourage them to seek group classes or instruction, live or online, that will challenge them with adult classics and facilitate the development of participation and communication skills that may be difficult to acquire on their own.

The Secondary Scholarly Adventure, Step-by-Step

The preparation stage of literary study (steps 1 through 4) is a time to organize and orient yourself to the task ahead. Don't rush through it. Good preparation will make your study easier and more pleasant.

Remember, studying a literary work is different from reading one for fun. When you prepare to study a book, you are readying yourself for a deep dive into not only the book but also the author's mind.

Step 1: Gather Supplies

To begin, you will need the following study supplies.

Notebook

Choosing and preparing your notebook involve the following steps:

1. Choose any notebook you like, from a three-ring binder to an expensive hardbound journal. I recommend a standard college-ruled composition book. The pages are sewn together for durability, the price is low, the size is easy to handle, and the smooth binding allows for easy storage on a shelf or in a stack.

2. You might like to make your notebook personal and fun by adding colors, stickers, doodles, and so forth.

3. If you're the kind of person who tends to jot notes and ideas on random paper scraps or index cards, you might consider pasting an envelope at the front or back in which to keep them until you're ready to copy or paste them into your notebook.

4. On page 1 write "Reading Notebook."

5. You can use page 2 for a table of contents, where you list the title of each book you study. Start each study on a fresh page.

6. Once you have chosen the literature you will study, turn to a clean page in your notebook and write the title at the top. Near the title add the date you are beginning your study. Now your notebook is ready for any notes and thoughts you choose to record as you study your chosen literature.

You will want to use this notebook only for your study of literature, because you will be doing a lot of writing in it. As you study your chosen book, record all your notes and thoughts about it in your notebook. Polished essays and your capstone project can begin in your notebook but should be finished on separate paper.

Writing utensils

The writing utensils you choose are a matter of preference. Color, style, and size do not matter. That said, you might consider using a distinctive color or a highlighter for recording unfamiliar words. It will help you find the words quickly when needed. More on that later.

Step 2: Buy—Do Not Borrow—Your Literature Selection

You may not always have the freedom to choose your own literature to study. When you do, however, try to choose books that are either at or above your reading level. This doesn't mean you can't read easier books sometimes; good books are good books, no matter how difficult they are. Unless you are choosing easier books for a specific purpose, however (i.e., you want to learn how to write picture books), they should not be your typical choices.

Choosing worthwhile literature to study is not just about difficulty, of course. It's also about quality and the book's place in your curriculum. Choosing quality material can be daunting, but the good news is that there are many wonderful books of all kinds available. Don't waste your time on junk!

This guide is all about reading the Children's Great Books, but the world of literature is vast, rich, and exciting. You will not be at a loss for good options. No matter what you choose, take the time to research the literature to make sure that it is right for you. Lists of good books abound, and older classics are usually safe choices. If you aren't sure about a book, read three or four chapters. Some books take time to engage your interest, especially older books, so it's important to give your choice a fair chance. However, if you dislike it after that and don't have a compelling reason to keep reading it, choose another book.

Finally, choose an edition with as much white space on the page as you can find without spending too much money, so that you can write in it during your study. That is the reason for buying and not borrowing it. If it's a student edition, so much the better, because they often have extra sections with helpful notes to aid your comprehension.

Step 3: Collect or Identify Reference Materials

To experience fully a literary work, it's a good idea to consider what others have to say about it. This is especially true if you are struggling to understand it. This is where reference materials are invaluable, and there are many types available to help you.

Long ago, students would have to spend a long time browsing card catalogs and shelves at their local libraries to find these materials. Even then, many of them could not be checked out. Bookstores often had helpful materials, of course, but reference materials could be expensive. Today, though, the Internet allows for quick, easy, and often free access to many literary reference materials. Students today have a gold mine of information at their fingertips, as well as the traditional offerings in bookstores and libraries. Not only that, students can access discussion groups and forums online, such as Goodreads. These can help as well.

None of this information will be useful to you, however, if you don't know what to look for. Here is a list to get you started:

- standard dictionary and thesaurus
- study guides, such as *CliffsNotes* and *SparkNotes*
- literary dictionaries
- literary encyclopedias
- literary handbooks and companions
- *Reader's Handbook: A Student Guide for Reading and Learning*, by Great Source
- author biographies
- critical essays and books
- historical books (to understand a story's context)
- annotated editions of your chosen literature

And don't overlook the introductions, prefaces, discussion guides, and other extras that are found in many editions of acclaimed literary works.

Step 4: Review the Basic Elements of Narrative Literature

Once you have gathered everything you will need for your study, review the building blocks of storytelling on the next page. The list covers the basic elements of narrative literature with which *all* literature

The Basic Elements of Narrative Literature

Characters	The people, animals, or animated objects in the story. They can be categorized as main characters (or protagonist), supporting characters, and minor characters. The protagonist often has an antagonist, a character or a force that works against the protagonist.
Point of View	The vantage point from which the story is told. Several possibilities:

First person—a character telling the story through his own eyes (I did, thought, said)

Second person—a character telling the story from the reader's or another character's perspective (You did, thought, said)

Third person omniscient—a non-character narrator telling the story through the eyes of multiple characters (He or they did, thought, said)

Third person limited—a non-character narrator telling the story through the eyes of only one character, sometimes switching between a small number of selected characters in separate chapters.

Setting	When and where the story takes place; can include one or more of the following: historical era, time of year, time of day, time of week, place on the planet, and place in the character's world.
Conflict or Inciting Incident	The problem that drives the story; what happens in the story to begin the plot; usually a struggle between the protagonist and the antagonist.
Plot	The main events of the story, usually told in chronological order.
Dialogue	The words spoken by the story's characters; usually set off by quotation marks.
Mood	The feelings that the story evokes in the reader such as sadness, joy, or fear.
Theme	The underlying message or universal ideas of a story; usually must be inferred by the reader through careful reading.

students need to be familiar. You need to be able to identify them in short stories and novels in order to analyze, discuss, and write about them.

Step 5: Do an Inspectional Reading

Once you have prepared your notebook, identified some reference materials that may be helpful, and reviewed the elements of literature, you are ready to open your book. A rich and meaningful experience of a literary work, however, happens on several levels. On the first level, we only need to skim the surface. That is what inspectional reading is all about.

Inspectional reading isn't much of a reading at all. It is intended to orient you to the literature and help your actual reading go more smoothly. It has two stages: prereading, also known as systematic skimming, and superficial reading. In systematic skimming you will examine the extraneous elements of the literature, such as the jacket blurbs and the copyright page. In superficial reading you will spend a little time scanning each page of the work, letting your eyes grab bits and pieces as you move from beginning to end.

Stage 1: Systematic Skimming

This stage, outlined below, will give you a sense of background context for your chosen literature.

1. Read all text on the front and back covers.
2. Open to the title page and read it.
3. Study the copyright page to understand when the book was *originally* published. Note how many editions it has had since the first edition, if any. Note where the original publisher was located and whether it has been re-published in other countries. This information will provide insight into how old the book is and its importance to the literary world.
4. Read the table of contents to get a sense of the book's structure and content.
5. If there is a preface or introduction, skim it for any general information about the book and its author.

6. If the book contains an index or a glossary, skim it to get a sense of the concepts or ideas addressed in the book.

7. Turn to chapters that seem to contain key aspects of the plot, characters, or setting (if fiction) or key concepts and ideas (if nonfiction). Skim any introductory material and subheadings.

8. When you feel like you understand the gist of the book, turn its pages. As you do, dip in to read any paragraphs or short sections that seem to contain key parts of the story (if fiction) or key information and ideas (if nonfiction). Of course, you may want to avoid the ending!

9. If the book has summaries or other closing remarks, skim them. Avoid epilogues if you don't want to know the book's ending yet.

10. When you are ready, move to stage 2, that is, if you still want to read this book.

Stage 2: Superficial Reading

In *How to Read a Book*, Adler advises that readers first do a superficial reading when tackling a work that is quite a bit over their reading level. "In tackling a difficult book [or poem, short story, or article] for the first time, read it through without ever stopping to look up or ponder the things you do not understand right away."[1] Your goal should be only to understand the basics of the story: plot, major characters, setting, and so on. It should be easy and quick reading. Don't become bogged down in the details during the superficial reading stage, and don't worry if you don't understand the story very well. Focus on the basic structure, the key events, the main characters, the author's style, and the kind of diction (vocabulary and phrases) you'll encounter.

Step 6: Do Structural Note-Taking

Once you have completed the inspectional reading, it's a good idea to complete one more step before you begin a slow reading of the literature. This step will take us closer to the story but not quite

[1] Mortimer J. Adler and Charles van Doren, *How to Read a Book: The Classic Guide to Intelligent Reading* (New York: Simon & Schuster, 1972), 36.

inside it yet. It is called structural note-taking, and it is all about establishing context for what we are about to read. Context is the circumstances that form the setting of something, which enables us to better understand it. For example, when you give your mom a present, it is probably within the context of her birthday, Christmas, or Mother's Day.

Structural note-taking is where we study the literature's external context, meaning its place in the world. In this step we are still in the prereading stage, but it takes us a little deeper than step 5. We look at when and why the literature was written, who wrote it, and how the work fits into the broader realm of literature. By gaining this sense of context, you may better understand the literature as you read it. This can be valuable for picture books, as well as complex novels, so don't skip this step even if your selection is easy. To complete your structural note-taking, you will need to gather the following information and record it in your reading notebook.

1. *What kind of literature is it?* What is its genre? Is it classic or contemporary (or neither), written for children or adults, influential in any way, etc.?

2. *What was the setting in which it was written?* This is different from the setting of the story! It has to do with the historical and cultural context *in which it was written.* Where was it written, and what was the culture of that place like? When was it written? What historical era does it belong to, and what major events occurred near its publication?

   For example, we know that the books of the New Testament were written in the first century. To understand more accurately what the books are saying, some scholars believe, we need to understand the authors' culture, historical setting, and people to whom they were writing. Another example is *The Adventures of Tom Sawyer*, by Mark Twain. Before we meet its characters, who speak in dialects that may be difficult to understand, we might find it helpful to study the historical era and culture in which he wrote the story.

3. *Who was the author, both as a person and as a member of his society?* Here we seek to understand what kind of person is telling the story or discussing the ideas that we are about to read, because it may give us insight into the literature itself. Was the

author male or female, rich or poor, recluse or socialite, family-oriented or single, career person or homebody, etc.? What are the basic facts of his life?

For example, returning to our New Testament source, if we understand who the apostle Paul was and some details about his life, we can better understand the reasons for some of his actions after his conversion on the road to Damascus, as well as his passion for his missionary work.

4. *What is the author's purpose in writing the literary work?* You may not be able to give an insightful answer to this until you read it, but you can get an idea by examining the book's cover and by skimming the content. Is it to examine an idea, to entertain and amuse children, to express a personal struggle, to make fun of a group of people, to inspire others to do something, etc.?

5. *Do you notice anything interesting or noteworthy?* If so, put the book aside temporarily to research more information. Both the Internet and reference materials at the library can be useful, as well as any extra information in your edition of the book. Such research may be especially helpful for old, difficult, or foreign literature. For example, to understand a Shakespeare play, it can help to research the historical, cultural, and physical settings of the play and those of the author before you begin to read it. You don't need to find out a lot at this stage, so don't try to go in depth with this research. You just need a quick sketch of information. Your sources may include the following:

- study guides—as provided by *CliffsNotes*, *SparkNotes*, Shmoop.com
- literary commentaries—as can be found on websites or books devoted to your title and at the end of study guides like *CliffsNotes*
- encyclopedia entries—from *World Book Encyclopedia* or Encyclopedia.com
- biographies—as in books, articles, and websites about the author

Step 7: Do a Slow Reading

In order to understand and learn from a written work, you need to read actively not passively. Passive reading is one-way communication.

The author speaks to you, but your mind is not engaged, so you don't fully absorb his words; therefore, you comprehend little of what you read and have no response to give. In contrast, active reading is two-way communication, a completion of the circle begun by the author—like a conversation. This means that your mind is engaged. You listen intently to what the author is saying and try to understand what he is trying to communicate. You think it through, and you respond. Your response may be only a quiet pondering, or it may be a heated discussion, musings in your blog, a formal analysis, or other forms of expression.

Of course, the author will probably not see your response unless you send a personal letter, but through your responsive writing you are still completing the communication the author began. Using a reading process and engaging your mind through annotating and note-taking will help you make thoughtful, insightful responses.

Recording Vocabulary

One way to read actively is to record words that are new to you. The first level of Mortimer Adler's reading theory is fluency, which means that you have the skills to read and comprehend the literature you have chosen. Your answer may be an immediate, "Yes, of course I can," but that doesn't mean that the need for greater fluency doesn't apply to you. Language is rich and complex, and it evolves over time so that outdated words are forgotten or used less, even as new words are introduced. This means that we all need to work continuously on improving our fluency.

When you encounter a word you don't know well, pause to mark it in your book or write it in your notebook. If you write it in your notebook, be sure to record the page number. Either immediately or later on, look up the definition and part of speech, and write them next to the word. Also, make sure that you understand how to pronounce the word. Learn how to use the pronunciation key in the dictionary; that is a basic reference skill all readers should have. If necessary, you can also listen to an audio file in an online dictionary.

So that you can easily practice your new vocabulary words, you will need a way to separate them from your literary notes. You may do this in one of three ways:

1. Use a different color pen or pencil for your vocabulary words when you record them.
2. Mark all vocabulary words with a symbol, or draw a box around them.
3. Create a section in your reading notebook just for vocabulary words.

Several times each week, practice a few words by covering up the definition and trying to remember the definition, spelling, and part of speech. Every time you remember correctly, place a checkmark next to the word. After you have earned three or four checkmarks, you have sufficiently mastered the word.

Making Annotations

One way to enrich your experience of literature is to annotate it, which means to jot notes on any thoughts and ideas that come to mind as you read. These may be useful later in your study. Annotations are best written in the margins of your book, but they can be written on sticky notes, index cards, or in your reading notebook. Be sure to add the page and paragraph number if not writing notes in the book itself.

Marking unfamiliar words in literature is a simple form of annotation. To annotate literature also means to record your thoughts, insights, ideas, and other kinds of responses to what you read *as* you read. This requires that you engage your mind in a deeper way than what you might do for recreational reading and thus is a form of active reading.

Although annotating sounds easy in principle, some students find it challenging. If you are one of them, keep in mind that it is a skill to be mastered like any other skill and takes practice. If you know what kinds of annotations are possible, though, you will find it easier. Here are some ideas:

- new vocabulary, along with their definitions
- questions you have about the text
- questions that the text sparks in your mind about bigger issues in life
- personal connections you make with a character or event or setting

- observations you make, such as foreshadowing or character traits
- agreements or disagreements you have with something in text
- things you like or dislike about something in the text
- beautiful or interesting sentences, phrases, or words
- interesting or thought-provoking quotes
- moral or faith-based questions and issues that come to mind
- predictions or questions about what will happen later in text

In addition to your annotations, consider using the following markings when you choose to write in the book. Be sure to create a key in your reading notebook, in case you forget what they mean! Don't think of this list as exhaustive; it is just a starting point. Feel free to make up your own marks for additional purposes.

- underline—to note major points or important statements to remember
- vertical lines in margins—to emphasize a statement underlined or to mark a passage too long to underline
- star, asterisk, or other symbol—to mark the most important passages
- numbers—to mark an important sequence, such as the points in an argument or chronological events
- numbers of other pages in the book—to record other places in the book that are relevant to the passage or idea. Use "cf." followed by a page number to mean "compare to" or "refer to" something similar on that page (cf. p.15).
- circling key words and phrases—same as underlining, so assign a specific purpose to each and stick with it (e.g., underlining for major plot points or arguments and circling for key terms)
- colors—different colors for different purposes (e.g., blue highlighter over a word can mean a word you don't know; yellow over a sentence may indicate where you think the author is developing a theme)

Annotating is necessary for active reading because it helps you engage more fully in the text by requiring you to respond to what you read. This is not all that annotations are good for, though. The more annotations you make, the more likely you are to remember and understand what you read. Annotations also help prepare you for discussions and essays. For example, if you write down your questions about the text, you will remember to ask them during a discussion with your teacher or classmates. Some of your questions might also be good starting points for essays you might write later.

Step 8: Take Notes

Annotations are a form of note-taking, but they are all about your personal responses. The term "note-taking" here refers to *objective* observations and comments about the text—character traits, plot points, setting descriptions, and so on. By developing this skill, you will better understand the structure, organization, and other elements that make up the text. When you take good notes, you are also more likely to remember and understand what you read, and you will be more prepared for literary analysis.

Note-taking methods are a personal choice; there is no right or wrong method. As you practice, you may even develop your own method. What matters is that you learn to take good notes, which means that they are detailed enough to be useful and meaningful but not so much that the key concepts and information that you need to learn are lost.

You may take notes in the margins of your book or in your reading notebook. You may want to use colors or some other system to distinguish between your notes and annotations, but it is not necessary. Create a system that works for you. The important thing is that you record both annotations and notes for a full, rich, literary experience.

Although you can record and store notes in any way you wish, two formal methods are commonly effective. I encourage you to try them both and figure out which you like best. If you like neither one, you can design your own method. Remember, the goal of note-taking is to help you learn and understand the material, so your method must work for *you*.

Cornell Note-Taking Method

Cornell notes can be used for any subject. They are easy to set up and study, so I highly recommend that you try the method for at least one book. The key with making the method work for you is to be very tidy. This is true of any note-taking method, perhaps, but it is particularly true of the Cornell method. If you are sloppy, your notes will be confusing when it is time to study them for discussions, essays, or tests.

The Cornell Note-Taking Method is visual, so you will understand it best by examining the following template based on the novel *Anne of Green Gables*.

Cornell Note-Taking Template

Title and author: *Anne of Green Gables*, by L. M. Montgomery

Key Words and Topics:	Notes about Key Words and Topics:
Main character	Anne Shirley
Main character traits	Bright, imaginative, dramatic, lover of beauty, talkative, loving, generous, slow to forgive
Main character goals	Early—to be adopted by a family that would give her a loving, permanent home, to have a bosom friend
	Later—to get top grades, to win academic awards, and to go to Queen's College to become a teacher

Summary of Notes:

The main character, Anne Shirley, is a vivacious, imaginative pre-teen (who is well into her teens by the end). She is loving and longing for friendship at the beginning, as well as ambitious in academics.

Created by the author based on the system invented by Dr. Walter Pauk of Cornell University in Ithaca, New York

---

Here are some basic instructions for using this method:

1. Use lined notebook paper, in your case, your reading notebook.
2. Put the title and author of the work at the top.
3. Draw a vertical line down the page, creating two columns: a narrower one on the left and a wider one on the right.

4. As you read, write the key terms on the left and definitions or explanations of them on the right. In the example, the book is a novel; therefore the key terms are the basic elements of narrative literature as found on page 167.
5. Use your time and paper space efficiently by using symbols, abbreviations, paraphrases, and bullet points.
6. Three-quarters of the way down the page, draw a horizontal line. Beneath it summarize the notes on that page in complete sentences.
7. To continue taking notes, create a new template on the next page.

Graphic Organizer Method

Some people do best with a form of note-taking that is even more visual than Cornell's. They like to organize their notes using a kind of diagram called a graphic organizer. Such diagrams sort your notes into visual groupings that can help you to understand and remember what you read. As you can see in the example on page 178, it uses boxes around a central element. In this case the element is the main character in the novel *Anne of Green Gables*; thus we call this graphic organizer a character map.

Step 9: Write a Summary or a Narration

Once you have completed a slow reading of your chosen literature, it is a good idea to strengthen your comprehension of what you read. You may even want to do this chapter by chapter, instead of after you've finished the whole work. Some literature programs ask you to complete comprehension questions or other workbook-style activities, and these can be helpful. An arguably more meaningful way to test your comprehension, however, is by writing summaries and narrations. This is because, in a sense, they require you to teach the literature you just read to someone else (real or imaginary), and teaching something is the surest way to tell how well you understand the material.

Summary

A summary is a kind of essay that has the typical introduction-body-conclusion structure. Its purpose is to describe briefly the beginning,

Graphic Organizer

Book: *Anne of Green Gables*, by L. M. Montgomery

Character Map of Anne Shirley

What character says and does: loves to chatter about all kinds of things; loves to share stories and gossip; enjoys taking walks and daydreaming; expresses herself dramatically	What others think about character: wild, unusual, peculiar, too talkative, friendly but slow to forgive, generous, interesting

ANNE

SHIRLEY

How character looks and feels: • red hair (like "carrots") • large, grey eyes • freckles • skinny • homely/plain • zest for life	What I think about character: She's fun and interesting and loyal, the kind of person I'd like to be friends with. She helps me see the beauty in nature. I wish I was more like her, except that I don't like how she holds grudges.

Created by the author based on the "character map" template in *Reader's Handbook* (red edition), published by Great Source.

the middle, and the end of a literary work, presenting only its key characters and events, as you can see in this example.

> In the story "William Tell", retold by James Baldwin, a Swiss tyrant makes a demand that everyone who enters the town must bow down before a pole on which was set his cap. William Tell refused to do this, which made Gessler, the tyrant, so angry that he decided to punish William as an example to others. Knowing that William was a great hunter, he forced him to shoot an arrow into an apple sitting on his young son's head. If William refused or missed, the tyrant threatened, his soldiers would kill the son. Yet William did not miss and thus saved his son's life that day. Not long after this, he killed the tyrant and freed his country.

Narration

A narration is a retelling of a story in the student's own words. This example shows you how:

> Once there was a man named William Tell, who lived in a kingdom of Switzerland that was ruled by a wicked tyrant named Gessler. Wanting to ensure his power over every citizen of his kingdom, he decided to force everyone entering the public square to bow to his cap, which was set atop a tall pole. William Tell only laughed, however, refusing to give the tyrant what he wanted. Fearing that he would lose power if other people followed suit, Gessler tried to think of a way to bring Tell to misery.
>
> Now, William Tell was a great hunter in those parts, so Gessler decided to put Tell's skill to the ultimate test. One day he ordered William Tell's young son to stand in the public square with an apple on his head. If Tell did not shoot an arrow into the apple squarely on the first try, Gessler threatened, the boy would immediately be killed by his soldiers. Tell begged for mercy but received none, so with a prayer he took aim and shot the apple right in the center. Then a second arrow fell from his coat, and Gessler fumed. "What is this under your coat?" he cried. Tell replied, "It is the arrow I would have shot you with if I had missed and harmed my child." Soon afterward, William Tell did, in fact, kill the tyrant Gessler with an arrow and finally freed his country.

Similarities between Narrations and Summaries

1. Both convey a sense of the entire story—the beginning, middle, and end.
2. Both may be done as an oral or written exercise.
3. Both focus exclusively on a single literary work.
4. Both are completely objective writing forms and thus don't allow the writer to insert personal opinions or other commentary.
5. Neither may quote from the original literature or from any sources outside of the literature.
6. Both must remain true to the original work without copying the author's words, and they may never add or change anything.

Differences between Narrations and Summaries

Summary	Narration
Good for testing basic comprehension but also for sharpening skills in discerning main, supporting, and detail parts of a literary work	Good for testing comprehension thoroughly, for developing skills in identifying all the important elements of a literary work, and for developing the ability to expand a composition with details
Must be brief—perhaps one paragraph to a couple of pages, depending on the length of the literature; gives only key characters, events, and information.	May be as long as necessary to retell the story or information in detail
Is a type of formal, analytical essay	Is an informal retelling in the same genre as the original literature
Writer speaks from outside the story, because he or she is writing *about* it.	Writer speaks from inside the story, because he is *retelling* it.
Has an impersonal, formal voice	Has an engaging storyteller voice

Refers to the title and author of the original work in the topic sentence	Does not refer to the title and author of the original work anywhere
Begins with a topic sentence that provides the title, author, and a general statement about the work	Begins with an opening sentence that pulls the reader into the beginning of the story—not a topic sentence

Step 10: Make a Freytag Pyramid Outline

Many teachers want students to learn the skill of outlining someone else's writing, because it offers several benefits:

1. It helps students learn how to identify and categorize main, supporting, and detail points, which in turn helps them do the same in their own writing.
2. It helps students see the structure and order of ideas in a literary work, as well as the relationships between ideas.
3. It aids comprehension of a plot or set of ideas.
4. It provides a helpful overview of the literature for quick and easy reference, especially for test preparation.

The kind of outline that schools have traditionally taught is often called a formal outline. It is formal because it requires the user to follow a universal set of rules that most people know and understand. A formal outline looks something like this:

I. Important idea for first major section (Subsequent important ideas will use next Roman numerals.)
  A. Supporting idea that explains or describes important idea above (Subsequent supporting ideas for same Roman numeral will use next upper-case letters.)
    1. Detail that explains or describes supporting idea above (Subsequent details for same letter will use next Arabic numerals.)
      a. Detail that explains or describes detail above (Subsequent details for same Arabic numeral will use next lower-case letters.)

This hierarchy can continue in a descending order with other labels that denote smaller and smaller details according to the complexity of the literature.

For outlining narrative literature I recommend a different kind of outline that I have developed using the Freytag Pyramid. The Freytag Pyramid is a diagram designed by Gustav Freytag in the nineteenth century to illustrate the structure of a theatrical play, but every short story and novel follows this basic structure, too. Novels often contain subplots that complicate the basic pyramid, and the slopes of the pyramid can be longer or shorter on one side or the other, but the principles and parts remain the same and are therefore useful for literary studies. On the next page you'll find a diagram of the Freytag Pyramid as I teach it.

Once you understand the pyramid, you can make use of it in your literary studies. In order to do so, you first need to familiarize yourself with these terms:

- *Exposition*: events or information that prepare the reader for the story to come.
- *Conflict or inciting incident*: the first thing that happens in a story; it moves the characters from a static state to the problem that will need to be resolved by the end. The conflict may be an internal one within the main character or an external one that happens to the character.
- *Rising action*: the events that occur as a result of the conflict or inciting incident; they deepen and complicate the story; may include one or more mini-climaxes.
- *Climax*: the pinnacle of action or the turning point in the story; it is the result of all the events of the rising action.
- *Falling action*: the events that occur as a result of the climax; may include one or more complications or may move directly to the resolution.
- *Resolution*: the point in the story when the conflict that began the story is resolved
- *Denouement (pronounced "day-nyoo-maw")*: the final part of the story when the loose ends of the plot are tied (usually) and the characters return to a static state (usually).

183

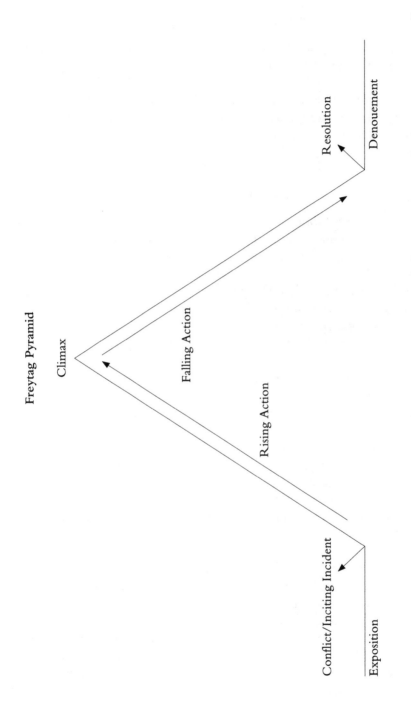

Freytag Pyramid

Climax

Falling Action

Rising Action

Resolution

Denouement

Conflict/Inciting Incident

Exposition

Created by the author based on Gustav Freytag's original 1863 diagram called "Die Technik des Dramas".

The Freytag Pyramid provides a convenient way to outline a story. Below I have provided a general template for using the outline, followed by an example outline of the story of "Cinderella" (see pages 185 and 186). Take some time to study the template and example. When you are ready, practice outlining a story you know by heart. Afterward you will be ready to outline the work of literature you are currently reading.

Step 11: Write a Personal Response Essay

This step may be done twice—once right after your slow reading and again at this point in your study. This is because your initial reactions and your reactions after you've studied the literature may be different. If you write a personal response essay only once, however, I suggest that you do it at this point in your study, when you've had time to make sure you understand the literature.

A personal response essay may be informal, written only in your notebook, or it may be typed and polished for a grade. Either way, this is your chance to express your own reactions (thoughts, feelings, opinions) to the literature. If you annotated the literature well, this kind of essay may even be easy and enjoyable for you. Here are some specific qualities of a strong personal response essay:

- It may include opinions, insights, connections to life, connections to the world or human experience, and reflections on how the text impacted you.
- It needs not only a strong statement of your reactions, but also a defense of them, preferably with quotations and other support how the text.
- It should show that you understand the literature.
- It must go beyond simply stating that you liked or disliked the text. This declaration is dull and avoids your deepest reactions.
- It must be specific, showing careful thinking about the text (see the example on page 188).
- It can focus on just one or two aspects of the story, not necessarily the whole thing. For example, you might have strongly connected to a character and want to discuss why that character is meaningful to you.

Template for Outlining Stories Using the Freytag Pyramid

Story and Author:

Beginning/Act One

Exposition
Important characters:
Setting:
Events:

Conflict or Inciting Incident
Important characters:
Setting:
Events:

Middle/Act Two

Rising Action
Important characters:
Setting:
Events:

Climax
Important characters:
Setting:
Events:

Falling Action
Important characters:
Setting:
Events:

End/Act Three

Resolution
Important characters:
Setting:
Events:

Denouement
Important characters:
Setting:
Events:

Sample Freytag Pyramid Outline Using "Cinderella"

Story and Author: "Cinderella" by Charles Perrault (adapted)

Beginning/Act One

Exposition

Important characters: Ella, father, stepmother, two stepsisters

Setting: large, wealthy household in a faraway land (in real life would be France)

Events: mother dies; father remarries, and Ella acquires stepmother and two ugly stepsisters; father dies, and stepmother and stepsisters show true colors; they make Ella servant and give her the name Cinderella.

Conflict or Inciting Incident

Important characters: stepmother, stepsisters, Cinderella, king's messenger

Setting: same house

Events: king's messenger delivers announcement about ball to be given in prince's honor, so that he can find a wife; Cinderella wants to go.

Middle/Act Two

Rising Action

Important characters: stepmother, stepsisters, Cinderella

Setting: same house

Events: Cinderella asks to go to ball, and stepmother tells her she may go only if she can finish work and find proper clothing; Cinderella works hard and does what stepmother says, only to be told she can't go after all; stepfamily goes off to the ball, and Cinderella gives up; fairy godmother appears and provides Cinderella with a gown and a coach to go to the ball with the warning that she must leave before midnight, when all will return to the way it was before.

Climax:

Important characters: Cinderella, prince

Setting: castle

Events: Cinderella and the prince dance at the ball and fall in love; at that moment the clock strikes midnight.

Falling Action

Important characters: Cinderella, prince

Setting: castle, countryside

Events: Cinderella runs away but loses her slipper just before the spell wears off and she is back in her old clothes; the prince runs after her and finds her slipper, vowing to search for her and marry her; the prince travels the countryside going from house to house.

End/Act Three

Resolution

Important characters: Cinderella, prince, stepmother and stepsisters.

Setting: Cinderella's house

Events: Prince arrives and tries to fit slipper on stepfamily; realizes someone else is present and demands to see her; Cinderella tries on slipper, and prince discovers she is his true love; stepfamily is outraged (or asks forgiveness, depending on version); Cinderella forgives family.

Denouement

Important characters: Cinderella, prince, stepfamily

Setting: Cinderella's house, castle

Events: The prince takes Cinderella away with him to the castle; they marry; depending on version, stepfamily is given husbands or a punishment; Cinderella and the prince live happily ever after.

- It assumes the reader is already familiar with the text, so it does not waste time summarizing it.
- It can be either positive or negative. Honesty and authenticity are important, so don't be afraid to tell the truth.
- If it is graded, well-founded opinions should not be criticized, only the thoroughness and quality of writing.

To write a strong personal response essay, be sure to open with the title and author of the work, as well as the main idea you want to communicate. Then spend the rest of your essay expanding on this idea. Remember, the main idea must be the opinion or reaction on which you want to focus your essay.

Some students don't find the above instructions sufficient, so if you aren't sure what to write about, try answering one or more of these questions:

1. How do you personally connect with the literature?
2. How much does the literature match or oppose your view of the world and what you consider right and wrong?
3. What did you learn, and how much were you challenged or changed by this literature?
4. In what ways did it address things that are important to you?
5. How well did you enjoy or appreciate the literature as a work of art? Do you think it is a meaningful and valuable contribution to literature, even if you didn't enjoy it? Why or why not?
6. What do you think the author is saying about life and living? Do you agree?
7. What do you notice about the illustrations or the author's language, word choice, or style? Do you think these were good choices?
8. How did you feel about the story's ending? Why do you think the author ended it that way? If you didn't like it, how would you have ended it differently?
9. What were your predictions about the story, and were they right?
10. Would you recommend the book to another reader? Why or why not?

Below is a sample personal response essay.

Robert Frost has long been my favorite poet, and "Stopping by Woods" is one of my favorite poems. I don't think it was at first; it has just grown on me over the years, since I've had occasion to read it often. The main reason I enjoy the poem so much is that Frost evokes a strong sense of mood and setting. As I read each line, I am transported in my imagination in an almost visceral way. I can almost see the snowy wood and hear the soft silence and feel the wintry cold. I hear the harness bells and imagine a warm house in a nearby village with some people—perhaps a grown-up daughter and her family—waiting for the narrator with supper almost ready.

Admittedly, the picture book version that I own has probably helped me experience the poem as vividly as I do, but I don't think I needed it. Frost's words work an enchantment all on their own, making me long for a quiet, chilly, white world with soft flakes falling all around me. There is much beauty in the world in many different settings, but experiencing such beauty as a wintry wood is the reason I would never choose to live anywhere that snow did not fall.

Step 12: Discuss the Work

One of the most important literary study activities is responding to discussion questions. Virtually every literature teacher values discussion, because it would be difficult, if not impossible, to get the most out of a literary work without discussing it in some way. Discussion questions are used in a variety of ways, but their purposes boil down to essentially three:

1. They help you develop the various analytical skills required for deep and insightful reading.
2. They deepen your experience because they allow you to consider the ideas and insights of others who are reading the same literature.
3. They help you apply the literature to yourself and your own life, which further deepens your reading experience.

All discussion question responses are technically short essays, if written, or short speeches, if oral. Some are only a sentence or two, and others are much longer, perhaps taking several paragraphs. You can expect to find such questions in both classes and on literature exams under the categories of "short essay" and "long essay." Sometimes, when posed to very advanced students, a single question may even require an answer that takes several pages to answer.

Long essays of several paragraphs or pages are typically called literary analysis essays. You will learn how to write one in step 13. To write a strong literary analysis essay, though, you must first learn how to respond to discussion questions clearly, thoroughly, and succinctly. Although this can be easier in a classroom setting, you can learn how to do it in an independent study, too.

You need to become skilled at answering three main types of discussion questions:

1. *Factual questions* ask *who, what, when, and where, and sometimes why and how.* These generally have one right answer, which can be given in one or two sentences. Factual questions about literature often focus on the literary elements in the story, such as plot, characters, setting, and so on.

2. *Interpretive questions ask why and how.* They require thinking about actions, conversations, or events in the story and determining their meaning or significance. Such questions often have more than one right or good answer, as long as those answers are thorough, specific, and supported by the text.

3. *Evaluative questions ask the reader what he thinks about the story.* These involve considering the actions of the characters in the light of one's own reasoning. These questions have no incorrect answers, but good answers require careful thought.

The Four Rules for Written Answers to Discussion Questions

When answering a discussion question in writing, follow these four rules:

1. *Answer in complete sentences that specify the subject.* Not only will this help prevent confusing responses, it will also help prepare you for the more complex responses of harder questions.

> *Example Question:* What are Anne Shirley's main goals in
> *Anne of Green Gables?*
>
> *Example of a Good Answer:* Anne's main goals are...

2. *Give not only a correct answer but also a thorough one.* One of the
   most important skills to cultivate in writing about any subject
   is how to support and expand upon a main idea. If you give a
   correct response to a discussion question, you have done well,
   but you are not yet finished. You must also consider whether
   you have supported your answer with details from the text that
   explain or defend your answer. Sometimes the questions are so
   simple there will be nothing more you can say.

3. *Answer the question directly.* This means first examining it carefully to determine exactly what the question is asking, and then
   answering only that question.

4. *Avoid opinion phrases, such as "I believe ..." or "I think ...".*
   Whether answers are opinion or fact, they should be stated as
   facts. This air of confidence will strengthen your writing.

Discussion Question Strategies

In addition to following the four rules above, be sure that all your
discussion question responses have these qualities:

1. *Focused*—They stay on-topic and address all parts; they also
   don't ramble or sneak in "padding" just to make them sound
   more substantial than they are.

2. *Organized*—The responses aren't haphazard; they show careful
   thought and planning with clear topic sentences. The sentences
   are logical and coherent. If the answers are complex paragraphs,
   they should also include conclusions.

3. *Supported*—A clear, direct response to the question is essential,
   but unless the question calls for just a quick, factual answer, it
   must be supported by evidence from the text. This may include
   both direct and indirect quotations.

4. *Polished*—Correct grammar and attention to style, spelling, and
   mechanics not only help to clarify your ideas but also give you
   credibility.

By now you may be wondering how to answer discussion questions without a formal curriculum to ask the questions. You can use several strategies in this case:

- Appendix H on page 263 is a selection of general discussion questions that can be applied to many different literary works. You can use these to create questions to ask yourself.
- Read the novel with someone else, such as a parent, and ask each other questions.
- Pretend you are a teacher who must create a test for your students. Develop questions and answer them in writing. This is an excellent study technique for any subject, by the way! Formulating meaningful questions deepens your learning, too, not just answering them.
- Join online book communities such as Goodreads, where you may be able to join a discussion about a book that interests you.
- Finally, study notes and study guides, such as *CliffsNotes* and Shmoop.com, often include sections with discussion questions. These tend to be deep questions that assume you already comprehend the story, so they can be excellent for helping you dive deeper into a literary work.

Step 13: Write a Literary Analysis Essay

The literary analysis essay is an important analytical skill that you should begin learning how to write in middle school. It is a formal essay commonly assigned in literature courses; however, it is more challenging than the personal response essay, so you need time to learn how to write a good one. The literary analysis essay typically answers "why" and "how" questions, and they are longer than answers to discussion questions. A good analysis is usually one or more pages when typed. This is because with literary analysis you must dive deeper into the text, developing arguments about the literature, encapsulating them in a thesis statement, and supporting them with extensive textual support.

To understand what a literary analysis *is*, it is helpful to first understand what it is *not*. The simple lists below will help you make sense of this kind of essay:

What a Literary Analysis Is Not

- *It is not a response essay.* This kind of essay does not discuss your emotional or intellectual reactions to the work.
- *It is not a critical review.* It does not present your opinions about its strengths and weaknesses.
- *It is not a research paper.* Though quotations are necessary, the only source allowed is the literature itself.
- *It is not a summary.* This kind of essay does not summarize the literature's main events or characters. Assume that your reader already knows the story.
- *It is not a narrative.* It does not retell the story in any way. Again, assume that your reader already knows the story.
- *It is not a report.* The literary analysis essay does not explain the literature's basic elements or provide commentary.

What a Literary Analysis Essay Is

- *It is a specific kind of argumentative essay.* It presents your ideas about the work along with supporting evidence from the work itself.
- *It is a formal essay.* The writing must be objective with a scholarly, serious tone. It may not use first-person references, and second-person references should be used formally and sparingly (see the example essay on pages 195 and 196 for how they might be used appropriately). It also does not try to entertain the reader.
- *It goes beyond comprehension to examine underlying subtext and artistic choices.* You must fully comprehend the story *before* you write the essay, because a literary analysis essay goes below the surface of the story.

The Importance of Textual Evidence

All literary analysis essays *must* include substantial textual evidence, which teachers sometimes refer to as "examples" or "support" from the text. Textual evidence is the equivalent of documented facts and quotations in a research paper. It includes quotations, details, and examples from the literature, all of which support the thesis statement and its supporting points. A good way to collect this evidence and take any other necessary notes is the Cornell Note-Taking System (step 8, pages 175–77).

Crafting a Thesis Statement for a Literary Analysis

Once you've determined what you want to discuss and have taken any necessary notes, it is time to develop a thesis statement and an outline. A good thesis statement will summarize your central argument in one sentence.

Below are some examples of weak and strong thesis statements. Use these as a guide when you write your own, and consider studying thesis statements using Internet guides or writing program lessons. This skill will be important for all formal papers that you write, not just literary analysis essays.

Weak thesis statements

- This essay will be about the villain in *Romeo and Juliet*.
- This essay will be about how the true villain of *Romeo and Juliet* is not Juliet's cousin Tybalt, but the ancestors of the Capulets and Montagues.
- *Romeo and Juliet* is a really depressing play about love and hate.
- In *Romeo and Juliet* Shakespeare presents themes of love and hate through a family feud and two teenagers who fall for each other.

Note how the first three examples simply announce what the essay will be about—never acceptable for a thesis statement in any essay. A couple of the sentences are also too casual. The fourth example does make a clear assertion and is certainly the strongest statement of the four, but it is too general and unoriginal. It simply summarizes what is generally known about the play.

Strong thesis statements

- In *Romeo and Juliet*, Juliet's cousin Tybalt represents the true villains of the play—the ancestors who began the Capulet-Montague feud.
- The danger of unsupervised adolescence is the theme at the heart of Shakespeare's tragic play, *Romeo and Juliet*.

- The true cause of Romeo and Juliet's deaths was not the Capulet-Montague feud, but Friar Laurence's short-sighted effort to help the couple elope.

A Method for Writing a Literary Analysis Essay

Once you have a thesis statement, with the help of your notes list the points you would like to make to prove it. Make sure that each point directly defends the thesis statement and can be supported with textual evidence.

Turn your list into an outline by collecting details, paraphrases, and indirect or direct quotations that illustrate your point. These should be taken directly from the literature, not secondary sources.

Write an introductory paragraph either beginning or ending with your thesis statement followed by a paragraph about each point using your evidence. You do not need to include the page number, unless the teacher requires it. Most classics have been published in multiple editions, so page numbers will be meaningless to most readers. Do, however, consider including the chapter, stanza, line number, or any other identifying information that might be helpful to your readers.

Wrap up your essay with a short conclusion. Ideally, it should summarize your main idea and make a final point. Avoid using phrases like "in conclusion" or "to summarize", because it states the obvious fact that you are wrapping up your essay and doesn't add any new information or insights.

You might be wondering about the length of an essay. It depends on your teacher, your purpose, and the topic itself. A literary analysis can be as short as several paragraphs and as long as several pages. A good rule of thumb for high school students is 1,000 words (three double-spaced pages of twelve-point type). For those in middle school, the paper could be half that length. But aim for quality, not quantity.

Prompts for a Literary Analysis

When assigning a literary analysis essay, most teachers will provide a prompt. The more advanced the class is, of course, the more challenging the prompts will be. Here are some examples of easy, intermediate, advanced, and college-level prompts, all using Shakespeare's *Romeo and Juliet* as their source:

- *Basic*: Compare and contrast Romeo's love for Rosaline with his love for Juliet.
- *Intermediate*: Prince Escalus is a distant but authoritative character in the play. How does he affect the events and outcome of the play?
- *Advanced*: Shakespeare uses cosmic imagery several times throughout the play, such as the term "star-cross'd lovers." Examine the role and function of this imagery.
- *College-level* (for literature majors): How do choice and destiny influence the fate of Romeo, Juliet, and other characters in *Romeo and Juliet*?

Sample Literary Analysis Essay

If you have never written or read a literary analysis essay, the above method may not be enough to guide you. To understand this kind of essay, it would be a good idea to examine examples on the Internet. Try to avoid those that use first-person references. Although some teachers may not mind this and although some prompts may lead naturally to first-person references, the literary analysis essay is typically a formal, argumentative essay that doesn't make any personal references. To prepare for college courses, it is important that you become comfortable with this kind of essay.

In addition to studying examples on the Internet, you might also like to examine the following example.

The Elements of Mood in "Stopping by Woods on a Snowy Evening"

A snowy wood may be a naturally peaceful setting, but in "Stopping by Woods on a Snowy Evening," Robert Frost evokes a mood of transcendent calm and wonder in several other ways, as well. The speaker is key to creating this mood, for through him we enter this wood that is "lovely, dark, and deep" and experience the beauty of the gently falling snow. Although, the speaker tells us, he must reach his destination miles away that same evening, he can't help stopping to watch the "woods fill up with snow." Real-life responsibilities are easily forgotten in the presence of such enchantment.

Frost also uses several literary devices effectively to evoke mood in his poem. Perhaps most subtly, the poem flows with a steady, yet gentle rhythm in iambic pentameter—for example:

> Between the woods and frozen lake
> The darkest evening of the year.

Because this meter is often reflected in natural English speech, the poem has an easy, almost sing-song rhythm. To enhance this rhythm Frost also uses frequent rhymes and alliteration, which help to convey the image of the wintry wood, as well as the mood. Most vividly, perhaps, is the rhyme "though/snow" in the first stanza, since it sets the scene, as well as lends the poem softness through the repeated "o" sound. Also, Frost adds sound effectively to the otherwise silent scene with the rhyme "shake/mistake," as the horse restlessly jingles his harness bells. Alliteration and repetition are perhaps the most important means through which Frost evokes mood, however, with his frequent use of the "s" sound, particularly in the third stanza:

> The only other sound's the sweep
> Of easy wind and downy flake.

Preceding this image are more "s" sounds in quick succession: harness, shake, ask, mistake. All of these "s" sounds together help us see the soft drifting of snow and hear the whisper of wind in the trees. In the end, Frost gently leads us deeper into his winter reverie with his closing lines:

> And miles to go before I sleep,
> And miles to go before I sleep.

The speaker drives away, reminding us that real life awaits, however reluctant we may be to rejoin it. With the gentle, soothing repetition of these lines, Frost keeps us rapt in the enchantment of the wood long after the speaker is gone.

Step 14: Complete a Capstone Project

In an independent literature study, it is up to you to decide how far to take it. You may have different goals for each literary work that you read. For one book your goal may just be to understand the story and its characters; for another book you may want to mine the depths of the literature as much as possible. For yet another you may just want to do some enrichment activities to round out your reading experience. A literary study can be as deep and complex as you choose, because literature is wonderfully rich in both ideas and connections to the human experience. With the best literature, especially, there is always something more you can mine from it.

If you come to the end of your study and want to wrap it up with a final project that ties everything together or that veers off onto a tangent that interests you, consider completing a capstone project. This can be as serious or as fun as you choose to make it, and you can take it in a variety of directions. In fact, there are so many delightful, creative ways to explore literature beyond a formal study that I cannot possibly list them all here. The best I can do is give you a sample list of ideas and some resources for expanding on those ideas. You can even develop your own project! The main purpose of a capstone project is to enrich your experience of the literature somehow. There isn't a "right" way to do this.

Once you settle on a project, be creative in how you complete and present it. Allow yourself to think outside the box, rather than worry about how a teacher would want you to do it (although if you do have a teacher or supervisor, he still gets the final say!). Choose a project that will be interesting and meaningful to you.

To give you a sense of the many possibilities for a capstone project, I have developed a list of ideas for one of my all-time favorite novels, the American coming-of-age classic *A Tree Grows in Brooklyn*, by Betty Smith.

- Write a formal research paper on the historical or geographical setting.

- Do a study of the American class system at the turn-of-the-twentieth century—maybe a visual project done on a tri-fold presentation board.

- Visit Brooklyn, New York, to walk the same streets as Francie, the protagonist, did. Write some journal entries to discuss my experience and observations.

- Visit the library weekly in the summer as Francie did; then spend all my free time reading my books and sucking pink peppermints.
- Compile a list of all the foods Francie ate as mentioned in the novel and try to live on them for a few days. Create some recipes based on how Francie's mother might have prepared them.
- Save all my loose change for a set period of time in a hidden can, as Francie's mother did. Invest the money in something meaningful to me as an American, just as Irish-born Katie saved for a small plot of land to establish her roots in this country.
- Make a list of all the street games children played in Francie's neighborhood. Research their origins, and present my findings in an interesting way—a small book, a tri-fold presentation, a picture album with captions, etc.
- Write a story based on a week in my childhood or on a meaningful incident that helped define my childhood. Bring my world alive through rich details and characterizations.
- Research my family's immigration story; create a visual presentation to show it.
- Go to a library with many photo archives or use the Internet to find images of New York City and Brooklyn around 1915. Study them to learn more about American life at that time.
- Watch a documentary about the beginnings of World War I and how it impacted Americans.

At this point I'm sure you are getting the idea of how to develop a capstone project and the limitless ways you can create one. Each book, story, or poem will lead to different ideas. If you would like yet more ideas, here are a baker's dozen of general ideas that you can use to spark your imagination:

1. Write a letter to a character you connected with or reacted to in some way.
2. Study critical essays and commentaries to see what others thought of the literature.
3. Study the author's life, and compile your findings in an oral, written, or visual presentation.

4. Create a video in which you recreate a scene from a historical novel adapted to our time to show how the human experience is the same from generation to generation—only the details change.
5. Write a new ending for the literature.
6. If your literature is a poem, try writing a poem of your own in the same form (sonnet, for example).
7. Choose an important theme from the literature, and write a story or poem of your own on the same theme.
8. Compare two literary works that deal with the same theme. Discuss how the authors viewed the theme differently.
9. Try one of the games or activities that a character in the novel did.
10. Visit a museum that has artifacts that relate to the literature, or watch a documentary.
11. Tour the setting of the novel, either in person or through photographs and videos.
12. Learn a handicraft that relates to the literature, such as knitting a scarf the way a character did.
13. Create a map of the character's world and trace his movement through it (like Middle-earth and Frodo's journey to Mordor).

APPENDIX A

Simplified Reading Lists

These simplified lists are to help with choosing literature after parents and perhaps older students have read the fuller lists at the beginning of the book. Those lists contain a lot of information for discerning which works are appropriate, especially among titles followed by *Parents Cautioned!*

Simplified Historical List

Ancient Times through the Early Middle Ages
1500 B.C.–A.D. 1000

Foundational

Old Testament from the Holy Bible (roughly 1500 B.C.–100 B.C.)
The Iliad, by Homer (c. 750 B.C.)
The Odyssey, by Homer (c. 725 B.C.)
Classical mythology (first recorded roughly between 700 B.C. and A.D. 8)
Fables by Aesop (probably first recorded by Demetrius of Phaleron about 320 B.C. but composed closer to 600 B.C.)
Aeneid, by Virgil (c. 20 B.C.)
New Testament from the Holy Bible (c. A.D. 50–A.D. 95)

Important

Beowulf, by anonymous (first known manuscript—c. A.D. 900–1000)
Norse mythology (recorded c. A.D. 900–1200 but composed much earlier)

The Middle Ages through the Protestant Reformation
1000–1620

Foundational

Lullabies and nursery rhymes of Europe (composed throughout the era)
King Arthur legends (A.D. 1485 and onward)
Robin Hood tales (first recorded in A.D. 1500)

Important

Play of Daniel, by the youth of Beauvais, France (mid-twelfth century)

Other Children's Classics of This Era

Colloquy, by Bishop Aelfric (c. late 900s)
Gesta Romanorum, author unknown (c. early fourteenth century)
Stans Puer ad Mensam ("Table Manners for Children"), by John
  Lydgate (early 1400s)
Mankind, by anonymous (mid-1400s)
The Book of Babees, by anonymous (c. 1475)
The Book of Curtesye, published by William Caxton (c. 1477)
The Schoole of Vertue, by Francis Segar (1557)
*A New Interlude for Children to Play Named Jack Juggler, Both Witty and
  Very Pleasant*, by anonymous (c. 1553–1558)
Actes and Monuments (also known as *Foxe's Book of Martyrs*), by John
  Foxe (1563) *Parents Cautioned!*
A Methode, or Comfortable Beginning for all Unlearned, by John Hart
  (1570)
Petie Schole, by Francis Clement (1587)

The Colonization of New England through
the Mid-nineteenth Century
1621–1849

Foundational

The Pilgrim's Progress, by John Bunyan (1678)
Folktales and fairy tales of Europe (first published 1696)
Robinson Crusoe, by Daniel Defoe (1719)

Important

The New England Primer, edited by Benjamin Harris (1690 with various editions)

The Thousand and One Nights, translated by Antoine Galland (1704)

Gulliver's Travels, by Jonathan Swift (1726)

The Children of the New Forest, by Captain Marryat (1847)

Other Children's Classics of This Era

Orbis Sensualium Pictus, by Johann Comenius (1658)

A Token for Children: An Exact Account of the Conversion, Holy and Exemplary Lives, and Joyful Deaths of Several Young Children, by James Janeway (1671)

A Little Book for Little Children, by Thomas White (c. 1671)

New Spelling-Book, by Thomas Lye (1677)

Divine Songs, Attempted in Easy Language for the Use of Children, by Isaac Watts (1715)

A Child's New Plaything, by Mary Cooper (1743)

Tommy Thumb's Song Book, by Mary Cooper (1744)

A Little Pretty Pocket-Book, by John Newbery (1744)

The Governess, or The Little Female Academy, by Sarah Fielding (1749)

Lives of the Noble Greeks and Romans, by Plutarch (1579 and Sir Thomas North's translation 1762)

The History of Little Goody Two Shoes, by anonymous (1765)

Adventures of a Bank-Note, by Thomas Bridges (1770)

Lessons for Children, by Anna Laetitia Barbauld (1778)

Hymns in Prose for Children, by Anna Barbauld (1781)

The Parent's Assistant, by Maria Edgeworth (1796)

Simple Susan, by Maria Edgeworth (1796)

Tales from Shakespeare, by Charles and Mary Lamb (1807)

The Swiss Family Robinson, by Johann Wyss (1812 in Switzerland; translated into English in 1814)

History of the Fairchild Family, by Mary Martha Sherwood (published in three volumes between 1818 and 1847)

"A Visit from St. Nicholas," by Clement Clarke Moore (1823—also known as "The Night before Christmas")

Struwwelpeter, by Heinrich Hoffman (published in German, 1845; English translation, 1848)

The First Golden Age of Children's Literature
1850–1928

Foundational

Alice in Wonderland, by Lewis Carroll (1865 and 1871)
Treasure Island, by Robert Louis Stevenson (serial—1881–82; book—1883)
The Adventures of Huckleberry Finn, by Mark Twain (1885)
Poems by Eugene Field especially "Wynken, Blynken, and Nod," "The Duel," "Little Boy Blue," and "The Sugar-Plum Tree" (late 1800s)
The Tale of Peter Rabbit, by Beatrix Potter (1902)
The Wind in the Willows, by Kenneth Grahame (1908)
Winnie-the-Pooh, by A. A. Milne (1926)
Millions of Cats, by Wanda Gág (1928)

Important

Poetry of Edward Lear (1846–1877)
Tom Brown's Schooldays, by Thomas Hughes (1857)
The Water-Babies: A Fairy Tale for a Land Baby, by Charles Kingsley (1863)
Little Women, by Louisa May Alcott (1868–69)
The historical fiction by G. A. Henty (1871 onward)
The Princess and the Goblin and *The Princess and Curdie,* by George MacDonald (1872 and 1883)
Black Beauty, by Anna Sewell (1877)
The Wonderful Wizard of Oz, by L. Frank Baum (1900)
Five Children and It (1902) and *The Railway Children* (1906), by E. Nesbit
Anne of Green Gables, by L. M. Montgomery (1908)
The Story of Mankind, by Hendrik Willem van Loon (1921)

Other Children's Classics of This Era

The Wide, Wide World, by Susan Warner (1850)
The Coral Island: A Tale of the Pacific Ocean, by R. M. Ballantyne (1858)
The science fiction novels of Jules Verne: *Journey to the Center of the Earth* (1864), *20,000 Leagues Under the Sea* (1869-70), *Around the World in 80 Days* (1872), et cetera

Hans Brinker, or The Silver Skates, by Mary Mapes Dodge (1865)

Ragged Dick, by Horatio Alger (1868)

The Brownies and Other Tales, by Juliana Horatia Ewing (1870)

At the Back of the North Wind, by George MacDonald (1871)

What Katy Did, by Susan Coolidge (1872)

The Adventures of Tom Sawyer, by Mark Twain (1876)

Heidi, by Johanna Spyri (published in two parts in German in 1880 and 1881; first published in English in 1884)

Uncle Remus, His Songs and Sayings, the Folk-Lore of the Old Plantation, by Joel Chandler Harris (1880)

Five Little Peppers and How They Grew, by Margaret Sidney (1881)

The Prince and the Pauper, by Mark Twain (1881)

The Adventures of Pinocchio, by Carlo Collodi (1883)

King Solomon's Mines, by H. Rider Haggard (1885)

Little Lord Fauntleroy, by Frances Hodgson Burnett (1886)

Kidnapped, by Robert Louis Stevenson (1886)

The Jungle Book, by Rudyard Kipling (1894)

Moonfleet, by J. Meade Falkner (1898)

The Story of Little Black Sambo, by Helen Bannerman (1899)

A Child's Garden of Verses, by Robert Louis Stevenson (1900)

Kim, by Rudyard Kipling (1901)

Just So Stories, by Rudyard Kipling (1902)

Rebecca of Sunnybrook Farm, by Kate Douglas Wiggin (1903)

A Little Princess, by Frances Hodgson Burnett (1905)

A Girl of the Limberlost, by Gene Stratton-Porter (1909)

A Secret Garden, by Frances Hodgson Burnett (first serialized in 1910; published in entirety in 1911)

Peter Pan and Wendy, by J. M. Barrie (1911)

Daddy-Long-Legs, by Jean Webster (1912)

Uncle Wiggily's Adventures, by Howard Garis (1912)

Pollyanna, by Eleanor Porter (1913)

Understood Betsy, by Dorothy Canfield Fisher (1916)

The Cambridge Book of Poetry for Children, edited by Kenneth Grahame (1916)

Raggedy Ann Stories, by Johnny Gruelle (1918)—first of a series

The Story of Dr. Dolittle (1920) and *The Voyages of Dr. Dolittle* (1922), by Hugh Lofting

Rootabaga Stories, by Carl Sandburg (1922)

The Velveteen Rabbit, by Margery Williams (1922)

Bambi, A Life in the Woods, by Felix Salten (1923)
The Boxcar Children, by Gertrude Chandler Warner (1924)
The Story of Rolf and the Viking Bow, by Allen French (1924)

The Great Depression through World War II
1929–1945

Foundational

The Story of Babar, by Jean de Brunhoff (1931)
Little House series, by Laura Ingalls Wilder (1932 onward)
The Hobbit, or There and Back Again, by J. R. R. Tolkien (1937)
The Yearling, by Marjorie Kinnan Rawlings (1938)
Curious George, by Margret and Hans Rey (1941)
The Little Prince, by Antoine de Saint-Exupéry (1943)

Important

Johnny Tremain, by Esther Forbes (1943)
A Tree Grows in Brooklyn, by Betty Smith (1943) *Parents Cautioned!*
Strawberry Girl, by Lois Lenski (1945)
Stuart Little, by E. B. White (1945)

Other Children's Classics of This Era

Smoky the Cowhorse, by Will James (1926)
Emil and the Detectives, by Erich Kästner (1929)
Hitty, Her First Hundred Years, by Rachel Field (1929)
The Little Engine That Could, by Watty Piper (1930)
The Secret of the Old Clock, by Carolyn Keene (1930)
Young Fu of the Upper Yangtze, by Elizabeth Foreman Lewis (1932)
The Story About Ping, by Marjorie Flack (1933)
Mary Poppins, by P. L. Travers (1934)
Caddie Woodlawn, by Carol Ryrie Brink (1935)
National Velvet, by Enid Bagnold (1935)
Ballet Shoes, by Noel Streatfeild (1936)
The Story of Ferdinand, by Munro Leaf (1936)
Roller Skates, by Ruth Sawyer (1936)
The Sword in the Stone, by T. H. White (1938)
Mr. Popper's Penguins, by Richard and Florence Atwater (1938)
Thimble Summer, by Elizabeth Enright (1938)

B is for Betsy, by Carolyn Haywood (1939)
Madeline, Ludwig Bemelmans (1939)
Mike Mulligan and His Steam Shovel, by Virginia Lee Burton (1939)
Betsy-Tacy series, by Maud Hart Lovelace (1940 onward)
Call It Courage, by Armstrong Sperry (1940)
Pat the Bunny, by Dorothy Kunhardt (1940)
Caps for Sale, by Esphyr Slobodkina (1940)
Blue Willow, by Doris Gates (1940)
Make Way for Ducklings, by Robert McCloskey (1941)
The Moffats, by Eleanor Estes (1941)
Paddle-to-the-Sea, by Holling Clancy Holling (1941)
Seventeenth Summer, by Maureen Daly (1942)
The Poky Little Puppy, by Janette Lowrey (1942)
Many Moons, by James Thurber (1943)
Homer Price, by Robert McCloskey (1943)
Rabbit Hill, by Robert Lawson (1944)
The Hundred Dresses, by Eleanor Estes (1944)
The Moved-Outers, by Florence Crannell Means (1945)
Pippi Longstocking, by Astrid Lindgren (1945)

The Second Golden Age
1946–1965

Foundational

The Diary of a Young Girl, by Anne Frank (1947)
The Chronicles of Narnia series, especially *The Lion, the Witch and the Wardrobe*, by C. S. Lewis (1950–1956)
The Catcher in the Rye, by J. D. Salinger (1951) *Parents Cautioned!*
Charlotte's Web, by E. B. White (1952)
The Cat in the Hat, by Dr. Seuss (1957)
A Wrinkle in Time, by Madeleine L'Engle (1962)
Where the Wild Things Are, by Maurice Sendak (1963)

Important

Goodnight Moon, by Margaret Wise Brown (1947)
Lord of the Flies, by William Golding (1954) *Parents Cautioned!*
Tom's Midnight Garden, by Philippa Pearce (1958)
Island of the Blue Dolphins, by Scott O'Dell (1960)

To Kill a Mockingbird, by Harper Lee (1960) *Parents Cautioned!*
The Phantom Tollbooth, by Norton Juster (1961)
The Snowy Day, by Ezra Jack Keats (1962)
Charlie and the Chocolate Factory, by Roald Dahl (1964)
Harriet the Spy, by Louise Fitzhugh (1964) *Parents Cautioned!*

Other Children's Classics of This Era

Mrs. Piggle-Wiggle, by Betty MacDonald (1947)
Happy Little Family (1947) and other books, by Rebecca Caudill
White Snow, Bright Snow, by Alvin Tresselt (1947)
The Twenty-One Balloons, by William Pène du Bois (1947)
Blueberries for Sal, by Robert McCloskey (1948)
My Father's Dragon, by Ruth Stiles Gannett (1948)
The Jennifer Wish, by Eunice Young Smith (1949)
The Door in the Wall, by Marguerite de Angeli (1949)
The Borrowers, by Mary Norton (1952)
Secret of the Andes, by Ann Nolan Clark (1952)
Children of Green Knowe, by Lucy M. Boston (1954)
Eagle of the Ninth, by Rosemary Sutcliff (1954)
Harold and the Purple Crayon, by Crockett Johnson (1955)
Frog Went A-Courtin', by John Langstaff (1955)
The Hundred and One Dalmatians, by Dodie Smith (1956)
Little Bear series, by Else Holmelund Minarik (1957)
A Bear Called Paddington, by Michael Bond (1958)
Chanticleer and the Fox, by Barbara Cooney (1958)
The Witch of Blackbird Pond, by Elizabeth George Speare (1958)
A Separate Peace, by John Knowles (1959)
My Side of the Mountain, by Jean Craighead George (1959)
Bedtime for Frances (1960) and other Frances books, by Russell Hoban
The Cricket in Times Square, by George Selden (1960)
Green Eggs and Ham, by Dr. Seuss (1960)
Are You My Mother? (1960) and *Go, Dog, Go!* (1961), by P. D. Eastman
James and the Giant Peach, by Roald Dahl (1961)
D'Aulaires' Book of Greek Myths, by Ingri and Edgar Parin d'Aulaire
    (1962)
The Winged Watchman, by Hilda van Stockum (1962)
The Wolves of Willoughby Chase, by Joan Aiken (1962)
Swimmy, by Leo Lionni (1963)

Amelia Bedelia, by Peggy Parish (1963)
The Giving Tree, by Shel Silverstein (1964)
The Chronicles of Prydain, by Lloyd Alexander (1964–1968)
The Dark Is Rising series, by Susan Cooper (1965–1977) *Parents Cautioned!*

The Noteworthy Books of the Late-Twentieth Century
1966–2000

Foundational

The Giving Tree (1964) and *Where the Sidewalk Ends* (1974), by Shel Silverstein
The Outsiders, by S. E. Hinton (1967) *Parents Cautioned!*
Ramona Quimby series, by Beverly Cleary (1968–1999)
Watership Down, by Richard Adams (1972)
The Giver, by Lois Lowry (1993)
Harry Potter series, by J. K. Rowling (1997–2007) *Parents Cautioned!*

Important

A Wizard of Earthsea, by Ursula K. Le Guin (1968) *Parents Cautioned!*
The Very Hungry Caterpillar, by Eric Carle (1969)
Are You There, God? It's Me, Margaret, by Judy Blume (1970) *Parents Cautioned!*
The Chocolate War, by Robert Cormier (1974) *Parents Cautioned!*
Roll of Thunder, Hear My Cry, by Mildred D. Taylor (1976)
Bridge to Terabithia, by Katherine Paterson (1977)
The House on Mango Street, by Sandra Cisneros (1984) *Parents Cautioned!*
Lincoln: A Photobiography, by Russell Freedman (1987)
Hatchet, by Gary Paulsen (1987)

Other Noteworthy Books of This Era

The Mouse and His Child, by Russell Hoban (1967)
From the Mixed-up Files of Mrs. Basil E. Frankweiler, by E. L. Konigsburg (1967)
Brown Bear, Brown Bear, What Do You See?, by Bill Martin, Jr. (1967)
Corduroy, by Don Freeman (1968)
The Pigman, by Paul Zindel (1968)
Sylvester and the Magic Pebble, by William Steig (1969)

Frog and Toad Are Friends (1970) and other *Frog and Toad* books, by Arnold Lobel

Summer of the Swans, by Betsy Byars (1970)

Corgiville Fair, by Tasha Tudor (1971)

The Best Christmas Pageant Ever, by Barbara Robinson (1971)

Mrs. Frisby and the Rats of NIMH, by Robert C. O'Brien (1971)

George and Martha, by James Marshall (1972)

Julie of the Wolves, by Jean Craighead George (1972)

Alexander and the Terrible, Horrible, No Good, Very Bad Day, by Judith Viorst (1972)

Summer of My German Soldier, by Bette Greene (1973)

M. C. Higgins, the Great, by Virginia Hamilton (1974)

Strega Nona, by Tomie dePaola (1975)

Tuck Everlasting, by Natalie Babbitt (1975)

The Snowman, by Raymond Briggs (1978)

Freight Train, by Donald Crews (1978)

The Westing Game, by Ellen Raskin (1978)

The Neverending Story, by Michael Ende (German—1979; English—1983)

Anastasia Krupnik, by Lois Lowry (1979)

Jumanji, by Chris Van Allsburg (1981)

Sweet Whispers, Brother Rush, by Virginia Hamilton (1982)

The Polar Express, by Chris Van Allsburg (1985)

If You Give a Mouse a Cookie, by Laura Numeroff (1985)

The People Could Fly: American Black Folktales, by Virginia Hamilton (1985)

Redwall series, by Brian Jacques (1986–2011)

Owl Moon, by Jane Yolen (1987)

The Devil's Arithmetic, by Jane Yolen (1988)

The True Story of the Three Little Pigs!, by Jon Scieszka (1989)

The Stinky Cheese Man and Other Fairly Stupid Tales, by Jon Scieszka (1992)

The Watsons Go to Birmingham, by Christopher Paul Curtis (1995)

Lily's Purple Plastic Purse, by Kevin Henkes (1996)

A Series of Unfortunate Events series, by Lemony Snicket (1999–2006) *Parents Cautioned!*

Because of Winn-Dixie, by Kate DiCamillo (2000)

Reading List by Genre

Poetry

The Iliad, by Homer (c. 750 B.C.)
The Odyssey, by Homer (c. 725 B.C.)
Aeneid, by Virgil (c. 20 B.C.)
Beowulf, by anonymous (first known manuscript—c. A.D. 900–1000)
Lullabies and nursery rhymes of Europe (composed throughout the era)
The Book of Babees, by anonymous (c. 1475)
The Book of Curtesye, published by William Caxton (c. 1477)
Divine Songs, Attempted in Easy Language for the Use of Children, by Isaac Watts (1715)
Tommy Thumb's Song Book, by Mary Cooper (1744)
"A Visit from St. Nicholas," by Clement Clarke Moore (1823—also known as "The Night Before Christmas")
Poetry of Edward Lear (1846–1877)
Poems by Eugene Field especially "Wynken, Blynken, and Nod," "The Duel," "Little Boy Blue," and "The Sugar-Plum Tree" (late 1800s)
A Child's Garden of Verses, by Robert Louis Stevenson (1900)
The Cambridge Book of Poetry for Children, edited by Kenneth Grahame (1916)
Where the Sidewalk Ends, by Shel Silverstein (1974)

Nonfiction

Old Testament from the Holy Bible (roughly 1500 B.C–100 B.C.)
New Testament from the Holy Bible (c. A.D. 50–A.D. 95)
Colloquy, by Bishop Aelfric (c. late 900s)
Stans Puer ad Mensam ("Table Manners for Children"), by John Lydgate (early 1400s)
The Schoole of Vertue, by Francis Segar (1557)
Actes and Monuments (also known as *Foxe's Book of Martyrs*), by John Foxe (1563) *Parents Cautioned!*
A Methode, or Comfortable Beginning for all Unlearned, by John Hart (1570)
Lives of the Noble Greeks and Romans, by Plutarch (1579; Sir Thomas North's translation 1762)
Petie Schole, by Francis Clement (1587)

A Little Book for Little Children, by Thomas White (c. 1671)

A Token for Children: An Exact Account of the Conversion, Holy and Exemplary Lives, and Joyful Deaths of Several Young Children, by James Janeway (1671)

New Spelling-Book, by Thomas Lye (1677)

New England Primer, edited by Benjamin Harris (1690 with various editions)

A Child's New Plaything, by Mary Cooper (1743)

A Little Pretty Pocket-Book, by John Newbery (1744)

Lessons for Children, by Anna Laetitia Barbauld (1778)

Hymns in Prose for Children, by Anna Barbauld (1781)

The Story of Mankind, by Hendrik Willem van Loon (1921)

The Diary of a Young Girl, by Anne Frank (1947)

Lincoln: A Photobiography, by Russell Freedman (1987)

Picture Books and Short Story Collections

Classical mythology (first recorded sometime between 700 B.C. and A.D. 8)

Fables by Aesop (probably first recorded by Demetrius of Phaleron about 320 B.C. but composed closer to 600 B.C.)

Norse mythology (recorded c. 900–A.D. 1200 but composed much earlier)

Gesta Romanorum, author unknown (c. early fourteenth century)

Lullabies and nursery rhymes of Europe (composed throughout the Middle Ages)

King Arthur legends (1485 and onward)—*Note: These are also included in the "novels" category, since they are usually published as one continuous story.*

Robin Hood tales (first recorded in 1500)—*Note: These are also included in the "novels" category, since they are usually published as one continuous story.*

Orbis Sensualium Pictus, by Johann Comenius (1658)

Folktales and fairy tales of Europe (first published 1696)

The Parent's Assistant, by Maria Edgeworth (1796)

Tales from Shakespeare, by Charles and Mary Lamb (1807)

Struwwelpeter, by Heinrich Hoffman (published in German, 1845; English translation, 1848)

The Brownies and Other Tales, by Juliana Horatia Ewing (1870)

Uncle Remus, His Songs and Sayings, the Folk-Lore of the Old Plantation, by Joel Chandler Harris (1880)

The Story of Little Black Sambo, by Helen Bannerman (1899)

Just So Stories, by Rudyard Kipling (1902)

The Tale of Peter Rabbit, by Beatrix Potter (1902)

Uncle Wiggily's Adventures, by Howard Garis (1912)

Raggedy Ann Stories, by Johnny Gruelle (1918)—first of a series

Rootabaga Stories, by Carl Sandburg (1922)

Winnie-the-Pooh, by A. A. Milne (1926)

Millions of Cats, by Wanda Gág (1928)

The Little Engine That Could, by Watty Piper (1930)

The Story of Babar, by Jean de Brunhoff (1931)

The Story About Ping, by Marjorie Flack (1933)

The Story of Ferdinand, by Munro Leaf (1936)

Madeline, Ludwig Bemelmans (1939)

Mike Mulligan and His Steam Shovel, by Virginia Lee Burton (1939)

Pat the Bunny, by Dorothy Kunhardt (1940)

Caps for Sale, by Esphyr Slobodkina (1940)

Curious George, by Margret and Hans Rey (1941)

Make Way for Ducklings, by Robert McCloskey (1941)

The Poky Little Puppy, by Janette Lowrey (1942)

Many Moons, by James Thurber (1943)

Goodnight Moon, by Margaret Wise Brown (1947)

White Snow, Bright Snow, by Alvin Tresselt (1947)

Blueberries for Sal, by Robert McCloskey (1948)

Harold and the Purple Crayon, by Crockett Johnson (1955)

Frog Went A-Courtin', by John Langstaff (1955)

The Cat in the Hat, by Dr. Seuss (1957)

Little Bear series, by Else Holmelund Minarik (1957)

Chanticleer and the Fox, by Barbara Cooney (1958)

Bedtime for Frances (1960) and other Frances books, by Russell Hoban

Green Eggs and Ham, by Dr. Seuss (1960)

Are You My Mother? (1960) and *Go, Dog, Go!* (1961), by P. D. Eastman

D'Aulaires' Book of Greek Myths, by Ingri and Edgar Parin d'Aulaire (1962)

The Snowy Day, by Ezra Jack Keats (1962)

Where the Wild Things Are, by Maurice Sendak (1963)

Swimmy, by Leo Lionni (1963)

Amelia Bedelia, by Peggy Parish (1963)

The Giving Tree, by Shel Silverstein (1964)

Brown Bear, Brown Bear, What Do You See?, by Bill Martin, Jr. (1967)

Corduroy, by Don Freeman (1968)

The Very Hungry Caterpillar, by Eric Carle (1969)

Sylvester and the Magic Pebble, by William Steig (1969)

Frog and Toad Are Friends (1970) and other *Frog and Toad* books, by Arnold Lobel

Corgiville Fair, by Tasha Tudor (1971)

George and Martha, by James Marshall (1972)

Alexander and the Terrible, Horrible, No Good, Very Bad Day, by Judith Viorst (1972)

Strega Nona, by Tomie dePaola (1975)

The Snowman, by Raymond Briggs (1978)

Freight Train, by Donald Crews (1978)

Jumanji, by Chris Van Allsburg (1981)

The Polar Express, by Chris Van Allsburg (1985)

If You Give a Mouse a Cookie, by Laura Numeroff (1985)

The People Could Fly: American Black Folktales, by Virginia Hamilton (1985)

Owl Moon, by Jane Yolen (1987)

The True Story of the Three Little Pigs!, by Jon Scieszka (1989)

The Stinky Cheese Man and Other Fairly Stupid Tales, by Jon Scieszka (1992)

Lily's Purple Plastic Purse, by Kevin Henkes (1996)

Novels, Novellas, and Plays

Play of Daniel, by the youth of Beauvais, France (mid-twelfth century)

Mankind, by anonymous (mid-1400s)

King Arthur legends (1485 and onward), often printed as one continuous story

Robin Hood tales (first recorded in 1500), often printed as one continuous story

A New Interlude for Children to Play Named Jack Juggler, Both Witty and Very Pleasant, by anonymous (c. 1553–1558)

The Pilgrim's Progress, by John Bunyan (1678)

The Thousand and One Nights, translated by Antoine Galland (1704)

Robinson Crusoe, by Daniel Defoe (1719)

Gulliver's Travels, by Jonathan Swift (1726)

The Governess, or The Little Female Academy, by Sarah Fielding (1749)

The History of Little Goody Two Shoes, by anonymous (1765)

Adventures of a Bank-Note, by Thomas Bridges (1770)

Simple Susan, by Maria Edgeworth (1796)

The Swiss Family Robinson, by Johann Wyss (1812 in Switzerland; translated into English in 1814)

History of the Fairchild Family, by Mary Martha Sherwood (published in three volumes between 1818 and 1847)

The Children of the New Forest, by Captain Marryat (1847)

The Wide, Wide World, by Susan Warner (1850)

Tom Brown's Schooldays, by Thomas Hughes (1857)

The Coral Island: A Tale of the Pacific Ocean, by R. M. Ballantyne (1858)

The Water-Babies: A Fairy Tale for a Land Baby, by Charles Kingsley (1863)

The science fiction novels of Jules Verne: *Journey to the Center of the Earth* (1864), *20,000 Leagues Under the Sea* (1869–70), *Around the World in 80 Days* (1872), et cetera

Alice in Wonderland, by Lewis Carroll (1865)

Hans Brinker, or The Silver Skates, by Mary Mapes Dodge (1865)

Ragged Dick, by Horatio Alger (1868)

Little Women, by Louisa May Alcott (1868–69)

At the Back of the North Wind, by George MacDonald (1871)

Historical fiction by G. A. Henty (1871 onward)

What Katy Did, by Susan Coolidge (1872)

The Princess and the Goblin and *The Princess and Curdie*, by George MacDonald (1872 and 1883)

The Adventures of Tom Sawyer, by Mark Twain (1876)

Black Beauty, by Anna Sewell (1877)

Heidi, by Johanna Spyri (published in two parts in German in 1880 and 1881; first published in English in 1884)

Five Little Peppers and How They Grew, by Margaret Sidney (1881)

The Prince and the Pauper, by Mark Twain (1881)

Treasure Island, by Robert Louis Stevenson (serial—1881–82; book—1883)

The Adventures of Pinocchio, by Carlo Collodi (1883)

King Solomon's Mines, by H. Rider Haggard (1885)
The Adventures of Huckleberry Finn, by Mark Twain (1885)
Little Lord Fauntleroy, by Frances Hodgson Burnett (1886)
Kidnapped, by Robert Louis Stevenson (1886)
The Jungle Book, by Rudyard Kipling (1894)
Moonfleet, by J. Meade Falkner (1898)
The Wonderful Wizard of Oz, by L. Frank Baum (1900)
Kim, by Rudyard Kipling (1901)
Five Children and It (1902) and *The Railway Children* (1906), by E. Nesbit
Rebecca of Sunnybrook Farm, by Kate Douglas Wiggin (1903)
A Little Princess, by Frances Hodgson Burnett (1905)
Anne of Green Gables, by L. M. Montgomery (1908)
The Wind in the Willows, by Kenneth Grahame (1908)
A Girl of the Limberlost, by Gene Stratton-Porter (1909)
A Secret Garden, by Frances Hodgson Burnett (first serialized in 1910; published in entirety in 1911)
Peter Pan and Wendy, by J. M. Barrie (1911)
Daddy-Long-Legs, by Jean Webster (1912)
Pollyanna, by Eleanor Porter (1913)
Understood Betsy, by Dorothy Canfield Fisher (1916)
The Story of Dr. Dolittle (1920) and *The Voyages of Dr. Dolittle* (1922), by Hugh Lofting
The Velveteen Rabbit, by Margery Williams (1922)
Bambi, A Life in the Woods, by Felix Salten (1923)
The Boxcar Children, by Gertrude Chandler Warner (1924)
The Story of Rolf and the Viking Bow, by Allen French (1924)
Smoky the Cowhorse, by Will James (1926)
Emil and the Detectives, by Erich Kästner (1929)
Hitty, Her First Hundred Years, by Rachel Field (1929)
The Secret of the Old Clock, by Carolyn Keene (1930)
Young Fu of the Upper Yangtze, by Elizabeth Foreman Lewis (1932)
Little House series, by Laura Ingalls Wilder (1932 onward)
Mary Poppins, by P. L. Travers (1934)
Caddie Woodlawn, by Carol Ryrie Brink (1935)
National Velvet, by Enid Bagnold (1935)
Ballet Shoes, by Noel Streatfeild (1936)
Roller Skates, by Ruth Sawyer (1936)
The Hobbit, or There and Back Again, by J. R. R. Tolkien (1937)

The Yearling, by Marjorie Kinnan Rawlings (1938)

The Sword in the Stone, by T. H. White (1938)

Mr. Popper's Penguins, by Richard and Florence Atwater (1938)

Thimble Summer, by Elizabeth Enright (1938)

B is for Betsy, by Carolyn Haywood (1939)

Betsy-Tacy series, by Maud Hart Lovelace (1940 onward)

Call It Courage, by Armstrong Sperry (1940)

Blue Willow, by Doris Gates (1940)

The Moffats, by Eleanor Estes (1941)

Paddle-to-the-Sea, by Holling Clancy Holling (1941)

Seventeenth Summer, by Maureen Daly (1942)

Homer Price, by Robert McCloskey (1943)

The Little Prince, by Antoine de Saint-Exupéry (1943)

Johnny Tremain, by Esther Forbes (1943)

A Tree Grows in Brooklyn, by Betty Smith (1943) *Parents Cautioned!*

The Hundred Dresses, by Eleanor Estes (1944)

Rabbit Hill, by Robert Lawson (1944)

The Moved-Outers, by Florence Crannell Means (1945)

Strawberry Girl, by Lois Lenski (1945)

Stuart Little, by E. B. White (1945)

Pippi Longstocking, by Astrid Lindgren (1945)

Mrs. Piggle-Wiggle, by Betty MacDonald (1947)

Happy Little Family (1947) and other books, by Rebecca Caudill

The Twenty-One Balloons, by William Pène du Bois (1947)

My Father's Dragon, by Ruth Stiles Gannett (1948)

The Jennifer Wish, by Eunice Young Smith (1949)

The Door in the Wall, by Marguerite de Angeli (1949)

The Chronicles of Narnia series, especially *The Lion, the Witch and the Wardrobe*, by C. S. Lewis (1950–1956)

The Catcher in the Rye, by J. D. Salinger (1951) *Parents Cautioned!*

Charlotte's Web, by E. B. White (1952)

The Borrowers, by Mary Norton (1952)

Secret of the Andes, by Ann Nolan Clark (1952)

Lord of the Flies, by William Golding (1954) *Parents Cautioned!*

Children of Green Knowe, by Lucy M. Boston (1954)

Eagle of the Ninth, by Rosemary Sutcliff (1954)

The Hundred and One Dalmatians, by Dodie Smith (1956)

A Bear Called Paddington, by Michael Bond (1958)

The Witch of Blackbird Pond, by Elizabeth George Speare (1958)

Tom's Midnight Garden, by Philippa Pearce (1958)

A Separate Peace, by John Knowles (1959)

My Side of the Mountain, by Jean Craighead George (1959)

Island of the Blue Dolphins, by Scott O'Dell (1960)

To Kill a Mockingbird, by Harper Lee (1960) *Parents Cautioned!*

The Cricket in Times Square, by George Selden (1960)

James and the Giant Peach, by Roald Dahl (1961)

The Phantom Tollbooth, by Norton Juster (1961)

The Winged Watchman, by Hilda van Stockum (1962)

The Wolves of Willoughby Chase, by Joan Aiken (1962)

A Wrinkle in Time, by Madeleine L'Engle (1962)

Charlie and the Chocolate Factory, by Roald Dahl (1964)

Harriet the Spy, by Louise Fitzhugh (1964) *Parents Cautioned!*

The Chronicles of Prydain, by Lloyd Alexander (1964–1968)

The Dark Is Rising series, by Susan Cooper (1965–1977) *Parents Cautioned!*

The Outsiders, by S. E. Hinton (1967) *Parents Cautioned!*

The Mouse and His Child, by Russell Hoban (1967)

From the Mixed-up Files of Mrs. Basil E. Frankweiler, by E. L. Konigsburg (1967)

The Pigman, by Paul Zindel (1968)

Ramona the Pest (1968) and other Ramona stories, by Beverly Cleary

A Wizard of Earthsea, by Ursula K. Le Guin (1968) *Parents Cautioned!*

Are You There, God? It's Me, Margaret, by Judy Blume (1970) *Parents Cautioned!*

Summer of the Swans, by Betsy Byars (1970)

The Best Christmas Pageant Ever, by Barbara Robinson (1971)

Mrs. Frisby and the Rats of NIMH, by Robert C. O'Brien (1971)

Julie of the Wolves, by Jean Craighead George (1972)

Watership Down, by Richard Adams (1972)

Summer of My German Soldier, by Bette Greene (1973)

M. C. Higgins, the Great, by Virginia Hamilton (1974)

The Chocolate War, by Robert Cormier (1974) *Parents Cautioned!*

Tuck Everlasting, by Natalie Babbitt (1975)

Roll of Thunder, Hear My Cry, by Mildred D. Taylor (1976)

Bridge to Terabithia, by Katherine Paterson (1977)

The Westing Game, by Ellen Raskin (1978)

The Neverending Story, by Michael Ende (German—1979; English—1983)

Anastasia Krupnik, by Lois Lowry (1979)

Sweet Whispers, Brother Rush, by Virginia Hamilton (1982)

The House on Mango Street, by Sandra Cisneros (1984) *Parents Cautioned!*

Redwall series, by Brian Jacques (1986–2011)

Hatchet, by Gary Paulsen (1987)

The Devil's Arithmetic, by Jane Yolen (1988)

The Giver, by Lois Lowry (1993)

The Watsons Go to Birmingham, by Christopher Paul Curtis (1995)

Harry Potter series, by J. K. Rowling (1997–2007) *Parents Cautioned!*

A Series of Unfortunate Events series, by Lemony Snicket (1999-2006) *Parents Cautioned!*

Because of Winn-Dixie, by Kate DiCamillo (2000)

APPENDIX B

Study Method Cheat Sheets

This appendix includes the following lists for your convenience. They may be reproduced for your students only.

The Leisurely Adventure Cheat Sheet
The Book Club(ish) Adventure Cheat Sheet
The Elementary Scholarly Adventure Cheat Sheet
The Secondary Scholarly Adventure Cheat Sheet

The Leisurely Adventure Cheat Sheet

Step 1: Skim through the reading list to get a sense of the whole. The list is organized chronologically, so choose the era in which you would like to begin.

Step 2: Choose a book that interests you.

Step 3: Purchase a notebook in which you will enjoy writing. Make sure the pages are blank. You will probably find it easier to use a lined notebook, but unlined pages are okay, too, especially if you enjoy drawing pictures or diagrams that relate to your reading.

Step 4: Choose a writing utensil you enjoy using, and keep it attached to your notebook, so that you always have it ready.

Step 5: On the cover of your notebook, add a title such as "Reading Notebook" or "Reading Record" or perhaps something similar but more creative.

Step 6: Label the first page on the inside with the same title. On the next page, write "Table of Contents" at the top. For your first entry, write the title and author of the book you will read. Every time you read a book, add to your table of contents.

Step 7: Read the book and from time to time write down your thoughts about it.

Step 8: After you finish the book, jot down your general reactions and thoughts about it. If you don't have much to say, at least write down what you liked and disliked about the book. Someday you will enjoy having this record, so fill it up and store it with your mementoes.

Step 9: Repeat steps 1–8 for as many books as you like!

The Book Club(ish) Adventure Cheat Sheet

Step 1: Find one or more members who will agree to meet regularly, participate faithfully, and hold you accountable for your reading.

Step 2: Decide what kind of books you'll read. Perhaps you might pick a certain genre or era, for example.

Step 3: Decide who will choose the first book. Then set a regular location and time for your meetings.

Step 4: Decide who will lead the meetings. That member could be responsible for preparing some discussion questions and providing snacks—or perhaps one member could host and the other members could provide food, et cetera. Alternatively, you could all sign up for different tasks, varying them from meeting to meeting. At minimum, you will need a leader to moderate each meeting, even if it's just an informal chat on a living room couch.

Step 5: Be faithful in keeping up your end of the agreement. If you don't, your book club won't be much fun. But if you do, you will not only deepen your appreciation of literature, but also deepen your friendships with the other members.

Step 6: Do an extension activity. Extension activities are meant to be just plain fun. You can find lots of ideas on the Internet or at your library, but these books offer a variety of foods, games, and activities related to classic children's books.

Cherry Cake and Ginger Beer: A Golden Treasury of Classic Treats, by Jane Brocket

Ripping Things to Do: The Best Games and Ideas from Children's Books, by Jane Brocket

Storybook Parties, by Penny Warner and Liya Lev Oertel

Turkish Delight and Treasure Hunts: Delightful Treats and Games from Classic Children's Books, by Jane Brocket

The Elementary Scholarly Adventure Cheat Sheet

Step 1: Gather supplies—reading notebook, writing utensils, and any other desired supplies.

Step 2: Choose a book. Consider buying, not borrowing, your literature selection, so that your student can write in the book. Choose an edition that has some visual beauty to enhance the experience.

Step 3: Do an inspectional reading. This involves systematic skimming.

Step 4: Do a slow reading. Vary the method—reading aloud and silent reading—to practice different skills. Write down new vocabulary words during the reading. Define them later and practice them frequently, until mastery is achieved.

Step 5: Narrate or summarize the story, either periodically during the slow reading or afterward.

Step 6: Discuss the story, either periodically during the slow reading or afterward. Questions may be answered in writing, through oral discussion, or both.

Step 7: Write one or more short essays.

Step 8: Complete one or more enrichment projects.

The Secondary Scholarly Adventure Cheat Sheet

Step 1: Gather supplies—reading notebook, writing utensils, and reference materials.

Step 2: Buy—do not borrow—your literature selection. Make sure it has as much white space on the pages as possible.

Step 3: Collect or identify reference materials. These may be books or websites.

Step 4: Review the basic elements of narrative literature (see page 167).

Step 5: Do an inspectional reading. This involves systematic skimming and, for especially challenging works, superficial reading to see the work as a whole.

Step 6: Do structural note-taking. This places the work in context.

Step 7: Do a slow reading. Record new vocabulary and jot annotations in the book.

Step 8: Take notes. Follow either the Cornell or Graphic Organizer method (pages 175–78).

Step 9: Write a summary or a narration. Summaries and narrations can also be given orally.

Step 10: Make a Freytag Pyramid outline (see pages 181–86).

Step 11: Write a personal response essay.

Step 12: Discuss the work.

Step 13: Write a literary analysis essay.

Step 14: Complete a capstone project.

APPENDIX C

A Secondary Scholarly Adventure Study Guide

Some students and parents may wish for more step-by-step guidance than what I have provided thus far without buying book-specific study guides from another source. For that reason, I am providing an adapted version of a general study guide that I have used in my live classes. This study guide is an expansion of the Secondary Scholarly Adventure Cheat Sheet and may be used with any story or narrative poem. The bolded instructions alert parents to the parts of the study that they may want to check for completion and to grade as they choose. The grading rubrics for each step are in appendix D. You may print as many study guides as you need for your students only, filling in the title for each study. You may also adapt the study guide to an elementary student, if you choose.

Literature Study Guide

Title: _____ Author: _____

If you will complete the study guide for a grade, print the rubrics in appendix D before you begin. Your parent can use these to evaluate your literature study. Alternatively, you may use them to evaluate yourself.

Steps 1–4: Preparation

Review pages 164–68 as needed.

1. Prepare your reading notebook, and gather any additional supplies you may want.
2. Buy—do not borrow—your literature selection, so that you can add it to your collection of good books and so that you can write in it.
3. Gather, or at least identify, helpful reference supplies. These may be books or websites.
4. Review the basic elements of narrative literature as needed, so that you can identify the fundamental parts of the story.

Show your work for steps 1–4 to your parent for approval (see rubric on page 236).

Step 5: Inspectional Reading

In step 5, you will prepare for a deep study of your chosen literature by doing the inspectional reading activity. Read pages 168–69. Follow the instructions for stage 1. If your book is above your reading level or otherwise very challenging, follow the instructions for stage 2.

Show your work for step 5 to your parent for approval (see rubric on page 236).

Step 6: Structural Note-Taking

Open this book to page 169. Review the section on structural note-taking. Then answer the questions on pages 170–71 in your notebook.

Show your work for step 6 to your parent for approval (see rubric on page 237).

Step 7: Slow Reading

Now it is time to experience the story fully by reading it slowly and thoroughly. As you do so, you will record annotations and new vocabulary words. Follow these steps to complete your slow reading:

1. Review pages 171–75.
2. Read the story at your natural pace. Try to experience it fully without distractions.
3. As you read, annotate as much as you can. Remember, annotations are gut responses that you record as you read. Aim for at least two annotations per page.
4. Since reading literature should also improve your fluency, or mastery of the English language, record any words you don't know and look them up in a dictionary. Avoid recording foreign words, unless you know they are commonly used by English speakers (e.g., *faux pas, burrito*). Record the part of speech and definition of each word as used in the story. You may record your new vocabulary words in one of two ways:
   a. Write them down as you annotate, perhaps using another color to distinguish them from the rest of your annotations.
   b. Create a section in your designated pages just for vocabulary.

Show your work for step 7 to your parent for approval (see rubric on page 238).

Step 8: Note-Taking

For this part, first review pages 175–78. Then create either a Cornell note-taking template or a graphic organizer. Fill in the following information on these seven literary elements:

- main characters
- setting (historical setting and place)
- main conflict or inciting incident
- major plot events
- point of view
- mood
- major themes (Leave this section blank for now; you'll fill it in later.)

If you use the graphic organizer, one of the boxes should be in the center of your paper and include the title and author of the story.

Show your work for step 8 to your parent for approval (see rubric on page 239).

Step 9: Summary or Narration

To help you fully grasp a story's plot, characters, and other literary elements, writing a summary or narration (or both) can be valuable. Remember, they are similar but different. When you are clear in your mind about which is which, follow these directions:

1. Review pages 177–81.
2. Choose which activity you would like to do—a narration or summary of the story. I suggest doing the one with which you are *least* comfortable, since you need the practice. If you would like to do both, feel free to do so.
3. If you choose a narration, aim for *at least ten sentences*. Remember that it should cover the beginning (exposition, conflict), middle (rising action, climax, and falling action), and end (resolution, denouement) of the story. Also, include as many details as you can to bring the story to life.
4. If you choose a summary, aim for *at least ten sentences*. Remember that you need a strong topic sentence that introduces the story and author and conveys its primary purpose (i.e., " 'Cinderella', retold by Charles Perrault, tells a magical tale of rags to riches.") Then present the entire story, focusing only on the main events and characters.
5. Revise, edit, and proofread your work.
6. Type your final draft, double-spacing it and giving it a title. Remember to label the top right corner of your paper.

Show your work for step 9 to your parent for approval (see rubric on page 240).

Step 10: The Freytag Pyramid Outline

Outlining a story helps the reader pull together all the parts of the story and grasp the "story arc"—the rise and fall of the plot. We will use the Freytag Pyramid and the outline template as our guide. Follow these instructions:

1. Review your notes and annotations, as well as pages 181–86.
2. Label a fresh page in your reading notebook "Outline for (title)."
3. Using the outline template as a guide (*not* the pyramid diagram), outline the *major* characters, settings, and events of the story. You do not need to include everything—only what's most important.

Show your work for step 10 to your parent for approval (see rubric on page 241).

Step 11: The Personal Response Essay

By this point you should fully understand the story and be able to answer many questions about it. Now you are ready for the next level, which is to make connections to yourself, your life, and the world around you. It also means that you are ready to mine the story for its themes, which are the universal, big ideas underlying the story. We can think of themes in two ways:

1. as general, broad topics, like friendship, coming of age, or survival; and
2. as specific, focused ideas like "Money can't buy happiness," "Love conquers all," or "Crime doesn't pay." (These examples are cliches for the sake of illustration. Yours shouldn't be.)

Both kinds of themes are valuable depending on the discussion at hand, so you should practice identifying them. To complete this part of the study guide, follow these instructions:

1. Take out the notes you completed in part 6. You were instructed to leave some space for notes about themes, and it is time to fill in that section. Think about the big ideas underlying the novel.
2. Then identify at least two "a" themes (broad topics) and one "b" theme (specific ideas). Jot these down in the space you set aside for themes in your notes.

Now it is time to step away from the story's elements and consider what you think about the story overall. When you examine your own experience of a literary work and what you think about it, this is called personal response. Your thoughts about the work are an important part of your overall study, because art of every kind is meant to be experienced in a personal, meaningful way. It is not a science experiment or math formula or history lesson; it is a communication between the artist and the audience. The artist speaks to you, and you get the chance to respond in some way. To write a personal response for your story, follow these instructions:

1. Review pages 184–88.
2. Open to a fresh page in the section of your reading notebook devoted to the story you are studying. Label it "Personal Response to (title)."
3. Think about your overall experience of this story—how you feel about it, reactions and thoughts you had while reading it, etc. If you have written personal response essays before, avoid discussing why you liked or disliked it, since this is too easy for an experienced student.
4. Write a one- or two-paragraph personal response essay. If you are a beginner, your essay should be a minimum of eight sentences. If you are more experienced, your essay should be double this length or longer, depending on your skill level. You may write this essay in your reading notebook or type it.
5. If you type it, especially if it's for a grade, remember to proofread and format it.

Show your work for step 11 to your parent for approval (see rubric on page 242).

Step 12: Oral and Written Discussion

Discussion, both oral and written, can help readers understand a story better, because the questions force them to examine it in ways that they might not otherwise. Oral discussion can be especially useful because readers have the opportunity to hear the insights and ideas of fellow readers. This can clarify confusing aspects of the work, correct misunderstandings, and deepen the reader's experience. Whichever you choose, follow these instructions:

1. Review pages 188–91 and the list of questions in appendix H.
2. If you choose to answer questions in writing, choose two from each category of the general questions listed in the chapter. Be sure to follow the instructions in the chapter for answering discussion questions thoroughly. You may refer to the story as needed as you answer each question.
3. If you choose to participate in an oral discussion, study the pointers for answering discussion questions effectively. Also, review the story before the discussion to make sure you fully understand it and know the story's main elements. You will not have much time to re-examine the story during the discussion, so you will need to be ready to answer questions and share insights on the spot.

Show your work for step 12 to your parent for approval (see rubric on page 243).

Step 13: The Literary Analysis Essay

Once you have fully examined a story's elements and connection to the world, you will analyze it. This is where you zoom in on specific aspects of the literature and examine them in more detail and depth. This examination leads to interpretations and a deeper understanding of the literature. Most analysis is done in class discussion and lectures, whether written or oral. Once this is completed, though, many teachers will ask you to show your ability to analyze and interpret the literature by writing a literary analysis essay.

The word "interpret" when used for a literary work (or any art) means to seek and to explain the deeper meaning of it. We can interpret small parts of the work, or we can interpret the work as a whole. Either way, interpreting a literary work takes us to new levels of understanding, especially when we compare our interpretations with those of other readers.

For the literary work you are currently studying, follow these instructions to write a literary analysis essay:

1. Review the literary work as well as your annotations and notes.
2. Ask your parent to provide you with a prompt or, if you are required to develop your own, choose an aspect of the story

that impressed you in some way—perhaps a complex character that intrigues you or an unexpected event. Then make an observation about that aspect that you can demonstrate with evidence from the text. If the story is classic, you might search for possible prompts on the Internet. Either way, the prompt should require you to examine a single aspect of the story in an objective way. Remember, there is no room for your personal response in a literary analysis essay. It should be formal and written in third person, and it should include plenty of textual evidence to support your ideas.

3. Review your notes to find those that help you examine the prompt to which you are responding. Then develop a thesis statement that matches the requirements described in the prompt. Show it to your parent for approval.

4. When your parent approves your thesis statement, develop an outline and write a literary analysis essay. It should be two or three paragraphs, typed and polished.

Show your work for step 13 to your parent for approval (see rubric on page 244).

Step 14: The Capstone Project

Exploring a tangential aspect of the story can be both an enriching and fun way to finish your study. It allows you to learn something new that you might never take time for otherwise. The project is open-ended. You design the project and its rubric, complete it on your own (but with supervision), and decide how long it should take. It can be easy and simple or challenging and complex, depending on the time you have to spend on it and the gaps you need to fill in your curriculum. To complete the capstone project, read pages 196–99. Then use the capstone project rubric and your reading notebook to design and plan the project. Be sure to determine a time frame in which to complete it. Enjoy!

Show your work for step 14 to your parent for approval (see rubric on page 245).

And with that, you are finished with this study guide!
Great job!

APPENDIX D

The Scholarly Adventure Grading Rubrics (or, How to Grade a Literature Assignment When You Haven't Read the Book)

To make the most of your secondary student's literature studies, you may want to give formal grades. Ideally, you will read the same books as your student, so that you have the necessary knowledge to discuss the books and grasp the true quality of your student's work. You may be in a situation, however, where you cannot read all the books your student reads. In that case, you need a way to grade his work that doesn't require you to read them. While reading and discussing the books along with your student is the only way to give truly thorough and accurate grades, the rubrics below will help you give more than mere completion grades when your student must study literature independently.

If you choose, you may photocopy the rubrics you need for your students only, fill them in when your student submits the assignment, and store them for your records. Be sure to give your student a copy of the relevant rubric before he begins the assignment, so that he knows what you expect. Also, feel free to simplify or add to the rubrics as needed. I have provided extra space in between each criterion to allow space for comments.

Please note that I have not included rubrics specifically for elementary students, since formal grading isn't usually important in the early grades, but you may choose to adapt these rubrics to suit your elementary student.

Name: _____

Date: _____

Steps 1–4: Preparation and Step 5: Inspectional Reading

_____ 1. Is the reading notebook set up according to the instructions?

_____ 2. Are the study materials prepared and organized for easy access?

_____ 3. Have helpful study resources been identified for the literature to be studied?

_____ 4. Have the basic elements of literature been reviewed and understood?

_____ 5. Has the entire inspectional reading process been followed thoroughly without missing any steps?

Name: _____

Date: _____

Step 6: Structural Note-Taking

_____ 1. Are the notes neatly organized on a separate, clearly labeled page in the reading notebook?

2. Has the student provided brief but specific information on each of the following topics?

_____ Genre and intended audience

_____ First edition publication date (not the date of your edition)

_____ City, state, country in which the book was *first* published

_____ Historical and cultural context in which the book was written (in other words, the author's setting, not the story's setting)

_____ Biographical sketch of the author

_____ Why the author wrote the book (stated by the author or reliable source, if possible, but guessing may be necessary)

_____ Any assigned additional research on the novel

Name: _____

Date: _____

Step 7: Slow Reading

_____ 1. Did the student read the entire book at a natural pace, rather than skimming or rushing through it?

_____ 2. Did the student record an acceptable number of new vocabulary words along with their definitions and parts of speech? (This assumes the novel is at or above the student's reading level.)

_____ 3. Did the student record an acceptable number of annotations for each chapter? (This number will be up to you, but a good rule of thumb for beginners is one or two annotations per page and two or three annotations per page for more advanced students.)

_____ 4. Did the student record several *kinds* of annotations?

_____ 5. If the student is skilled at annotating, are at least some of the annotations insightful and meaningful?

Name: _____

Date: _____

Step 8: Note-Taking

_____ 1. Did the student choose or design a structured method for note-taking? If you required a specific method, did the student follow it correctly?

_____ 2. Did the student take the amount or type of notes required for the assignment? (If you aren't sure how much or what type to require, a good rule of thumb is to ask for a complete description of all the story's basic elements—plot events, character traits, setting information, and so on.)

_____ 3. Are the student's notes detailed enough to facilitate understanding?

_____ 4. Are the notes neat and legible? (Don't underestimate the importance of this if you intend to have the student use them for other activities.)

Name: _____

Date: _____

Step 9: Summaries and Narrations

_____ 1. Does the student's piece show an understanding of the difference between a summary and a narration?

_____ 2. If a summary, does it contain a topic sentence, supporting details that relate the sequence of events in the plot, and an idea of who the main characters are?

_____ 3. If a summary, is the style formal and told in third person?

_____ 4. If a narration, does it tell the story from beginning to end *as if* the student were the original storyteller? Is it in the student's own words, and does it convey all the important parts?

_____ 5. If a narration, is the style informal and engaging?

_____ 6. Does the piece meet the length you required, or is it a good length in proportion to the literature?

_____ 7. Is it handwritten or typed neatly?

_____ 8. Is it sufficiently free from grammatical or mechanical errors according to your standards?

Name: _____

Date: _____

Step 10: The Freytag Pyramid Outline

_____ 1. Did the student complete all the sections in the template?

_____ 2. Is the information provided in the outline detailed enough to be useful and meaningful for a full comprehension of the story?

_____ 3. Does the student show a sufficient understanding of the different parts of the Freytag Pyramid? Can the student identify each part in the story and identify its place on the pyramid?

_____ 4. Is the outline handwritten or typed neatly? (Don't underestimate the importance of this if you intend to have the student use it for other activities.)

Name: _____

Date: _____

Step 11: The Personal Response Essay

_____ 1. Does the essay show an understanding of the personal response essay form? Does it discuss personal opinions and observations about the story?

_____ 2. Does the essay have a main idea? (In this kind of essay, this may be stated or implied.)

_____ 3. Does the essay respond directly to the prompt you assigned and stay focused until the end?

_____ 4. Does the essay provide enough details and supports to fully explain the main idea?

_____ 5. Is the style conversational, introspective, and honest?

_____ 6. Does the piece meet the length you required, or is it a good length in proportion to the literature?

_____ 7. Is it handwritten or typed neatly?

_____ 8. Is it sufficiently free from grammatical or mechanical errors according to your standards?

Name: _____

Date: _____

Step 12: Oral and Written Discussion

_____ 1. Do the student's answers directly respond to the question asked?

_____ 2. Are the student's answers correct or (if you're not sure or if it's open-ended) at least thorough and detailed?

_____ 3. Does the student provide sufficient support for the answer?

_____ 4. Does the student answer in complete sentences and in such a way that anyone could understand it without knowing the prompt?

_____ 5. If the answers are written, are they neat and error-free according to your standards?

Name: _____

Date: _____

Step 13: The Literary Analysis Essay

_____ 1. Does the essay show an understanding of the literary analysis essay form? Does it examine a single aspect of the story?

_____ 2. Does the essay have a stated topic sentence or thesis statement?

_____ 3. Does the essay respond directly to the prompt and stay focused until the end?

_____ 4. Does the essay provide enough details and supports to fully explain the main idea?

_____ 5. Does the essay provide ample textual evidence to support the student's ideas?

_____ 6. Is the style formal and objective?

_____ 7. Does the piece meet the length you required? (Depending on the student's age and ability, as well as the prompt itself, this may be from half a page to several pages.)

_____ 8. Is it handwritten or typed neatly?

_____ 9. Is it sufficiently free from grammatical or mechanical errors according to your standards?

Name: _____

Date: _____

Step 14: The Capstone Project

Because this project is student-designed, I have offered only two basic require-ments to score. The blanks are for you to fill in with your own requirements. I suggest that you fill it in and give it to your student before he begins working on the project, so that the requirements are clear.

_____ 1. Is the project complete according to your requirements?

_____ 2. Is the project presented neatly and formatted according to your requirements? Is it reasonably free from technical errors?

_____ 3. _____

_____ 4. _____

_____ 5. _____

_____ 6. _____

_____ 7. _____

_____ 8. _____

APPENDIX E

Four Short-Term Study Plans

If you are using *Before Austen Comes Aesop* as a homeschool literature program, you can use it for as long as you wish. Some families, however, may have only a year or two to spend on it before they need to begin a different path. If you anticipate this limitation, consider following one of the short-term plans outlined below.

Plan 1

When you select works for formal study, focus on giving your student a strong foundation. This groundwork will be important for future academic studies in literature. Therefore, begin at the beginning of the reading list, having your student study age-appropriate versions of the "foundational" works. If your student has already read one, skip to the next one. For this plan, avoid the "important" books for your student's formal study. You're trying to fit the big rocks into your homeschooling jar, and time is precious, so limit your study to the most important literature.

Don't worry if you must choose a simple adaptation of a foundational book because your student is not ready for the original. These are not ideal, but great books are best read more than once, so it is all right for this first reading to use the best and most faithful adaptation that you can find to help your student absorb the characters, setting, and storyline. This will make studying the original in high school and college easier.

Step 1

Decide which books to read during the year. Also decide which "adventure" you will use for each book, factoring in significantly more time for any Scholarly Adventure books.

Avoid overplanning. It is better to read slowly and deeply than to rush and skim. I suggest limiting your choices to only as many as you can study thoroughly and meaningfully. If you want your student to read more books than that, it is okay to use some as leisure reading.

Step 2

Purchase the books your student will read. I suggest ordering only one semester's worth of books at a time. Avoid library copies for the Scholarly Adventure. Your student needs the freedom to write in the books and to go at his own pace. If library copies are your only option, your student can annotate using sticky notes or index cards.

Step 3

Purchase any supplies your student will need, such as a dictionary and a reading notebook.

Step 4

Copy any reproducible pages that you might need, and store them in a handy place.

Step 5

As you begin each selection, place flags or sticky note labels on any pages of *Before Austen Comes Aesop* to which you might want to refer often.

Plan 2

Let your student expand his literary experiences while giving him some choices. To do this in an organized way that allows you some behind-the-scenes control, use the Children's Great Books Project as your guide, which you'll find in appendix F. You can choose any adventure with this project, but the project will work best with the Leisurely or Book Club(ish) Adventures. If you use the Scholarly Adventure, you will want to reduce the number of "stars" required.

Plan 3

Consider what your student is studying in history. Then choose the corresponding era in the reading list. Focus on as many books in that era as you have time for. Make historical connections wherever you can, so that your student can understand the context for the book. You may want to plan extra projects to facilitate the history–literature connection.

For this plan you may use any adventure you wish. If you want to place a heavy emphasis on history in your curriculum, however, you may want to use the Leisurely and Book Club(ish) Adventures more than the Scholarly Adventure. Otherwise, your student may become overwhelmed. In addition, your student may not get the rich literary experience of your chosen era that you hoped for.

If you are studying American history, I encourage you to add American folktales to your student's literature program. Although folktales are not included in the reading list after the Middle Ages, they are an important part of American history and culture and can help illuminate the people and the regions from which they come. In addition, modern literature alludes to them often.

My favorite resource for American folklore is *From Sea to Shining Sea: A Treasury of American Folklore and Folk Songs*, by Amy L. Cohn.

Plan 4

If your goal is that your student experiences the *crème de la crème* of the Children's Great Books within a single school year, I suggest that you focus on the following top ten foundational works before moving on to any others. These tales have had a particularly strong impact on Western civilization.

- Bible stories of the Old and New Testaments
- Greco-Roman mythology
- *The Odyssey*
- *Aeneid*
- King Arthur tales
- Robin Hood tales

- European fairy tales and nursery rhymes
- *Treasure Island*
- *Alice in Wonderland*
- *The Hobbit* or *The Wind in the Willows*

As a bonus idea to round out your student's reading, you may want to add a generous helping of American folktales, such as those about legendary heroes like Paul Bunyan and larger-than-life historical figures such as Davy Crockett. Although folktales are not included in the reading list after the Middle Ages, modern American literature alludes to them often; thus they are an important addition to any American student's curriculum. If you are not American, consider introducing the folktales of your own country as well.

APPENDIX F

The Children's Great Books Project:
A Student-Led Approach to Literature

In the live version of this course, which was designed for middle-school students, I assigned this project with satisfying results. For some students it was a challenge with which they struggled, but for others it was a motivator. The students were introduced to some of the Children's Great Books while having some say in what they read. Below is the project as I gave it to my students. It may be especially useful if you are following the Leisurely or Book Club(ish) Adventure, although it could be used for the Scholarly Adventure, too.

You will notice that many books on the reading list are not listed for the project. This was due to the limitations of my class. I have not given rating stars to every book on the reading list, but I encourage you to use the list below as a benchmark for "starring" other books. For example, I did not include *The Hobbit* on the list. If you would like to make that an option for your student, consider his ability and the list below for comparison to determine the number of stars you will assign that novel. You may also use the method I used to determine the number of stars for each selection: look up its "Lexile reading level" on the Internet, consider its length and general content, and then combine those factors to determine the number of stars you feel the book is worth.

Finally, keep in mind that the project was designed for middle-school students, although I did have a couple of ninth and tenth graders take the class who were appropriately challenged by the project. This information may help you adapt the project if you have an elementary or high school student. I made only slight modifications for the sake of clarity. The project is reproducible for your use only, and again, feel free to adapt the project to suit your needs. One change you might want to make is giving a special reward at the end of the project, in addition to or instead of a grade.

The Children's Great Books Project

Throughout this semester, you will read several books of your choice as you learn strategies for studying literature of various kinds. The selections from which you may choose are listed below. Each one is what I consider a Children's Great Book. Like the Great Books of Western civilization, these books and poems were chosen for their impact on the development of children's literature, on the literary experience of young people throughout history, and on Western culture. Reading as many as you can will not only help you learn to discern quality literature, but also prepare you for the study of adult classics—and possibly even the adult Great Books—later in your education. To complete the two-part project, follow the instructions below

Part 1

Choose any work of literature from the list below *that you have not read or have read but don't remember well.* Each selection has been assigned a value from one-half star to five stars, which indicates its difficulty. The entire project will comprise half of your semester grade, so take it seriously! After you complete a selection from the list below, record it on the log.

Your grade will be based not only on your reading but also on your completion of the reading notebook portion, as described below. If you read twenty stars' worth but don't follow the instructions for the journal, your grade will be lowered. The letter grades assigned to numbers of stars are the following:

More than 20 stars—extra credit

20 stars—A+	14 stars—C
19 stars—A	13 stars—C-
18 stars—A-	12 stars—D+
17 stars—B+	11 stars—D
16 stars—B	10 stars—D-
15 stars—B-	9 stars and under—F

Part 2

The second part of the project is your journal. For each selection that you read, you will complete the following tasks:

- In the front half of your reading notebook at the top of a clean page, record the title and author, as well as the number of stars awarded.
- Tell two or three things that you liked about the book in *complete sentences*. Please be specific and provide explanations. For example:

    One of my favorite parts was _____, because _____.
    Even though _____ was a villain, I liked his character best because_____.

- Tell two or three things you didn't like about the book in *complete* sentences. Again, be specific and provide explanations.
- Have your parent sign the log sheet on the back page for each book or poem.

Answers to Possible Questions You May Have

What is Western civilization and these Great Books you mentioned—and why are they important?

Western civilization is the term we give to the culture that originated in Ancient Greece and spread throughout Europe via the Roman Empire as it was being influenced by Judaism and Christianity. When Europeans colonized the Americas, Africa, Oceania, and parts of Asia, they took Western civilization with them.

"The Great Books" is the term for the written works that have shaped the thought and art of Western civilization. These include many works of both fiction and nonfiction, and they are studied more often in college than in high school due to their difficulty. The movement to read the Great Books in American colleges and universities began in the 1920s. Lists were made of those books that allow readers to enter the "Great Conversation of Great Ideas," the ongoing process of writers and thinkers referencing and building on each other through time.

How are the books assigned stars?

I have ranked them partly according to their reading level and partly according to the length and the maturity of the content.

What if I am a slow reader?

First, begin the project right away, so that you have the most time available to work on it. Second, many of the selections may come in an audio format. This is okay, too. You may also have your parent read part of your selections to you. If you do your best and still can't reach twenty stars by the deadline, please ask your parent for help.

Can I read a book I have read before, if I remember only some of it?

If you remember some parts, then no. If you know you read it but don't remember anything about it, you may read it again. The purpose of this project is to expand your experience of the Children's Great Books, so choose books you don't know.

What if I have read so many of these selections that I can't read enough to earn twenty stars?

If you are that well-read, kudos to you! Ask your parent for additional selections.

Why are picture books included when I'm able to read novels?

Literature is an art, and art can be created for any age level. Picture books are just as much art as novels are and have made important contributions to Western culture.

Why are some adult books included?

Some books began life as adult literature and were embraced by children and teens over time. A few of these, such as the adult, Pulitzer

Prize–winning novel *The Yearling*, are now even marketed as children's or young adult literature.

Do I have to read any introductions or prologues?

You do not have to read introductions, which are not part of the story, but you should read prologues, which are part of the story. Introductions are important, however, as they can deepen your reading experience.

Does it matter which edition I choose?

As long as the edition includes the complete and original text, then no, it doesn't matter. Do not choose adaptations or abridgments without getting approval from your parent first. Some of them change the story so much or are so poorly written that they are not worth reading. If you need an adaptation and your parent can find a good one, that is okay.

The Children's Great Books Project Reading List

Half-Star Selections

> *Goodnight Moon*, by Margaret Wise Brown
> *The Very Hungry Caterpillar*, by Eric Carle
> *The Cat in the Hat*, by Dr. Seuss

One-Star Selections

> *The Story of Babar*, by Jean de Brunhoff
> *Millions of Cats*, by Wanda Gág
> *The Snowy Day*, by Ezra Jack Keats
> *The Poky Little Puppy*, by Janette Lowrey
> *The Tale of Peter Rabbit*, by Beatrix Potter
> *Curious George*, by Margret and Hans Rey
> *Where the Wild Things Are*, by Maurice Sendak
> *The Giving Tree*, by Shel Silverstein
> Collections of *classic* lullabies and nursery rhymes

At least ten poems of Eugene Field, particularly "Wynken, Blyn-ken, and Nod," "Little Boy Blue," "Sugar-Plum Tree," and "The Duel"

Two-Star Selections

Beezus and Ramona, by Beverly Cleary
Ramona the Pest, by Beverly Cleary
The Little Prince, by Antoine de Saint-Exupéry
The Outsiders, by S. E. Hinton *Parents Cautioned!*
Strawberry Girl, by Lois Lenski
The Giver, by Lois Lowry
Winnie-the-Pooh, by A. A. Milne
The Railway Children, by E. Nesbit
Where the Sidewalk Ends, by Shel Silverstein
Charlotte's Web, by E. B. White
poetry of Edward Lear—choose one: *A Book of Nonsense, Nonsense Songs* (contains "The Owl and the Pussycat"), *More Nonsense, Laughable Lyrics*, or another collection of his poems

Three-Star Selections

Little Women, part one—by Louisa May Alcott (original novel)
Little Women, part two—by Louisa May Alcott (sequel that was later added to first part)
Charlie and the Chocolate Factory, by Roald Dahl
Johnny Tremain, by Esther Forbes
Lincoln: A Photobiography, by Russell Freedman
The Water-Babies: A Fairy Tale for a Land Baby, by Charles Kingsley
A Wrinkle in Time, by Madeleine L'Engle
The Phantom Tollbooth, by Norman Juster
The Chronicles of Narnia series, by C. S. Lewis (one book equals three stars)
Five Children and It, by E. Nesbit
Island of the Blue Dolphins, by Scott O'Dell
Bridge to Terabithia, by Katherine Paterson
Hatchet, by Gary Paulsen
Tom's Midnight Garden, by Philippa Pearce
Black Beauty, by Anna Sewell

Roll of Thunder, Hear My Cry, by Mildred D. Taylor
Stuart Little, by E. B. White
Little House series, by Laura Ingalls Wilder (one book equals three
   stars)

Four-star selections

Watership Down, by Richard Adams
The Pilgrim's Progress, by John Bunyan
The Diary of a Young Girl, by Anne Frank
The Wind in the Willows, by Kenneth Grahame
Books by G. A. Henty (*Out on the Pampas* is suggested)
Tom Brown's Schooldays, by Thomas Hughes
Children of the New Forest, by Captain Marryat
The Princess and the Goblin, by George MacDonald
The Princess and the Curdie, by George MacDonald
At the Back of the North Wind, by George MacDonald
Anne of Green Gables, by L. M. Montgomery
The Yearling, by Marjorie Kinnan Rawlings
The Hobbit, Or There and Back Again, by J. R. R. Tolkien
The Adventures of Huckleberry Finn, by Mark Twain

Five-star selections

Robinson Crusoe, Daniel Defoe
Gulliver's Travels, by Jonathan Swift (An adaptation is strongly
   recommended.)
Play of Daniel—performance must be found and viewed online

Varied-star selections

Should you choose any of the following classics the "star" value of
your particular edition will be determined by your teacher. Age-
appropriate adaptations are recommended, which can be found in the
full lists in the front of the book.

Beowulf (original author unknown)
Aeneid, by Virgil
The Iliad, by Homer
The Thousand and One Nights, or *The Arabian Nights*

Tales of Greek mythology—stars will vary, depending on the edition you choose

Tales of Norse mythology

Aesop's fables

Collections of folk and fairy stories as close to originals as possible (but if original, parents should preview first)—Andrew Lang's series is suggested

The Children's Great Books Project Log Sheet

Title	# of Stars	Date finished
TOTAL STARS EARNED (fill in all blanks)		

APPENDIX G

Major Awards for Children's Literature

Because the children's literature market is so chock-full of books of all kinds, parents often don't know how to guide their children. This is one reason, perhaps, that many parents fall back on the tried-and-true older classics. Another way to seek out quality literature, though, is to use awards lists for ideas. I am hesitant to say that, because there are many good books that don't win awards, but we have to start somewhere!

This approach can be daunting, too, because the number of awards is huge. Only a few of the most important ones are listed below. Still, using awards lists can narrow down the field a bit. Most readers know about the Newbery Awards, because winners are announced every year and are easy to spot in libraries and bookstores, but other award lists celebrate quality books, too. Some have specific goals in mind, such as honoring Jewish authors or translations from other languages. All seek to honor great writing, however.

As helpful as award-winners can be, a caution is in order. Readers cannot assume that award-winners are "safe" in the sense that they will not conflict with your family's moral and religious values. Some winners are clean and appealing to readers of various religious and political backgrounds. The Newbery and Caldecott winners are good examples; I have not come across one, yet, that caused me concern. Not all lists are like this, though, and even the Newbery might surprise me someday. In fact, I have read some award-winners from other lists that have truly shocked me with their mature and sometimes deeply offensive content. As much as I hate to say it, especially since I work in this field myself, we are past the era of trusting publishers, authors, teachers, and librarians to protect our children!

American Awards

Boston Globe-Horn Book Awards—since 1967; an award determined by a joint agreement between *The Boston Globe* and the children's literary magazine *The Horn Book Magazine* (fiction and poetry, nonfiction, and picture book)

Caldecott Medal—since 1938; most distinguished picture book; award goes to illustrator

Coretta Scott King Award—since 1970; for African-American author and illustrator "who made an outstanding contribution to literature for children in the preceding year"; memorializes Dr. Martin Luther King and his wife

Laura Ingalls Wilder Award (now renamed The Children's Literature Legacy Award)—since 1954; most significant contribution to children's literature over the career of the author or illustrator

Michael Printz Award—since 2000; recognizes literary excellence in young adult literature

Maud Hart Lovelace Award—since 1980; a children's choice book award for middle-grade books

National Book Award—since 1950; a set of U.S. literary awards in several categories, including young people's literature

Newbery Medal—since 1922; most distinguished contribution to children's literature published in the United States

Scott O'Dell Award for Historical Fiction—since 1984; most distinguished work of historical fiction set in the New World and written by a citizen of the United States

International Awards

Carnegie Medal—since 1936; honors outstanding new book for children or young adults that was first published in English in the United Kingdom

Hans Christian Andersen Award—since 1956; honors one living author and one living illustrator whose works have had a lasting, significant, international impact on children's literature

Kate Greenaway Medal—since 1955; honors the most distinguished illustrations in a new book first published in the United Kingdom

APPENDIX H

Useful Questions for
Literature Study

Who Questions

- Who are the characters? Protagonist? Antagonist? Supporting?
- Who is the story about?
- From whose point of view is the story told?
- Who is the narrator of the story?
- Which character(s) do you like the best? Dislike the most?
- In the story, who said/felt/thought _____?
- In the story, who caused the conflict that initiated the action? Who resolved or helped resolve the conflict?

What Questions

- If someone asked you what the book is about, what would you say?
- What happened in the beginning of the story? Middle? End?
- What was the conflict that made things start to happen in the story?
- What was the most important or most exciting part of the story?
- What are the most important events in the story?
- Discuss an event that had important consequences.
- Which events had an important effect on the main character?
- What did the author mean by _____?
- What big idea is the story about? What did it make you think about?

When and Where Questions

- Where does the story take place?
- When in history does the story take place? What do you know about this period?
- When during the day does this event take place?
- Describe the setting's time and place.
- Name the historical events that took place during the story. Why are they important to the story?
- Is the setting realistic or meaningful to the story? Why or why not?
- Can you visualize the setting? If not, what might help you do that?
- Does the setting affect the mood of the story? If so, how?
- Where does most of the action in the story take place? And when?
- How did the setting affect the character's thoughts and feelings?
- Did you have to infer the setting, or was it specified?

How Questions

- How did this event happen?
- How did the character(s) react to this event or another character's actions or words?
- How did the problem in the story affect the main character?
- How did the main character change throughout the story?
- How have the characters changed by the end of the story?
- How do these two characters differ from each other?
- How did the author create suspense in the story?

Why Questions

- Why do you think the character made that choice or did that action?
- Why did this event have to occur for the story to make sense?
- Why did the event affect the character so much?
- Why do you think the author chose this setting?
- Why doesn't the character make the right choice in this situation?

Questions of Prediction (guessing a future part of the story)

- What do you think this book will be about? What kind of characters do you think we'll meet?
- What do you think will happen next?
- What do you think the character will do next?
- How do you think the story should end? How do you think it *will* end?
- If the story had a sequel, what do you think might happen?

Questions of Inference (using context clues and real-life knowledge to figure out something in the story)

- Why do you think the character made this choice or did this action?
- What is the character feeling? How do you know?
- What is the author not telling us about this character or situation? Why do you think the author left us to fill in the blanks ourselves?
- What do you think the author is trying to say through this story? Why do you think that?

Questions about Drawing Conclusions

- Based on evidence from the story, what kind of person do you think the character is?
- If the story doesn't specify the time and place setting clearly, what details lead you to your best guess?
- What conclusions can you draw from this event in this story?

Questions about Making Connections

- What do you know or what is your experience with the setting or situation in this book?
- Has anything like this ever happened to you? What was your experience or feeling about it?
- Do you know anyone like this character?

- How are you like or different from this character?
- Is this story or situation meaningful to you? How?

Questions about Comparing and Contrasting

- Compare and contrast character one and character two (or another literary element that varies throughout the story).
- How would you compare and contrast _____ and _____?
- Do you see any similarities or differences between this book and that one?
- How does the movie version differ from the book? How is it the same?

Questions about Cause and Effect

- Who or what caused the character to behave or speak as he did? What was the character's response?
- Name an important event in the story, and then explain how it happened. What was the outcome of the event?
- What caused the story's main conflict?
- How did the main conflict of the story affect each of the important characters by the end?

Summary Questions

- Summarize what you have read today.
- Summarize the entire story.
- Describe the characters as you understand them so far.
- What has happened to this character so far?

Sequencing Questions

- How is the book organized?
- List the main events from beginning to end.
- What are the main characters and events from least important to most important?

Response Questions

- What questions about the story do you have so far?
- Is there anything you are wondering or hoping will happen?
- Do you think this story is important for other students to read? Why or why not?
- How do you wish the story had ended? Why?
- Did you think the ending was a good one? If so, why? If not, why not?
- What did you learn or take away from the story?
- How did the story make you feel and why?
- What would you have done differently from what the character did?

RECOMMENDED RESOURCES

Recommended Literature Programs and Reference Materials

The market is rich in literary and homeschool resources, far too many to address here. In the lists below, however, you will find the resources I most recommend to students. The "Reference Materials" list is a collection of useful study aids. The "Literature Programs" list is a collection of my favorite homeschool programs for those who would like more structured, direct guidance than what *Before Austen Comes Aesop* provides.

Reference Materials

CliffsNotes (cliffsnotes.com; also in book format)

Essential Literary Terms: A Brief Norton Guide with Exercises, by Sharon Hamilton

Glossary of Literary Terms (literaryterms.net)

LitCharts.com—literature guides, dictionary of literary terms, and Shakespeare translations

Literary Devices: Definitions and Examples of Literary Terms (literarydevices.net)

Merriam-Webster's Encyclopedia of Literature, by Merriam-Webster

Oxford Dictionary of Literary Terms, by Chris Baldick

Reader's Handbook: A Student Guide to Reading and Learning, by Great Source (a multi-level resource)

SparkNotes (sparknotes.com; also book format)

Literature Programs

CenterForLit (centerforlit.com)

Excellence in Literature, by Janice Campbell (https://excellence
-in-literature.com/)

Hewitt Homeschooling (many literature education resources, such as
Lightning Literature) (https://www.hewitthomeschooling.com/)

Memoria Press study guides (memoriapress.com)

Memoria Press online courses (memoriapressacademy.com)

Progeny Press (stores.progenypress.com)

Total Language Plus (totallanguageplus.com)

SELECTED BIBLIOGRAPHY

For this book I consulted many, many resources. I have listed here the most comprehensive ones and have also starred those that formed the backbone of the book.

* Adler, Mortimer and Charles Van Doren. *How to Read a Book: The Classic Guide to Intelligent Reading.* Revised and updated edition. Simon & Schuster, Inc., 1972.

Anderson, George Parker. *Research Guide to American Literature: American Modernism, 1914–1945.* Facts on File, Inc., 2010.

Anderson, Patricia. "Bloom's Taxonomy." Vanderbilt University, https://www.cft.vanderbilt.edu/guides-sub-pages/blooms-taxonomy/.

CliffsNotes. Houghton Mifflin Harcourt, 2016, www.cliffsnotes.com.

Craig, Amanda. "Why This is a Golden Age for Children's Literature: 'Children's Books are One of the Most Important Forms of Writing We Have'." *Independent,* June 24, 2015, www.independent.co.uk/arts-entertainment/books/features/why-this-is-a-golden-age-for-childrens-literature-childrens-books-are-one-of-the-most-important-10340568.html.

D'Addario, Daniel, Giri Nathan, and Noah Rayman. "The 100 Best Children's Books of All Time." *TIME.* www.time.com/100-best-childrens-books.

Encyclopaedia Britannica, Britannica Group, Inc., www.britannica.com.

Galda, Lee, Lawrence R. Sipe, Lauren A. Liang, and Bernice Cullinan. *Literature and the Child,* 8th ed., Cengage Learning, 2012.

* Hunt, Peter, editor. *Children's Literature: An Illustrated History.* Oxford University Press, 1995.

Hunt, Peter, editor. *The International Companion Encyclopedia of Children's Literature, Volume 1.* 2nd ed., Routledge Ltd., 2004.

Kline, Daniel T., editor. *Medieval Literature for Children.* Routledge, 2003.

*Lerer, Seth. *Children's Literature: A Reader's History from Aesop to Harry Potter.* The University of Chicago Press, 2008.

Mendlesohn, Farah and Michael Levy. "The Most Influential Children's Fantasy Books." *fifteeneightyfour* (Cambridge University Press blog), June 13, 2016, www.cambridgeblog.org/2016/06/the-most-influential-childrens-fantasy-books/

Mickenberg, Julia L. and Lynne Vallone, editors. *The Oxford Handbook of Children's Literature.* Oxford University Press, Inc., 2011.

* *The Norton Anthology of Children's Literature Web Student Companion.* W.W. Norton and Company, 2005, wwnorton.com/college/english/nacl/timeline/index.html.

O'Sullivan, Emer. *Historical Dictionary of Children's Literature.* The Scarecrow Press, Inc., 2010.

Parini, Jay. *The Oxford Encyclopedia of American Literature, Volume 3.* Oxford University Press, 2004.

"Questions to Ask Your Student Before, During and After Reading." Katy Independent School District, www.katyisd.org/campus/KDE/Documents/Before%20During%20and%20After%20Questions%20-%20ELA.pdf.

Renaissance Accelerated Reader Bookfinder. Renaissance Learning, 2017, arbookfind.com/default.aspx.

Reynolds, Kimberley. *Children's Literature: A Very Short Introduction.* Oxford University Press, 2011.

Root Jr., Shelton L. and Barbara Z. Kiefer. "Children's Literature: History, Literature in the Lives of Children, Environment, Awards." *Education Encyclopedia—StateUniversity.com,* education.stateuniversity.com/pages/1829/Children-s-Literature.html.

Rudd, David, editor. *The Routledge Companion to Children's Literature.* Routledge Ltd., 2010.

*Russell, David L. *Literature for Children: A Short Introduction.* 7th ed. Pearson, 2011.

Silvey, Anita, editor. *The Essential Guide to Children's Books and Their Creators.* Houghton-Mifflin Company, 2002.

Silvey, Anita. *100 Best Books for Children: A Parent's Guide to Making the Right Choices for Your Young Reader, Toddler to Preteen.* Houghton Mifflin Company, 2004.

SparkNotes. Barnes & Noble, sparknotes.com.